This edition first published in 1996 by Motorbooks International Publishers & Wholesalers, 729 Prospect Avenue, PO Box 1, Osceola, WI 54020 USA

Previously published by Amos Press, Inc. under the title of SUZY Q. RESTORING A '63 CORVETTE STING RAY. Compiled by the staff of *Cars & Parts* Magazine. Amos Press Inc., 911 Vandemark Rd., Sidney, OH 45365.

Motorbooks International books are also available at discounts in bulk quantity for industrial or sales-promotional use. For details write to Special Sales Manager at the Publisher's address.

Library of Congress Cataloging-in-Publication Data Available.

ISBN 0-7603-0270-7

Printed and bound in the United States of America

1

'OH SUZY Q. ...'

By Eric Brockman

We knew the job was formidable when we took it. But *Cars & Parts* elected to return to the restoration scene with a third project car in 1993.

In fact, Peggy Sue, the '57 Chevy convertible that preceded this project, had barely departed our presence when plans were formulated for a third give-away project car. The debate on what to pick was hot and heavy when it came to selecting a model. A Chrysler product seemed to be the logical choice, since previous projects had been a '55 Ford (known as Vicky) and a '57 Chevy. A small but vocal contingent of readers lobbied for an orphan make. But we also had to consider what make and model might have the broadest appeal — something that could transcend brand loyalties and grab the imagination of the vast majority of readers. In other words, a dream car ... such as a Corvette!

So we decided to face the potential backlash of doing another Chevy and picked the '63 Corvette split-window coupe as the subject of our search. The '63 represented a real turning point in Corvette history, as an all-new design debuted with ultra-modern styling and all-independent suspension. The '63 helped silence the critics who felt the Corvette wasn't a real sports car. And the one-year-only split-window body style is one of the most collectible of Corvettes.

As the search began, we also re-evaluated the method by which we had handled the previous two projects. Many readers felt our approach of having one

2

shop do the majority of the work didn't realistically represent how the average hobbyist with a limited budget would tackle a restoration. So this time, we set out on our project with the notion that we would attempt to do some of the work ourselves, and farm the large portions out to separate shops. It was a noble idea, but, as we later found out, having parts of a car spread over three states also created a few logistical nightmares

as story deadlines loomed and critical pieces ended up at the wrong shop.

We announced we were looking for a '63 Vette before even beginning the search. Subsequently, we were deluged with leads and began the long, sometimes frustrating, search for just the right combination. As our deadline for getting things underway approached, we finally located what seemed to be the perfect car in Florida — a silver blue number

1. *Our time with the completed car was painfully short, but we did manage to get some time behind the wheel. Suzy Q. wasn't even fully completed when Staff Writer Dean Shipley got to give her a short test-run.*

2. *Suzy Q. was a complete, but tired, old girl when we purchased her from Classic Chevy International in Florida.*

3. *How to disassemble a car, in four easy lessons .... Art Director Ken New, with help from other members of the C&P staff, handled most of the job of dismantling Suzy Q.*

4. *It's alive, it's alive! After more than a year of work, Suzy Q. finally returned to life during the summer of 1995. Even after the car was running, there was still a lot of last-minute work to be completed.*

with the optional 300-hp engine and four-speed transmission. It needed a total restoration, but it was mostly complete and in running condition.

Despite a harrowing trip in an ice storm, Editor Bob Stevens and Bruce Henderson, of the advertising department, delivered our girl, subsequently dubbed Suzy Q., to her temporary new home in Sidney, Ohio.

Once the project got underway, this writer soon became the point man for much of the writing and photography, with extensive help from editor Bob Stevens, art director Ken New, staff writer Dean Shipley and publisher Walt Reed. Keeping to our promise to do some of the work ourselves, New and the author dismantled Suzy Q. in a garage at parent company Amos Press. Drafting everybody on the staff of *Cars & Parts* to help, we even managed to remove the body from the frame ourselves.

Then the body, chassis and engine went their separate ways for restoration. With Suzy Q.'s pieces scattered across Virginia, Kentucky and Ohio, keeping everything organized and on track became a real challenge at times — as did finding places to store all the parts piling up in our offices.

But eventually everything started coming together, and it was an incredible feeling to watch the new and rejuvenated pieces form a car once again. All the shops, rebuilders and parts suppliers involved in the project (see the "Honor Roll" at the end of the book) did a fantastic job of seeing us through, even when our deadlines and realistic goals for completion diverged ("You want it done *when*?!?!").

Whenever Suzy Q., or at least part of her, made a public appearance, she always drew a curious crowd. A Corvette was definitely the right choice, from the standpoint of garnering attention. Driving (or pushing as was often the case) a '63 Corvette off an enclosed trailer is guaranteed to instantly draw a crowd, most of whom want to know if it's for sale. At one point, we cynically considered calling the car "Not For Sale."

The months rolled on, 1994 gave way

to 1995, and we began approaching the deadline to complete the car for the giveaway at Hershey that year. As with most projects of this caliber, things began running behind schedule, sometimes due to unforeseen problems, sometimes due to miscalculation on our part as to how long it would take. Things were really getting down to the wire when Suzy Q.'s 327-cid V-8 finally returned to life during mid-summer 1995. No matter how much hair-pulling you've done (both yours and other people's!) during a project, that's always the point when you know it was all worthwhile. You've reduced a car to its individual pieces, reassembled it, and gotten it to run again, hopefully better than it did before! Words can't describe the thrill of getting to take Suzy Q. on her first short shakedown run.

Unfortunately, we couldn't keep Suzy Q. and enjoy her for very long. Even as the sweepstakes winner's name was drawn, we were desperately still trying to

work out all the last-minute bugs and gremlins. Far too quickly after her completion, we said goodbye to Suzy Q.

But we know she's got a good home, in the hands of Doyle Kash, of Kingman, Ariz. She'll be right at home cruising legendary Route 66, which runs through Kingman on its way west to Los Angeles.

Suzy Q. may be gone, but she's definitely not forgotten around the offices of *Cars & Parts*. In fact, we've still got a large pile of used parts cluttering up the office, and we think of her every time we trip over one of those pieces! But seriously, we *will* miss her, although we're certain there'll be a replacement at some time in the future.

5. *"Oh Suzy Q., baby I love you, Suzy Q. ...."*

Suzy Q.
Restoring a '63 Corvette Sting Ray
Contents

Selecting C&P restoration project 1

No resto. project car yet, but we're getting warm 2

The hunt continues; how about a fuelie 3

Surveying the field at Bloomington Gold 5

Sorting through dozens of leads 7

Still no project car, but we're getting warmer 8

Still enjoying the hunt 9

Our six-month hunt nears end 12

At last our project car is found 13

Taking delivery of our new car 18

Hauling the car home 21

The morning after 22

Researching a resto., the software side of things 25

The name game 27

Let's just call her ... not for sale 28

We find a shop ... and it's ours 29

Building a body dolly 30

Body disassembly, part 1 31

Body disassembly, part 2 36

Removing the body 40

Pulling the engine and transmission 42

Final disassembly 44

The engine doctors 46

Engine teardown reveals past rebuilds 47

Removing a bolt broken in block 54

Align boring 55

Reboring the cylinder block 57

Decking the block 59

Honing the block 61

Grinding the crank 64

Resizing the connecting rods 66

Balancing the engine 70

Installing cam bearings 75

Installing freeze plugs 76

Head bolt boss repair 77

Installing valve guide inserts 79

Rebuilding the heads 81

Decking the heads 85

Resurfacing the flywheel 88

Decking the exhaust manifolds 89

Coating the exhaust manifolds 92

Engine reassembly, part 1 93

Engine assembly, part 2 98

Antique Auto: Peggy Sue to Suzy Q. 104

Disassembly of rear suspension 105

Final chassis teardown 107

Chemical derusting: Suzy Q.'s rust is 'zapped . 112

Painting the frame and chassis parts 115

Springing to action 119

Rebuilding the rear end 123

Rear suspension reassembly 130

Rebuilding the gas tank 133

Piper's a Corvette specialist 135

Trannie teardown, trans rebuild, part 1 136

Transmission rebuild, part 2 139

The Vette stops here 144

Installing the engine and trans 145

Viscous fan clutch build-up 146

Fan clutch alternative 149

Suzy Q. goes to Broadway ... Virginia 150

Suzy Q. unmasked 152

Plastic surgery 155

Painting the body 159

Gauge restoration, part 1 162

Gauge restoration, part 2 166

Restoring the radio, part 1 168

Restoring the radio, part 2 172

Restoring the clock 177

Mid-America Designs 179

Chrome plating 180

Corvette Central 184

Introducing D&D Restoration 186

Custom parts fabricating at D&D Resto 189

Spare wheel refinishing 192

Fitting the brakes 193

Final chassis assembly 194

Remounting the body 197

Baby needs a new pair of shoes 200

Mounting knock-off wheels 202

Building the wiring harness, Lectric Limited 203

Installing the wiring harness 205

Installing headlight motors 207

Fitting a repro hood 209

Hood trim installation 212

C.A.R.S. West settles in L.A. 214

The dash specialist 215

Molding a new dash pad 217

Installing the dash 220

Installing the dash instruments 221

O.E.M. Glass 223

Installing a new windshield 224

Installing the side and rear glass 226

Trim parts 230

Installing exterior trim and bumpers 232

Cooling system resto 235

Installing the ignition shielding 237

Al Knoch Interiors 239

Recovering the seats 241

Installing carpeting, door panels 244

Installing the headliner 246

Suzy Q. goes home 248

The first Sting Ray (color feature article) 249

Project review 256

STAR SEARCH 3

SELECTING CARS & PARTS' RESTORATION PROJECT

By Bob Stevens

The recent '57 Chevy convertible restoration project left our staff exhausted, our finances depleted ... and our readers begging for more. So, after a brief vacation of sorts from the resto shop scene, we're plunging back into yet another full-scale restoration effort.

Vicky, the '55 Ford Crown Victoria that was restored and given away by *Cars & Parts* some five years back, and Peggy Sue, the '57 Chevy ragtop awarded in the 35th *Cars & Parts* Anniversary Sweepstakes last fall, were both very successful projects. It would be hard, we surmised, to top those two exciting ventures. But, we'll try.

Selecting the candidates for the third project car wasn't difficult, narrowing it down to a short list of five or six, however, was tough. At first, the staff discussions regarding the next project car were limited basically to postwar models, simply because that's where most of the restoration action is these days, and general hobby interest is now focusing on the newer special interest cars.

Since we'd restored a '55 Crown Vic and a '57 Chevy Bel Air convertible, the mid-year Fords and Chevys were excluded from the process at the outset. A few '40s cars were proposed, including a couple of interesting woodies, a '49-51 Merc coupe (the author's favorite), late '40s Chevy or Ford convertible, and even a Hudson pickup. But it was determined that interest might be more limited in this era, so we opted to further limit our project to the '50s, '60s or early '70s.

Shortly thereafter, following a review of such potential candidates as the '58 Chevy Impala, the Ford Skyliners of 1957-59, Packard Caribbean convertibles, etc., it was decided that we should vacate the '50s altogether since both of our first two projects featured cars from that era. And, since the '60s have been coming on strong, it was a natural to focus our search on cars from that decade (and into the early '70s).

Suddenly, the list became shorter; now it was at least manageable. The first logical choice to come to mind was the first-generation Mustang, the car that launched the pony car revolution. However, the Mustang is the exclusive subject of several magazines, numerous books and many one-marque car shows. The general hobby media has also covered the Mustang in great detail. Several early models of Ford's premier pony car have been the subject of complete or partial restoration projects covered in serial form in various magazines; books have been authored on the subject. So, the popular Mustang was eliminated in the early rounds.

In fact, the Camaro and Firebird suffered much the same fate. They've been restored by other magazines, or via independent projects covered by club or commercial publications. In fact, the only pony cars to survive the final cut were the Dodge Challenger and Plymouth Barracuda, both in convertible guise and with a gutsy motor under the hood. Since we used a Ford and a Chevy the first two times around, a Mopar would be a sound choice for project number three.

Several independents – now all orphan cars – were summarily dismissed for such reasons as too limited in appeal, problems in finding parts, too expensive to buy and/or restore, etc. We had to have a car with great general appeal across all party lines. Among the orphans considered were the Studebaker Hawk and GT, American Motors AMX and Javelin, Studebaker Avanti, etc. (Also mentioned earlier in the process were Packards and Hudsons from the '50s such as the Caribbean convertibles, the Hornet, and so on.)

At this point, we were basically considering cars from the Big Three – General Motors, Ford and Chrysler. From Dearborn, we were looking at Shelby Mustangs, about any year or body style, although our budget, which has been replenished but is still limited, precluded us from an early convertible (only six were made in 1966). The Shelby then would be a '65-67 fastback or a '68-70

convertible. Any of these would make a super exciting project.

Also in the Ford camp was a second finalist, the 1964-66 Thunderbird convertible. Only a couple of the six or seven staffers involved in the decision liked the idea of doing a mid-'60s T-bird, so it fell out of favor early.

Another car still standing in the final leg of the selection process was Pontiac's GTO of 1964-67. We favored a convertible, of course, and one with an array of neat accessories. We even pondered the possibility of buying a LeMans and "creating" our own GTO (only kidding, folks).

All of the different candidates had their own unique qualities, and each would make a super project car. But after lengthy deliberation, it became clear to most on staff that the final candidate was the overwhelming favorite. That model, as some may have already guessed, is the 1963 Corvette coupe. Yep, the ideal candidate for *Cars & Parts'* next restoration project is the world-famous split-window coupe. It was the only year that the Vette had the divided rear window; it was such a nuisance for the driver when backing up that Chevy eliminated it the following year.

Before our Ford and Mopar readers start flooding our office with hate mail, accusing us of favoring Chevy over everything else (not true, incidentally), please review the facts. The Corvette is a universally recognized and loved automobile. Even hobbyists who dislike Vettes can appreciate their slick design, sports car heritage, superior performance, etc. Also, to our knowledge, no major magazine has performed a complete, ground-up, body-off restoration on a split-window coupe and covered the entire process step-by-step. Besides, who wouldn't want to win a split-window Corvette? Even if you don't care for Chevy's little sports machine, you could easily trade it for a Shelby Mustang, if you're into Fords, or a Challenger or 'Cuda ragtop, if you're a Mopar guy, and probably pocket some change.

In respect to the car itself, the '63 Corvette is a certified milestone car (it assuredly would be a genuine classic, if the classic period extended beyond 1948, which it doesn't). It was the first of the famous Sting Rays and sported an all-new body, a new frame and suspension setup, hidden headlamps, a totally redesigned dash and instrument cluster, etc. Most important of all, though, was the addition of a coupe to the line for the first time.

Chevy built 10,594 coupes in '63, plus 10,919 convertibles, for a total production of 21,513. Each and every one is a proven collectible, but the split-window coupes command the most attention.

Of the 10,594 '63 split-window coupes produced by Chevy, there has to be one in an acceptable original color (Riverside red, Daytona blue, silver blue or Sebring silver) and still powered by its original mill that needs a total restoration, including frame, body, paint, interior and drivetrain. And, we're going to find it!

No Resto Project Car Yet, But We're Getting Warm

By Bob Stevens

Photos by the Author

1. *We got excited about this black-on-red split-window coupe when we discovered that it was originally a red car, according to its tag. But our enthusiasm was tempered when we learned that it had a late model engine in it, a Chevy 350 V-8. At $17,000 it would have made a super driver, though.*

2. *Although it was priced at only $19,800, this red coupe was actually too nice to fully restore. It was detailed underneath, had decent paint and ran super. It also had a non-original engine, a 327 V-8 from a '66 Corvette and was originally painted Sebring silver. A good buy, indeed, but not quite the candidate for the next Cars & Parts' project.*

We haven't located our new Peggy Sue or Miss Vicky yet, but we sense that we're getting close to finding the car that will serve as the subject of *Cars & Parts'* next restoration project. There's nothing concrete on which to base that piece of speculation; it's just a feeling. At press time, we were no closer to latching onto a suitable candidate than we were six months ago when we got the "go ahead" for resto project number three, except that we've more or less focused our search on a '63 Corvette coupe.

As announced last month, the new restoration project will begin as soon as we locate the right car, and will culminate with the presentation of the keys to the fully restored split-window to the winner of the next *Cars & Parts'* sweepstakes. It could be you!

Armed with piles of data collected during years of Corvette ownership and enjoyment, plus books, manuals and other materials from Chevrolet, the National Corvette Restorers Society (NCRS) etc., we began our search in earnest back in March of this year. Unfortunately, an ideal candidate was unearthed a few months before our project began. It was a silver blue '63 coupe that had been in storage since 1981 in Cincinnati, Ohio. A couple of staff members inspected the car last summer with thoughts of buying it themselves as a personal project. The author was one of those staffers who let the car slip by. It was, believe, it or not, a one-owner car. That's right, the guy who took delivery of the car back in 1963 still owned it. It was thoroughly documented and still had its original 340-hp engine, four-speed transmission, etc. We couldn't find a single number (radiator, intake, carb, exhaust manifolds, intake manifold, alternator, etc.) that wasn't correct. It needed a total restoration. It was perfect. It also sold before any of us got serious about it. It was priced at $13,000, but sold for even less.

But by the time the project received the endorsement of top management, the silver blue split window was long gone. We even tried to track it down and offer a bounty to the individual who was smart enough to spot a real bargain. But the seller had moved and his phone was disconnected; other inquiries went unanswered. Oh, well, onward and upward; we still had plenty of leads to follow up.

Trips to Corvette Expo in Knoxville, Tenn., and the Corvette Nationals in Indianapolis turned up a few prospects, but no solid candidates. The leads turned into dead ends. The cars found at the shows themselves were either already restored, or had too many incorrect components. We were searching for a Vette that still had its original engine, and most of its major components correct in terms of numbers, codes, dates, etc. We had decided that if all else failed, we would consider one with an engine that was substantially correct but whose numbers were not matching (not coded to the car's serial number). Still, an original car with an original numbers-matching engine was preferred.

Among the cars we uncovered but disqualified for various reasons were (all 1963 split-window coupes):
• Silver blue/dark blue coupe, but no motor and mounted on a '64 frame, $8,400 (too many problems).
• Black on red, incorrect 350-cid V-8, originally a red car, $17,000 (bad color; black and white are not on our preferred list of paint colors).
• Real red car, black interior, incorrect '66 model 300-horse engine, nice interior and frame, etc., $19,800 (too nice to restore, plus wrong engine).
• Silver car with dark blue interior, nice, only $20,000 (too nice; fresh paint, new interior, new tires, etc.)
• Black, 340-hp engine with correct numbers and dates, $21,900 (wrong color, and too nice a car to be redone).
• Silver blue with black interior, 300-hp 327, original engine, very nice condition, $20,000 (a good deal, but too nice a car for a project).
• Red-on-red, California car, perfect frame, base 250-hp engine, four-speed, radio, power windows, needed general restoration, good driving car, $17,500 (sold for $17,000 a few days before we got through to the Indiana owner).
• Complete yellow car (originally tan), needing total resto, original engine, runs, $14,000 (car was sold before ad appeared).
• California car, straight frame and body, missing motor, hood, wheel covers, spare tire carrier, etc., $12,800 (not enough there, missing too much).

Obviously, we've investigated quite a few cars, and without much success. But things would look more promising for us, and soon.

1

2

THE HUNT CONTINUES;
'HOW ABOUT A FUELIE?'

By Bob Stevens

Photos by the author

3

1. *One of the more intriguing split-window coupes we've checked out so far was this toothless wonder buried under a lot of dust. The car's missing engine, which had been yanked and safely stored away, was its biggest attraction...a genuine fuelie!*

2. Cars & Parts *publisher Walt Reed peers inside the old coupe. The Vette seemed ideal for our project needs.*

3. *The hood was in pretty decent shape, although it obviously needed complete refinishing. The car was amazingly complete, even though a number of key parts were not stored at the resto shop.*

L ocating a '63 Corvette coupe is not a particularly difficult task, but finding one that is complete, correct and in need of a total restoration is quite challenging. Challenging almost to the point of frustration.

Restored split-window coupes fairly abound. As reported last month, we found a lot of choice examples in various colors and in different states of originality. Basically, a well restored car was bringing from the high 20s up to about $32,000 with nice street/show machines selling for $23,00 to $28,000. Cars with non-original engines were available from about $17,000 to $21,000, depending on restoration quality, options, etc.

All this was fine, but we needed a car with an original numbers-matching engine that also required a total restoration ... a real project car. We had followed up on a number of tips, most of which were empty. One lead I checked out personally produced zero results, as the guy had already sold the car ... two years ago!

Then, out of the blue, I received a phone call from a good friend of mine. He'd just visited a small restoration shop with a friend of his whose '62 Corvette was being restored there. While snooping around the shop, he spotted this '63 coupe over in the corner. He inquired about it and discovered that the car had a really interesting history, and that, yes, it might be for sale; at least it had been a few months back. The resto facility, inci-

dentally, was less than 10 miles away. My friend telephoned me that evening; I visited the shop and inspected the car the very next day.

The Daytona blue coupe was ordered new as a race car – primarily drag racing. That explained the radio delete, and the lack of creature comforts.

The coupe was very solid, complete, and in need of a total restoration. Best of all, it was a real fuelie! In fact, the 360-hp fuel-injected 327 V-8 and four-speed manual transmission were about the only options on this car originally. Naturally, it was modified some for drag racing, and then altered more for street running at a later date. What a find; a genuine fuel-injected '63 split-window Corvette in an acceptable color combination!

I hurried back to the shop to run the numbers. The VIN – 30837S113563 – broke down this way: 3 = model year (1963); 08 = series (Corvette); 37 = body style (two-door sport coupe); S = assembly plant (St. Louis, Mo.); 113563 = sequential production number, beginning with 100001. This was car number 13,563 out of a total production of 21,513 (there were 10,594 coupes and 10,919 convertibles produced that year). It was built, according to my own calculations, on or about Wednesday, March 27, 1963.

Also checking out 100 percent was the trim tag, which showed a paint code of 916A (Daytona blue), trim number 490A (dark blue vinyl), style 63837 (1963 model year, coupe body style), and body production number 7,293. All the codes

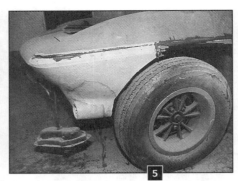

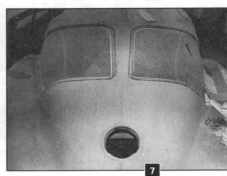

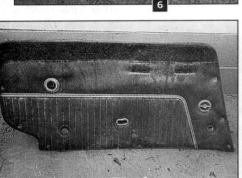

4. Missing in action, the fuel-injected 327-cid V-8 carried a factory rating of 360 hp. This car's original engine, complete with fuelie unit, had been removed and placed in storage many years ago. We wanted to reunite the two after fully refurbishing the body and chassis. We detected no serious frame problems at all; the car was basically well preserved.

5. The body showed signs of former repairs, but nothing all that dramatic.

6. Body parts were found on the floor around the car, and most seemed to be in very good condition. Virtually everything was restorable.

7. The famous, or infamous, split rear window instantly identifies the coupe as a '63 model. The upper structure was in excellent original condition.

8. The old door panels would have been discarded for new ones.

9. A minor accident tore up the right rear quarter panel, but basic repairs had already been made. There was still a fair amount of work to do on this panel, though.

10. Since it was ordered new as a race car, this '63 coupe came without a radio, or a hole for one.

11. While it looked a bit nasty, the interior was at least complete, save for the clutch pedal and transmission shifter, which went away when the transmission was pulled.

and numbers we could check proved to be correct, although we were not able to inspect the engine as it was stored 25 miles away.

We anxiously contacted the owner of the little coupe. He assured us that all of the engine numbers and codes were correct and that the mill and fuelie unit were the original ones that came with the car. He said that the coupe was sold new at Hopkins Chevrolet in New Carlisle, Ohio, and that he was the fifth owner of the car. Also, he had talked to all four previous owners.

The '63 coupe was last on the road in 1977, at which time it struck a guardrail, which caused the right rear quarter damage we had spotted at the shop. He had purchased the car in 1981. After pulling the engine to have it rebuilt at a shop in his hometown, he hauled the car to the Corvette restoration business near us. The shop had just started working on it when he had to call a halt to the progress due to financial difficulties. He then put the car up for sale, asking $20,000. But he had no takers and, after a number of months, his personal finances had shifted back into the black and he had just instructed the shop to resume work on the car. But, he might still be interested in selling it, he said, asking that we give him a few days to think about it. We did.

Several days after, he called to thank us for our interest and inform us that he had decided to keep the car. Disappointed but undaunted, we called him a couple of days later, but he was adamant. It was the find of a lifetime for him, and he was going to follow it through to completion. Being car people ourselves, we could understand the emotional attachment he had developed for the car he'd owned more than a dozen years. After all, we'd become attached to it in just a few days!

We had missed another one, but we were still quite optimistic because the biggest Corvette meet in the country was just weeks away.

SURVEYING THE FIELD AT BLOOMINGTON GOLD

By Bob Stevens

1

2

Where else would one expect to find the Corvette of his dreams but at the most prestigious and famous Corvette meet in the world, Bloomington Gold? The 21-year-old show relocated from Bloomington to Springfield, the Illinois state capitol, in 1993, but retained its highly recognized and trademarked name.

Fulfilling the basic needs of our '63 split-window coupe resto project is as simple as attending Bloomington with your checkbook in one hand and your car specs in the other. Just pick your color, equipment, engine, transmission, and then decide which one of the several cars fitting your description is the best buy. Naturally, that's a little polyanna, but we still had high hopes as we saddled up and headed out for Abe Lincoln's favorite town.

Having attended Bloomington Gold for nine consecutive years before this season's transition meet, the author knew in advance that there would be many '63 coupes for sale in Springfield, especially with the economy still sputtering along in second gear. And there were ... probably somewhere around 30 or more.

With his mission well defined – the boss said "don't come back without a project car in tow" – the author loaded up the *Cars & Parts* hauler and pointed it west. In less that six hours, he was strolling among the hundreds of cars offered in the Corvette–only car corral at Bloomington Gold.

In just a few hours, more than a dozen split windows had been spotted. Unfortunately, not one satisfied our project requirements. Most were already restored, or needed only a partial restoration to be street/show quality.

To reiterate, *Cars & Parts* was searching for a '63 Corvette coupe that needed everything – including body work, paint, chrome, interior, tires, engine, transmission, rear end, body trim, some glass, etc. Nothing in the car corral qualified, so we waited for the auction, which was scheduled for Saturday.

The auction came and went, without depositing a '63 resto project at our feet. The '63 Sting Ray coupes offered during the auction were also too nice to be restored – actually re-restored. There were some nice solid cars present in both the car sales lot and the auction, but not one met the basic criteria established for the project.

The best buys today, as underscored at Bloomington, are in restored cars – especially ones that were done a number of years ago, when restoration costs were lower, parts more readily available, etc. It's clear that the best buy in a Corvette today is in one that is finished, not one that needs finishing.

But then we're not shopping for the best buy, we're on a very special mission ... to save another car and show the world how others can do the same thing.

The hunt intensifies!

Photos by the author

1. *This nicely refinished split-window coupe sold for $22,250 when the seller dropped his $25,000 reserve. It was painted silver, had a red interior, and was powered by a strong sounding 327 base V-8. It was far too nice to serve as a project car.*

2. *At the top of the heap among '63 coupes for sale at Bloomington Gold this year was a rare Z06, one of only 199 Vettes made that year with the special high-performance package that retailed for $1,800 and included the 360-hp fuelie engine, M20 four-speed manual transmission, special suspension, knock-off wheels, 36-gallon fuel tank, etc. The seller was asking $79,500 for his five owner, numbers-matching Z06. It was silver blue with the standard dark blue interior, a pretty combination.*

3

4

3. Representing a great buy in a non-original coupe, this Daytona blue '63 sported a frame-off restoration, including a rebuilt 370-hp LT-1 engine and a fresh four-speed transmission. The fuelie tags, of course, were for show only, and the engine, side pipes and knock-offs were not original; but the good looking Vette was priced at just $20,000, a steal in a sharp, good running split-window coupe that was ostensibly correct in general appearance.

4. This little number, painted red with a saddle interior, had the 300-hp engine, four-speed transmission, radio, etc., but no price tag.

5. Beautiful Riverside red '63 fuelie coupe was on the lot at $37,500. It was very nice – too nice for our purposes. So was an all-black 340-horse coupe with 82,000 original miles, fresh paint, new carpet, repro seat covers and a price of $26,900.

6. An NCRS (National Corvette Restorers Society) Top Flight car, this all-black '63 coupe had the optional 340-hp engine, four-speed, tinted glass, knock-offs, whitewalls, radio, etc. All numbers and codes were correct. It was

We never did catch up with the car's owner, who was from Iowa.

bid to $33,500 but seller was looking for $39,000. He did agree to take $38,000, but there were no takers. Once again, the car was much more than we needed, and priced way out of our league.

7. This red-on-saddle coupe came the closest to being a legitimate project car. It needed everything, including some body work, paint, interior, etc. But it had an incorrect grille and a non-original motor, a later model 350 V-8. The price was $16,900, and that was negotiable. We thought about it, but passed, still hoping to find an example with its original engine still on board.

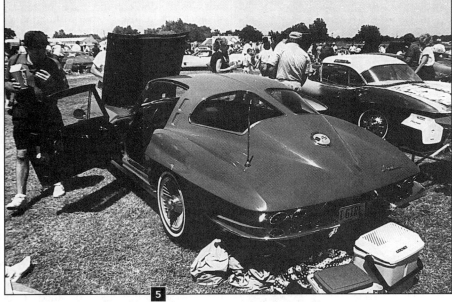

5

6

7

SORTING THROUGH DOZENS OF LEADS

By Bob Stevens

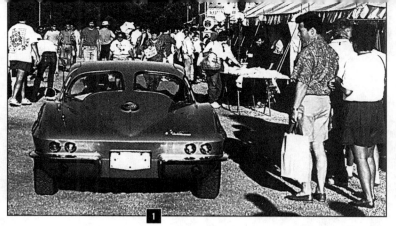

1. *Another one gets away: This Sebring silver '63 coupe sold for $24,500 at the Auburn '93 auction in Auburn, Ind.*

It's often suggested in car circles that the search for a collector car, whether one is looking for a project car or a restored jewel, is more satisfying than the actual purchase. This is like the sportsman who derives more enjoyment from tracking down wild game than bagging his limit; in other words, the thrill of the hunt exceeds the thrill of the kill!

In our case, the actual hunt has been very interesting, and quite rewarding. However, we may have short-circuited the entire process by sharing the early stages of the adventure with our readers.

Announcing our project car search through the pages of the magazine was an open invitation for owners of '63 split-window Corvettes to approach us about their cars. And, yes, we have entertained a significant number of proposals. They include several from car owners who volunteered their pets as restoration candidates, with us sponsoring the restoration and following along with a series of articles. However, they would *keep* their Corvettes at the conclusion of the project. We respectfully declined all such offers, since we planned from the beginning, upon completion of the restoration project, to give the car away in another *Cars & Parts* sweepstakes or a raffle of some sort.

Aside from that, though, we did receive a number of solid leads. In fact, more than a dozen proved to be of serious interest, at least to the point of checking them out in person. And, that's what we intend to do in the weeks ahead.

Among the cars on our current prospect list are: White-on-red split-window coupe with a 350-cid V-8 out of a Chevelle, in Canada, but comes with a correct 340-hp engine; a battered but complete old fuelie in the Midwest for $25,000; a Daytona blue coupe that's partially disassembled in Pennsylvania; a silver '63 with base engine, four-speed and all correct codes and numbers, located in the East with a price in the mid-teens; and, believe it or not, a genuine Z06 (one of only 199 made) that needs a total remake but is complete and the real thing (fuel-injected racer with

the big brake package but not the 36-gallon tank). What a project that would make – a genuine Z06 Corvette, one of the rarest and most desirable of all Corvettes, and the king of the '63 line! At press time, though, we had not yet received a price on the car, and we're quite confident that it will be substantially beyond anything we could handle without donating our own paychecks to the cause.

Some other candidates that have surfaced and may soon be checked out are an automatic-equipped coupe in northern Ohio that is 85 percent complete and priced under 20 grand, and a Sebring silver split window with the 300-hp 327 and four-speed powertrain. The latter is located in Michigan and is in the possession of its owner of 17 years, who just completed a 500-mile trip in his original engine coupe.

Also a prime prospect is a silver blue '63 in nice original condition. It has the 300-horse motor, four-speed and a dark blue interior, and not much else. While the author will be checking out the cars located in Michigan, Pennsylvania, New York, etc., this little number will be personally inspected by the publisher ... it's located in Florida and the weather up north is becoming sort of cool this time of year ... rank has its privileges.

Also, at press time we learned of an el cheapo split window, one priced under 10 grand. Obviously, it needs a total remake, but that's what we want, anyway. It's in New York – Long Island, to be specific – but we also have a candidate hidden away in Massachusetts. This one also needs a complete resto, and is powered by a 350-cid V-8 (originally, it was a 300-hp 327). It's on its third owner and has all new brakes, an incorrect hood, solid frame, four-speed tranny, and a clean, non-hurt body that was originally silver blue but has been completely stripped.

There are another dozen or so on our shopping list, any one of which could prove the chosen one.

Originally, we thought that such an extensive field trip would not be necessary, since we were attending Bloomington Gold, the huge Corvette meet held annually in Illinois. But we fired nothing but blanks at Bloomington this year. Last year, if memory serves, there were several ideal candidates for sale at the granddaddy of Corvette

meets. But then, approximately two months later, we also had Corvettes at Carlisle, which is staged every year in Carlisle, Pa. This event, held toward the end of August each season, is actually a bit bigger than Bloomington (at least in terms of the swap meet, general attendance, etc.), but no match for Bloomington in respect to prestige. Still, the car corral is typically heavily patronized by sellers, and this year, true to form, it bulged to the limits with some 300 Vettes for sale.

Only two of the Corvettes in the corral were split-window coupes. One was a silver fuelie in pretty decent shape, but needing general cosmetics. It was priced at $26,900, which was too much for our budget to accommodate.

The second '63 Sting Ray coupe was white, had an automatic transmission (a definite minus), and was in very nice condition (recent paint, chrome, etc.). It was way too nice for us to strip and restore. But it was certainly priced right for a claimed original engine car in A-1 driving condition and street/show quality paint and chrome. The seller needed only $19,900, and probably would have taken a little less.

This is definitely the prime time to invest in a split-window Corvette; more so if someone is searching for a car that is done, or needing just a little restoration work. It's a buyer's market. Prices and availability are better than they've been in five or six years, or longer. Unfortunately, most '63 Corvette coupes needing a full restoration cannot today be restored for the difference between a restored and unrestored example. Unless, of course, one "steals" the project car.

Due to the notoriety already realized with our project, it's unlikely we'll "steal" anything, but we'll certainly strike the best bargain we can. And, we'll go anywhere in our search for just the right car. In fact, we have a friend in southern California who's checking out two cars for us right now, and another associate in the northern reaches of the Golden State who will soon inspect a split-window coupe on our behalf.

Hopefully, we'll be able to announce a successful conclusion to our search soon, possibly in the next issue. Remember, we're as eager as anyone to get started on "Yvette," "Cora Vette," or whatever we decide to call her ... or him!

1

2

Photos by author

1. *This silver split-window coupe was very nice – way too nice for our project. It had an automatic transmission, power steering and brakes, power windows and genuine Chevy knock-off wheels. Originally powered by a 300-hp 327, this slick little number now carries a fuel-injected 327. The fuelie unit is off a later model. It was priced at $29,500, complete with fuel injection and the set of knock-offs.*

2. *Under the hood of the silver car was the surprise of the month ... a fuelie system, dating to 1965. It obviously wasn't correct or original on the coupe, but was a topic of conversation, nonetheless. And, we're told, it functioned beautifully.*

STILL NO PROJECT CAR,
BUT WE'RE GETTING WARMER

By Bob Stevens

There's no concrete evidence to support the contention that we're getting close to finding our next project car, but we can feel it. The '63 split-window Corvette that we're going to restore is not parked in our garage yet, but it's just a matter of time before we connect with the right car at the right price. We can sense it.

With dozens of leads to chase down, and precious little time between meets (Auburn, Hoosier, Fall Carlisle, Hershey, etc.), we've made little progress in the past month. However, we contacted a number of dealers specializing in vintage Corvettes, and we've had several interesting possibilities served up. One dealer in California had two '63 Corvette coupes, but both were a bit too nice for our needs. The same was true of another West Coast dealer, except that he had three of the special coupes available, two in stock and one coming in on consignment.

We also had conversations with dealers from several midwestern and eastern cities, including one in Florida that has a pretty interesting candidate. That coincides nicely with our plans since we already have one car to be checked out in the sunshine state.

Right in our own backyard, the great State of Ohio, there were several Corvette dealers who offered up examples, but all were either too nice, too expensive or had an incorrect engine or undesirable paint color.

At one Ohio dealer's showroom, we found three '63 Corvette coupes, while yet another Ohio dealer had no fewer

3

4

3. *In the showroom at one dealership, we found this all-tan coupe sporting an off-frame restoration. It was equipped with an automatic, original 300-hp 327 V-8, power steering and power windows. The price was a digestible $28,900. It was definitely too nice for our project, though.*

4. *On one dealer's lot, we found this tan '63 coupe with a tan interior, 340-hp 327 engine, four-speed, and radio delete. It needed paint and detailing, but not much else. The dealer was asking $26,900 for this high-horsepower version. We passed on it; it was too nice to be completely disassembled and restored.*

than five in his inventory. A nice selection, and just an hour or two from home. But none of them were quite right – not even the silver car with the '65 fuelie unit mounted on its 300-hp 327 engine. That car, admittedly, was an appealing novelty, if nothing else. It also had an automatic trans (an instant deductible), power steering and brakes (both pluses), and a set of nice original knock-off wheels (get out the checkbook). At $29,500, it wasn't too bad a deal; and, it could have been bought for considerably

less money, minus the wheels and fuelie system.

Although we enjoyed talking with the major Corvette dealers around the country, our phone inquiries and in-person visits produced no solid results. But, we're about to embark on a couple of weeks of roadwork that will carry us to several midwestern and eastern states as we inspect some 15 split-window coupes that we have ferreted out in recent months. One, we're sure, is meant for us.

By Bob Stevens

Recent stories describing our newest restoration mission, and specifically our search for a '63 Corvette coupe, have generated an avalanche of leads. We've literally been inundated with new prospects; some have proved promising, while others have already been dismissed for one reason or another. The latest batch, though, should produce the winning candidate.

The examples presented in the accompanying photos are all solid prospects, but we have several more to check out yet. We learned of a couple in Tennessee, but one had been badly mangled by a customizer, and the other was a fuelie that was missing not only the fuelie unit but the engine as well. Yet a third one from the Volunteer State had a correct but non-original engine in place, and was complete, running and ready for restoration. It was priced at "about $15,000."

A reader put us onto a fuelie in New Jersey, but it was priced at $33,000, a bit rich for our project needs. We also stumbled onto an original Z06 Corvette, one of only 199 made. The $1,818 option included, among other things, the 360-hp fuel-injected engine, 36-gallon fuel tank, and knock-off wheels. However, the owner of this car knows what he's got, and has priced it accordingly ... in the mid-thirties.

Other possibilities included a red-on-red 340-hp coupe in Milwaukee, priced at $24,500; a 300-hp silver blue '63 in Norwalk, Mass., at $15,000; a stripped split-window with non-original engine for $9,500 in northern Ohio; a '63 coupe needing a complete restoration in Long Island, N.Y., owner was asking $9,800, but it sold before we learned of it (half a dozen readers advised us of this one); a silver coupe in California priced at $23,900, but too nice for our needs; an 85-percent complete coupe with new tires and suspension for $19,000 on an Ohio Chevy dealer's used car lot; a nice red-red coupe in San Jose, Calif. priced at $21,000, including a set of original knock-off wheels; and an $8,000 restorable '63 coupe that sold in the Cleveland area before we could get to it.

Obviously, there is a lot of potential out there for anyone wanting to restore a '63 Corvette coupe. We even found a genuine parts car, complete with body frame, suspension and differential, all for $3,200. The availability of unrestored or partially restored '63 split-window coupes is actually much better than we had anticipated. The selection process will therefore be a bit tougher now that we're narrowing it down to several very promising candidates. Among them are the cars from Michigan, Pennsylvania, Florida and Ohio pictured in this report.

With everything from parts cars to restorable fuelies and Z06 coupes coming our way, we're bound to net one...and soon! Meanwhile, we're still enjoying the hunt.

STILL ENJOYING THE HUNT

Photos by the author, except where noted.

1. Jack Smith, an insurance agent in Litchfield, Mich., has owned this spiffy little split-window for 17 years. It's an 85,000-mile coupe with its original running gear, shifter, engine shielding, etc. The car was repainted 20 years ago and needs to be painted again, but is otherwise pretty decent. In fact, it's far too nice to be totally restored.

2. The interior of the car in Michigan is serviceable, but could use some freshening. The black interior complements the Sebring silver exterior. Options include the 300-hp 327, four-speed, AM-FM radio, whitewalls, tinted windshield and the paint (a premium of $81 was charged for Sebring silver). All codes and numbers were correct and matching on this car. It was fairly priced at $21,500.

3. The 300-horse engine in Smith's Vette started and ran fine. This prospect needs little to be a nice street/show coupe, probably too little for our purposes.

4. Another candidate for our project surfaced in Pennsylvania. The owner is Jack Miller, who owns a body shop in Elizabeth, Pa., which is where we found this neat old coupe about ready to undergo some body work. Miller had just started disassembling the car and stripping the body when he read about the Cars & Parts project and thought his car would be excellent for that purpose. It's definitely a strong contender.

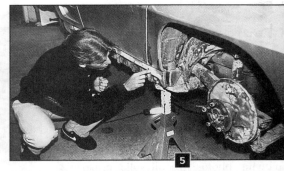

5. Staff writer Eric Brockman examines the lower body of Miller's car. The car is very solid and straight, although some major body work will be needed, mostly on the front clip.

6. Unfortunately, Miller's car has the base 250-hp engine. Fortunately, it's original with matching codes and numbers.

7. All gauges, including the tach, are correct and in working order. The black interior does need a complete refurbishment, though, but that's what a resto project is all about. One thing with this car, it is 99-percent complete and comes with a lot of new parts, including stainless steel exhaust, grille, mirror, antenna, rocker moldings, tires, etc. Original wheel covers are also included. Miller wants $16,900 for everything.

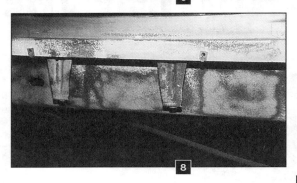

8. The frame on the Pennsylvania car was very solid ... no serious problems anywhere.

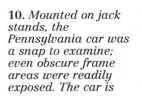

9. Up against a wall in Miller's body shop, the hood was easy to inspect. It's fine.

10. Mounted on jack stands, the Pennsylvania car was a snap to examine; even obscure frame areas were readily exposed. The car is loaded with options, including Powerglide automatic, power steering and brakes, AM-FM, whitewalls, Sebring silver paint, etc.

11. *Close to home, although we caught up with the car at Corvette Expo Fall in Knoxville, Tenn. this past October, this black '63 coupe is the property of Jerry Black, Dayton, Ohio, who is seen here with his son Brandon in the car corral at Expo. The car was hit once in the left rear quarter and repaired, but not very well. Otherwise, it's a super straight, solid split-window that needs very little. Priced at $18,900, it's road-ready now, but could use some cosmetic freshening, but not enough to suit our goals. The car is very correct in terms of numbers, codes, etc., and has had only three owners. It was built on Jan. 15, 1963. It has a saddle interior, and lots of new parts, including exhaust, battery, air cleaner, fuel pump, etc.*

12. *Located in Florida, this sweet little number is the silver blue color. It's straight, solid and ready for restoration. It's in the temporary custody of Classic Chevy International, Orlando, which took it in trade on a restored '57 Chevy Bel Air convertible. It's priced at $17,900. (Photo by Joe Whitaker, Classic Chevy Int.)*

13. *The dark interior is complete, serviceable, correct and presentable. Options include the AM-FM radio and four-speed. (Photo by Joe Whitaker)*

14. *The original engine is still on board, and it's the optional 300-horse number. It runs, but needs to be rebuilt. (Photo by Joe Whitaker)*

15. *The car shows no evidence of ever being hurt in a catastrophic way. It's also complete and running, and all numbers and codes are correct. The wheels, of course, are incorrect, being later model Chevy rally wheels. (Photo by Joe Whitaker)*

OUR SIX-MONTH HUNT NEARS END

By Bob Stevens

The barn door creaks open and falls to the ground with a startling thud as the top hinge surrenders to years of rust, use and Midwestern winters. A few streaks of light slicing through the barn's weathered boards dimly illuminate the huge, dark interior. Barely visible in a far corner is that unmistakable shape of a vintage Vette ... a first generation Sting Ray ... a split-window coupe! At last, our search for the elusive *Cars & Parts* project car has struck gold ... the mother lode, in fact. Before our eyes as a crumbling old tarp is peeled away, appears a complete, original, red-on-red fuelie coupe. What a find ... and it's all ours!

That's the scenario we'd conjured up in our dreams and played over and over again in our minds as we searched diligently for our latest project car. But, alas, our mental fabrications have been dashed. It just hasn't happened, and we can't wait any longer.

The last few weeks of our search have been filled with a grand assortment of potential winners. There was the 300-horse red-on-red car in San Francisco, but it was too expensive at $21,000 and too far away (another $1,200 or so to ship it back to Ohio, not to mention the grand it would take to send a staffer to the coast for a personal inspection). Another car that was too far away was one in Richland, Wash. There was also a split-window coupe in New Mexico, but while the price of $12,000 was appealing, the logistics were again an expensive proposition. Besides, it had a non-original motor, and we would still like to latch onto a car that had its original mill in the engine room.

Also having a newer powerplant under its hood was a '63 coupe in Northern Ohio that was available at just $9,500, complete and running but needing everything. In the same category was a Corvette coupe with a modern 350 Chevy V-8 in it from Eastern Pennsylvania, and a modified '63 coupe in nearby Lima, Ohio. In addition to having a 350 engine out of a '70 Corvette, along with the automatic transmission out of the same late-model Vette, this example also had a custom one-piece nose minus the retractable headlights.

One car that we tracked down seemed ideal, on the surface at least, but it turned out to be another dead end. Located in Albion, Mich., the car seemed perfect as it was being described over the phone. It was red with a red interior and

had a numbers matching optional 340-horse engine partnered with a four-speed. Just what we wanted, and priced at $20,000 or best offer. Imagine our disappointment when the seller added that his '63 Corvette also had a new top. Yes, it was a convertible, not the fabled split-window coupe we'd decided on for our project. For a few moments, at least, the adrenalin was pumping.

There were several features we didn't want. One was the base 250-hp engine, and another was the Powerglide two-speed automatic transmission, which killed off a Sebring silver coupe in Flint, Mich. that had both features, and no other options. It also had a frame in need of repair, but that would make an interesting sidelight of the project, and new frame pieces are available. Two more coupes with the slushbox tranny were a silver blue number from Muskegon, Mich., and a white split-window from Dallas, Tex. The latter example had two strikes against it, since white was a color on our "no" list. Also, the Michigan car was not silver blue originally, but rather black, another color not on our recommended list.

Oh, yes, we did find another parts car, or possible builder, in eastern Pennsylvania. The ad stated that the purchase included a '63 coupe body, frame and miscellaneous parts. In the same city, Johnstown, Pa., there was a Daytona blue coupe with the 300-hp 327, but it was a bit to nice with all rebuilt running gear. The nice driving coupe was priced reasonably enough at $19,500.

A rare, low-priced Corvette project car of mid-year vintage was located in Rochester, Minn., but it was white and already had its engine rebuilt. The price, though, was just $12,000. An other bargain basement special was a silver 340-horse coupe for only 10 grand, but it had been hit, and hard. Two more spotted recently were just $15,000 each, but one had a non-original motor and the other had been about 30 percent restored already.

Also crossing our trail this past month was a pair of real fuelies. Only 2,610 fuel-injected Corvettes were assembled in '63; it was a $430 option. Unfortunately, the one, a black coupe in Butte, Mont., now carries a late model 350 where a 360-hp fuelie once ruled. It's also set up for vintage racing, which is correctable, but its original engine was parted out years ago. The second fuelie,

a silver blue coupe needing a total restoration, sold several days before we heard of it and called the seller in Coral Springs, Fla. Both were priced at $22,000.

Wearing an identical price tag was a black-on-saddle '63 Corvette with its original 300-hp 327 still at home. It had been repainted red in 1976 and non-authentic side exhaust was added four years ago. It now wears reproduction knock-off wheels. The original color, black, was a problem, though.

We also found an ad for another Z06 Corvette, the big-tank fuelie coupe of 1963. But this one was minus its engine and fuel-injection system, so we didn't even waste a call. The same lack of response was afforded a matching-numbers coupe in Ypsilanti, Mich., that was priced at $29,500 – too much for our budget to handle, and quite pricey for a non-show-quality coupe with the base 250-hp engine. Another Michigan car, a silver one in Northville, also pushed the envelope price-wise at $20,000 for a car needing restoration.

Surfacing close to home were two '63 coupes that were pretty strong contenders, at least initially. The first was a black-on-black coupe with the 340-hp 327, four-speed, knock-offs, AM-FM, etc. It was located just 60 miles away and was worth the trip to see it in the flesh, but it left the factory wearing a coat of saddle tan paint and a saddle interior. Also, it had been modified to accept side exhaust, which was not available in '63.

The second local car, which was about 90 miles down the road, was an even better bet. It was Daytona blue and a black interior and had come from the factory that way. All codes and numbers matched perfectly. It was complete, original, running, non-modified and had the desirable 340-horse motor with the optional four-speed. It needed a total restoration, but was very solid. There was some frame rot and undercarriage rust and the interior was in just serviceable condition, but we were prepared to give it everything it needed, and then some. It was priced fairly at $15,900. But the timing wasn't there. We were on deadline and couldn't get down to Cincinnati to see the car for a few days. In the interim, it sold.

If nothing else, Star Search 3 has produced dozens and dozens of restorable '63 Corvette split-window coupes, given us a good education in the first-year Sting Ray, and introduced us to many new friends. It's been fun! 📷

Yes, we have a project car!

Right at press time, *Cars & Parts* hammered out an agreement over the phone to acquire one of the '63 Corvette coupes described during our multi-part Star Search 3 series. The car is ideal for the project at hand, and will be introduced next month.

1

At Last ... Our Project Car Is Found

By Bob Stevens

Photos by Joe Whitaker, Classic Chevy International

1. *Cars & Parts Magazine's newest restoration project car is this 1963 Chevrolet Corvette coupe, representing the first year of the sensational Sting Ray. This is the third such project undertaken by the magazine in the past 10 years, but the first Corvette.*

It all started with a phone call from Joe Whitaker, vice president of Classic Chevy International, the Orlando, Fla. based 31,000 member club for owners of 1955-57 Chevys. We knew Joe from his help as a technical advisor on our last project, the '57 Chevy Bel Air convertible restoration.

"We've been following the series of articles on your search for a '63 Corvette coupe project car," he said. "Well, we took a '63 Corvette coupe in trade on a restored full-size '57 Chevy ragtop, and we think it might be a good candidate for your project."

As he described the car, he piqued our interest. It was one of our chosen colors, silver blue, with one of our favorite interior shades, dark blue. This meant it would photograph well in color, as well as black and white, all the way through the project.

Even better, all of its major numbers and codes matched precisely. The engine was the original 327 that the factory installed back in '63, and it was the optional 300-horse edition, another plus. Also adding to the excitement was a four-speed manual transmission, although it's controlled by an aftermarket shifter, a superior Hurst unit that will be simple to replace with a stock system. The wheels are also wrong, he added, identifying

them as Chevy rally wheels off a later model car. A set of wheel covers from a '64 model also comes with the car.

Other than the 300-horse V-8 and the four-speed manual, the car had only a few options: an AM-FM radio, whitewalls, and Positraction real axle. When new, the car stickered for $4,748, which included $491 in options added to the base coupe price of $4,257.

It was one of 21,513 Corvettes made in

2. *The '63 Corvette coupe, which celebrated its 30th anniversary this past year, has been a favorite of collectors because of its distinctive "split" rear window. It was the only year that the Corvette coupe featured the famous, or infamous, split, which was deleted in '64 because it distorted and obstructed the driver's rear view. Today's vintage Vette driver isn't concerned with what's trailing him, so it's no longer a problem.*

2

3. *Powering this car is the optional 300-horsepower engine. It reportedly runs okay, but needs an internal update, as well as an upgrade for lead-free fuel. At least the car won't have to be towed or pushed everywhere in the early stages of the project.*

4. *Emblems are in good to very nice condition, but will be replaced by new-old-stock or repro items so as to not detract from the beautiful body and paint work that will grace this little number in a year or so.*

5. *The '63 model was the only one to feature small decorative trim plates on the hood. The rectangular sheets were originally checked, but time and the elements have faded the black squares. The plates reside in indentations that have built-in drain holes.*

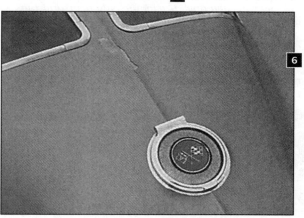

6. Large chunks of paint are separating from the body. The body itself, though, is very straight and solid, not showing any evidence of major problems, old or new.

that first year of the Sting Ray, 1963, which was also the first year of the coupe body style in the Corvette series. The breakdown between the two versions in 1963 was 10,594 coupes vs. 10,919 convertibles. The coupe, of course, featured a slender panel through its rear window. That styling feature would separate it from other Sting Rays, as it was dropped for the '64 model year.

After some deliberation, and comparison with other cars under consideration, a staff member was dispatched to inspect the car. His report was positive in all respects. The car was a very strong candidate, indeed. It was sound, straight and fairly complete, and had never been seriously modified. It also appeared to be free of any major accident damage. The frame was solid and intact. The body showed no evidence of major problems.

This candidate, unlike many we looked at, even ran pretty well. It

was fully roadable, in fact. As we were told, it would make a nice driver as is, but to be really nice a total restoration would be in order.

It showed its age. The paint was bad and the interior was in need of upgrading. The mechanics were old and worn and it had an incorrect rear end gear. That, of course, will be changed. The wheels were wrong, but they will also be changed. (A nice set of knock-off wheels would certainly add a lot more pizzazz than an original set of wheels and caps.)

The major numbers and codes are all matching, and the serial number indicates that the car was a late one, number 20,317 out of the 21,513 cars built that model year. Also, the body was the 10,114th made out of the 10,594 coupe bodies built that season. The car, according to its date code, was assembled in the fourth week of July, 1963.

The fact that this is a late car is

7

8

7. *Some splotches can be detected as one gets closer to the car. At a distance, though, it doesn't look bad at all. The wheels are incorrect, but that will be rectified.*

8. *Corvette Sting Ray emblem appears on the right rear of the coupe. It was the first year for the use of the Sting Ray name.*

9. *The cockpit-style interior is very inviting, and this one is still pretty serviceable. Still, it will be thoroughly refurbished as needed to bring it up to street/show condition.*

fortunate. Because early ones had certain peculiarities that make them much more difficult, and expensive, to restore. Some of these differences between early and late models were seat bottoms, gas filler door mechanisms (nylon slide catches replaced roller-type units in later models), painted (early) vs. vinyl (later) dash area around the radio and speaker grille, fiberglass buckets gave way to metal units for the headlights very late in the model year. The source for the four-speed manual tranny was changed from Borg-Warner to Muncie during the model year, and an outside mirror of a different design was adopted about midway through the model year.

Tackling a later model would be a simpler, less frustrating task, so we've been told by several '63 models, but they can't be documented to everyone's satisfaction. We'll explore this area more as the project progresses.

Since the car is located in Orlando, Fla., at Classic Chevy International headquarters, we'll have an opportunity to road test our new towing system, the Chevy Suburban and Trailer World enclosed hauler depicted in last month's issue. Also, we'll be able to exchange some Ohio snow and freezing cold for Florida sunshine.

But we'll be back ... at least by the spring thaw, and with our new project car in tow. Then the real fun starts!

**Next Month
Taking delivery**

9

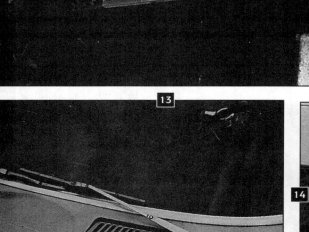

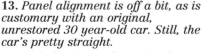

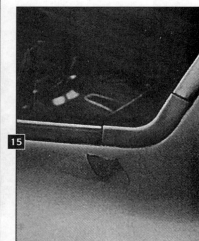

10. *Destined to be replaced by a stock unit, the shifter is a superior Hurst unit. When properly restored and set up, though, the original Chevy system works fine. Fortunately, this example is fitted with the optional four-speed transmission, a necessity to squeeze all that power out of the 327 V-8.*

11. *In the storage area behind the seats are the wheel covers that come with the car: a set for a '64 model. We'll trade for a set for a '63.*

12. *The VIN plate and trim tag reside on a bar under the dash, right below the glove box. The VIN - 30837S120317 - is decoded in this fashion: 3 = model year (1963); 08 = series (Corvette); 37 = body style (coupe); S = assembly plant (St. Louis, Mo.); 120317 = sequential production number (beginning with 100001; 20,317th car built that model year). The trim tag shows that the car is a '63 model coupe, with body number 10114 (10,114th coupe body made that model year), paint silver blue (paint code 912A) and featuring a dark blue interior (trim code (490J). The K4 date code, which is also found on the trim tag, indicates that the car was assembled in the fourth week of July, 1963. This would be right at the end of 1963 model production, which coincides with the production sequence number (car number 20,317 out of 21,513 built that year).*

13. *Panel alignment is off a bit, as is customary with an original, unrestored 30 year-old car. Still, the car's pretty straight.*

14. *Door fit is actually pretty decent for an unrestored car. With the coupe in particular, door alignment is critical.*

15. *The paint is cracking, peeling and chunking ... just that much less for us to have to strip away!*

16. *The all-important engine block casting number seen here - 3782870 - is correct for all 327 Corvette engines used in 1963 (as well as 1962 and 1964).*

17. *Door panels are in decent shape and could be used, but a total restoration means just that ... total!*

18. *All the instruments are original, and will be rebuilt as necessary. It's certainly a nice car to start with though.*

19. *The '63 Corvette coupe sits pretty well. It doesn't appear to ever have been hurt in a major way.*

Classic Chevy Int'l.

Photos by the author

1. *The new* Cars & Parts *project car prepares to bid Classic Chevy International farewell. A call from one of the outfit's officers advised the* Cars & Parts *staff of the availability of the silver blue split-window coupe, which had been taken in trade on a restored '57 Chevy Bel Air convertible, the car that is the organization's number one celebrity. Classic Chevy Int. is dedicated to the 1955-57 Chevrolet, and CCI's 30,000 members who collect, restore and drive the so-called tri-Chevys.*

TAKING DELIVERY OF OUR 'NEW' CAR

By Bob Stevens

Classic Chevy International, Orlando, Fla., served as the primary technical consultant of the Peggy Sue project, where a '57 Chevy Bel Air convertible was restored. It was a natural since 1955-57 Chevys are the club's sole purpose for being. But when I learned that Classic Chevy's President Joe Whitaker wanted to talk to me about our new project, I was a bit confused. It turned out, though, that Whitaker didn't have advice for us, but rather a candidate for our project ... and a good one.

The car, as revealed last month, was a matching-numbers '63 split-window coupe, per our project specifications. It came with the optional 300-hp 327 engine, four-speed transmission and a photogenic color scheme of silver blue paint with the contrasting dark blue interior. The price, which was special to our project since we would be doing a service to the old car hobby by restoring the car and covering it in the magazine for the benefit of all, and then giving it away to some lucky reader, was $16,000. The only other car that came close to meeting the basic parameters of our project, was a red Z06 coupe in the Cleveland, Ohio area, but it needed many more parts, a lot more restoration and was more than double the price.

We bought the silver blue number over the phone, after staff writer, Randy Moser, had a chance to eyeball the car in between rounds of golf in the Orlando area.

A major side benefit of buying the silver blue car that Classic Chevy had taken in trade on a restored '57 Chevy Bel Air convertible was that I would get a chance to visit the headquarters of Classic Chevy Int., which counts me among its nearly 30,000 members. It would be an opportune time to see the organization's huge 80,000-square-foot facility, including its beautifully appointed showroom and its massive storage facilities that rival the biggest and best in the parts reproduction business.

Behind the fancy, modern facade of CCI's building lies a real car-guy's paradise. Up front is the spacious, well-lit showroom, where cars for sale are offered. Actually, there are two adjacent showrooms; one features everything from original cars and street-show machines to projects, while the other is reserved for fully restored, high-dollar rides. One of the latter on display during our visit was a fully restored red '57 Bel Air convertible with the dual-four setup. It was tagged at $70,000 and was just about perfect.

Sharing space in the showroom was a restored chassis for a '57 Chevy that is fitted with a variety of modified equipment, such as rack and pinion steering, a big-block mounting kit, custom wheels, power brake conversion, etc. Also present as a demonstration unit was a dash that showcases Classic Chevy's digital instrument display, tilt wheel, quartz clock, AM-FM cassette player, etc. – all custom touches that make the old Chevys more driveable.

While most of the club's parts activities are still focused on stock restorations, about 25 to 30 percent of all CCI sales are realized in modified parts, and club President Jim Bruce thinks that percentage will soar to 50 percent very soon, possibly by the end of 1994. A new rack-and-pinion steering setup for 1955-57 Chevys has attracted a wave of interest. The club works closely with manufacturers in developing such upgrades to make sure that they do not alter the basic structure of the car or dilute its design integrity. Also, all such updates can be deleted and the car returned to stock at some future date.

Classic Chevy International is a commercial club, a for-profit organization that is professionally managed and provides its members all the normal benefits of a national car club, such as a monthly magazine, *Classic Chevy World*, technical help available by phone or fax, national meets, more than 200 local chapters, and free classified ads for members. But it also offers a full range of parts, more than 4,500 of them, including many made exclusively for the club.

Membership in the club, which costs $30 a year in the U.S. ($39 in Canada, Mexico, and overseas), follows the car. In other words, when a member sells his 1955-57 Chevy and leaves the club, the membership moves along with the car, as Classic Chevy follows up with phone calls to solicit the new owner of the car as a member. The club had a growing membership overseas, especially in Germany, Sweden, Australia, etc., and foreign membership now accounts for 10 to 15 percent of all parts sales. Also, a couple of dozen cars are sold and shipped to members overseas each year.

Speaking of shipping, Classic Chevy sends out 300 to 500 packages a day from its Orlando warehouse, making the club one of the largest UPS customers in northern Florida. The shipping department operates two shifts, and all orders received by 3 p.m. are out that day, as long as the parts are in stock, of course. On extra busy days in the shipping department, all 30 full-time employees may be called on to help package orders, up to and including president Jim Bruce.

The shipping department will be getting even busier soon, as another 1,000 to 1,500 new parts will join the line of modified components being offered by

2. Jim Bruce (right) president, and Joe Whitaker, vice president, love to show visitors the '56 Corvette convertible that the club is giving away in a raffle this year. The spacious and brightly decorated showroom has a real nostalgic feel about it, thanks in part to all the 1955-57 Chevys on display and the checkerboard floor reminiscent of the '50s.

3. Heading up a line of 1955-57 Chevys for sale in the main showroom is a pristine '57 convertible wearing a price tag of $70,000. It's a beauty, powered by the optional dual-carb engine. They don't come much nicer than this.

4. A nicely restored '57 Chevy chassis gives the club a chance to show off many of its high-performance aftermarket products.

5. Step right up, grab a stool and order whatever you need to finish that 1955-57 Chevy restoration. This is the official parts counter, where cash is traded for shiny chrome trim, rebuilt generators, detailed engines, or something as simple as a Classic Chevy T-shirt. Anyone can visit the showroom and buy parts, but only club members get the big discounts.

6. Steering units are reconditioned to perfection, functionally and cosmetically, for either stock installation or an upgrade.

7. *The used parts business is big business for the Florida-based operation. That's particularly true of parts that are not reproduced, such as wheels, air conditioning components, radios, transmissions, engines, certain convertible pieces, etc. Also, a good deal of demand is still evident for rust-free original sheet metal, everything from doors and fenders to deck lids.*

8. *Joe Whitaker points out certain custom features on Classic Chevy's test mule. All club-sponsored parts are mounted and tested for fit and function before they're released to the membership, and the public at large. Non-original power steering and brake setups, rack and pinion steering systems, big-block mounting kits, etc., are representing a bigger and bigger part of Classic Chevy's business. No components are offered, though, if they change the basic structure or physical integrity of the automobile.*

9. *Classic Chevy's newest restoration project is this 1955 Chevy two-door sedan. The car has some typical rust in the usual areas and will be turned into a roarin' street machine with the entire project chronicled through the pages of the club's monthly magazine,* Classic Chevy World. *At the conclusion of the program the entire series of articles on the restoration/modification project will be packaged in book form, in a fashion similar to what the club did a few years ago on a '57 Chevy convertible it restored.*

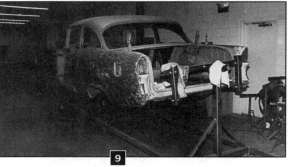

Classic Chevy. Some 20,000 square feet of space will be devoted to the new line of parts.

In addition to all the reproduction parts, the club has a complete inventory of used items, most of which are not reproduced yet. Among the used items commonly sought by the club and stocked are wheels, transmissions, power seat systems, air cleaner units, power window setups, sheet metal, steering wheels, trim pieces, seats, bumpers, jacks, flywheels, etc.

Some of the used items are restored, either cosmetically or functionally, or both, and resold to members, For instance bumpers are rechromed, steering boxes are rebuilt, engines are sent out to be machined then detailed in Classic Chevy's in-house shop, generators with correct date codes are rebuilt and sold outright or on an exchange basis, and special kits are packaged with all components, hardware and installa-tion instructions sold as a single item. There's also an in-house glass shop where correctly styled and coded glass is mounted in frames.

The showroom in Orlando is open to the public, but club members get a substantial discount on all purchmases, including new, used and repro parts, reprinted shop and owner's manuals, wearing apparel, etc. The same discounts apply to mail order, and the club's booth at car shows. Incidentally, the club sponsors five or six major meets a year, including a Winter National in Old Town, Fla., just down the road from its headquarters in Orlando, and its annual international convention, which is rotated to different sites around the country. In 1994, which marks the club's 20th anniversary, the big one for Classic Chevy will he held in Nashville, Tenn., July 3-7, 1994.

In addition, there are dozens of local meets sponsored by Classic Chevy chapters around the nation. Also, the club's big trailer can be found at about 25 swap meets a year from coast to coast. Also delivering the club's message to the public is a race car campaigned by Classic Chevy. It's a '55 Chevy powered by a 509-cid V-8 (a punched out 454) that will do the quarter in 9.5 seconds at 130 to 135 mph. Amazingly, the car is streetable.

Since the club was formed in 1974, it has dedicated itself to the active hands-on hobbyist ... those 1955-57 Chevy owners who restore their own cars, service them, drive them and show them. And many of the club's employees are car enthusiasts themselves. In fact, an area inside the club's headquarters is set aside for employees' project cars. They can store them in heated/air conditioned comfort, with full-time electronic security, and work on their cars on weekends and in the evenings after work. Club management subscribes to the theory that only true car people can understand the problems and frustrations that collector car restorers and owners face. During our visit, about 10 project cars in various stages of restoration lined the wall of the indoor reserved parking lot for employee collector cars.

Also reflecting the club's philosophy of hands-on involvement are test mules used to evaluate various products offered by the club, or being considered for inclusion in the club's huge parts catalog. Components are checked for quality, fit and finish, and where feasible, durability. The club's officers also work closely with various manufacturers to ensure that repro and custom parts are engineered and manufactured to fit properly.

A number of years ago, Classic Chevy International restored a '57 Bel Air convertible to like-new, factory-stock condition and published a book on its project. The club has launched a similar venture, but this time the car is a '55 Chevy two-door sedan that will become a street machine. As with the first project, articles in the club's magazine will chronicle the restoration, and then a complete book will be published at the conclusion of the project. The car has typical rust problems and truly needs a total restoration. The car is the type of vehicle the average guy starts with on the typical project.

As Classic Chevy International celebrates it 20th anniversary, its officers and members look forward to yet another two decades of camaraderie. The brotherhood of 1955-57 "classic" Chevy owners is as strong as ever, and like the cars they worship, will enjoy prosperity well into the next century. 📷

About the club

Classic Chevy International is located at 8235 N. Orange Blossom Trail, Orlando, Fla., and can be reached by writing CCI, Box 607188, Orlando, FL 32860-7188, or phoning 407-299-1957, or by sending a fax to 407-299-3341. Office hours are 8 a.m. to 5 p.m. Monday thru Friday.

HAULING THE CAR HOME

By Bob Stevens

Picking up the '63 Corvette project car in Florida and hauling it back to Ohio was delayed by a severe winter storm that closed all major arteries south through Kentucky and Tennessee. The freeways were closed for several days, so the trip south was rescheduled for a couple of weeks later. On the second try, we got through to Florida without a problem.

The new Chevy Suburban and Trailer World enclosed hauler were good partners, providing a stable rig with enough power, cargo space and auxiliary equipment to get the job done. Once in Orlando, Fla., the car was quickly and easily loaded, everything was checked and double-checked and then we hit the road, leaving behind beautiful 80-degree weather. We had no hint of the misery that awaited us in the mountains of Tennessee and Kentucky.

The weather turned sour in Tennessee, just north of Knoxville, and remained fierce for a hundred miles or so, keeping highway speeds at about 20 mph and putting a lot of vehicles in the ditch. The roads were iced over and freezing rain pelted the rig. Though the freeway was very treacherous, we managed to keep the rig on the road and headed in the right direction. We witnessed several accidents, including one right in front of us that claimed a Ford pickup truck. The driving was pretty tricky, but the crew returned everything safely to Ohio. The project car was shaken up a bit, but unhurt, thanks to the excellent protection of the enclosed trailer.

Hopefully, the balance of the project will go more smoothly.

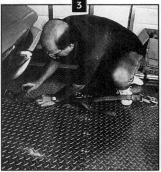

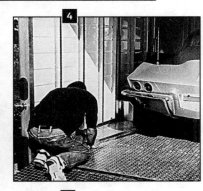

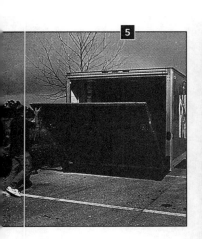

Photos by the author

1. The split-window Corvette is driven into the comfortable confines of the Trailer World enclosed hauler.

2. As the car enters the trailer, it's clear that there will be plenty of room to accommodate the little sports car.

3. Bruce Henderson of the Cars & Parts ad staff tightens down a front strap. Built-in tie-down hooks simplify the job. All four straps are secured before they're ratcheted down.

4. The rear straps are secured, one to each side. It's necessary to check the straps for tightness at every stop, as they loosen while driving.

5. Henderson closes the ramp door. The entire loading exercise can be handled easily by one person.

6. Stopping at a Shell station in Corbin, Ky., the crew found the walking a bit treacherous, with one of the staffers taking a bad fall while exiting the Suburban. The freeway was finally opening up as the salting was taking effect, but secondary roads and parking lots were ice-covered.

THE MORNING AFTER

By Eric Brockman and Bob Stevens

By the cold light of day, it would seem our new-found '63 Corvette perhaps needs a bit more work than we first anticipated. But that's always the way restoration projects seem to go.

The old Vette looked pretty decent sitting in the trailer, but looks can be deceiving in the tight, poorly-lit confines of an enclosed environment. So recently when Ole Man Winter relaxed his icy grip for a day, we jumped at the opportunity to get the car out and inspect it more closely. We wanted to have an inkling of what we'll be up against once we ship it off to the restoraton shop.

Edco Automotive, just down the road from *C&P*, gave us access to a lift, allowing us to inspect the underside of the car. What we found was typical for an unrestored car that's been on the road for 30 years – remnants of the undercoating, along with lots of dirt and grease. But the frame looks solid so far; disassembly will determine just how solid it truly is. There is evidence of some repair to the frame above the rear axle, and it looks like the rear end was removed from the car at some point.

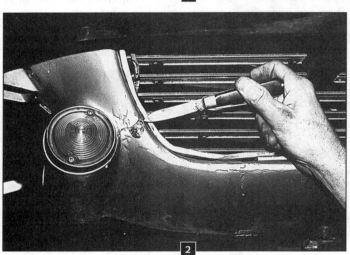

Photos by C&P staff

1. *Edco Automotive of Sidney, Ohio graciously let us use its lift to inspect the car's underside. The misaligned front bumpers give indication of an altercation with a solid object in the car's past.*

2. *Poor bodywork and a damaged grille indicate further the car was involved in a minor accident. But that's not unusual with an unrestored, 30-year-old car, so we're not too worried.*

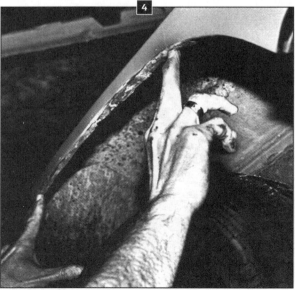

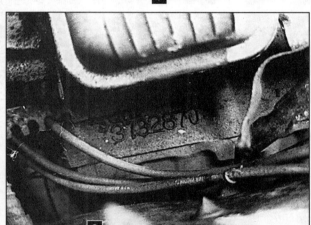

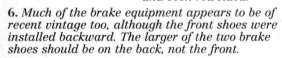

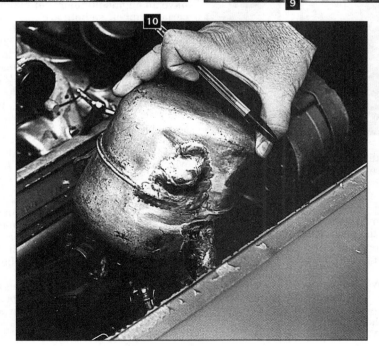

3. *The battered grille is no longer connected to the front bodywork of our Vette.*

4. *More amateur bodywork is evident in the passenger side wheel opening. The body filler seems to get thicker closer to the nose of the car.*

5. *Out back, it appears that the rear end has been out of the car at some point. This driver side mounting point appears to have cracked and been rewelded.*

6. *Much of the brake equipment appears to be of recent vintage too, although the front shoes were installed backward. The larger of the two brake shoes should be on the back, not the front.*

7. *The Carter carburetor is wrong for the car; it's apparently off a later model Vette, possibly a '65 or '66 model, judging by the intake manifold, which is also wrong for a '63. The carb should be a model 3461S Carter AFB.*

8. *The intake manifold number is 3844461, which is an aluminum intake for the 365-hp engine of 1964 and the 350 and 365 hp engines of 1965. The correct intake for 1963's 300-horse engine was 3799349, and it was a cast iron unit.*

9. *The block casting number - 3782870 - is the right one for 1963 (it's also correct for 1962 and 1964).*

10. *The surge tank is one of many items that will have to be replaced. Some major patch-work has been performed on the underside of the unit.*

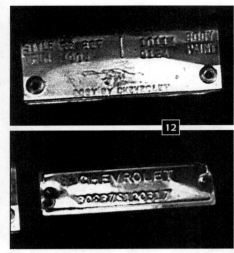

11. *At first attempt, only the right side headlights would rotate into the open position. After a couple of tries, the driver's side headlamps moved into the open position. But alas, neither side would close!*

12. *The serial number plate is mounted on a bar underneath the glove compartment. This car's VIN - 30837S120317 - decodes this way: 3 = model year (1963); 08 = series (Corvette); 37 = body style (coupe); S = assembly plant (St. Louis, Mo.); 120317 - sequential production number (beginning with 100001). The trim tag, which is found alongside the VIN plate, on the same bar beneath the dash, shows a K4 date code, which indicates that the car was assembled in the fourth week of July 1963. The body number is shown as 10114 (10,114th coupe body made that model year), and the paint code as 912A (silver blue), while the trim code is 490J (dark blue).*

13. *The interior will need complete refurbishing.*

14. *The speedometer doesn't work, but the tachometer does.*

15. *After a little fiddling, the factory AM/FM came to life.*

Up on the lift, some of our prior suspicions were confirmed; the car appears to have suffered some minor accident damage to the passenger-side front corner. The body work, as can be seen in the accompanying photos, wasn't quite up to par, and the grille still wears scars from the accident.

Back in the *C&P* parking lot, we took stock of what works and what has expired over the years. With a bit of poking and prodding, both headlights opened — but refused to close. After jostling the speaker wires around, the factory AM/FM radio came to life. The oil pressure and temperature gauges *seem* to function, but the others are dead.

One of the first steps in buying a collector car is checking the vehicle's vital numbers, particularly the VIN. The serial number on the car must match the number on the title, digit for digit. Also, certain models, such as the Corvette, have an engine number that matches the serial number, so both are important.

In our case, the numbers did, indeed, "match." The serial number - 20317 - also appears on a small pad on the front of the engine block, on the passenger side. The block number - 3782870 - is also correct for 1963. Having the original block is important to Corvette purists, and has a major impact on the overall value of the car.

We knew right away that the carb was off a later model car, and that the intake was incorrect. And, of course, the valve covers, mounting bolts, ignition wiring, etc., were all incorrect. The exhaust manifold numbers are correct.

The 327 purrs like a kitten, and overall, the car seems real strong mechanically. One noticeable exception is the brakes, which when applied pull hard to the right. But that problem can be remedied with little trouble.

We may be faced with a car possessing more "non '63" parts than we originally thought, but it's still better than a lot of the Vettes that could've followed us home.

RESEARCHING A RESTORATION ...THE SOFTWARE SIDE OF THINGS

By Bob Stevens

Paperwork is not much fun for a real car guy; he'd rather plunge into a restoration and start enjoying the parts hunt, the disassembly, the restoration of different pieces, and then putting everything back together again in like-new condition. But success in any restoration is contingent on good research. Even before a wrench is turned, the smart restorer has done his homework.

The first items to acquire are a shop manual and an owner's manual. In our case, since the car of choice is a Corvette, there is a third indispensable reference source ... the assembly manual. All three of these factory-inspired sources are chock full of vital specs, component performance data and critical disassembly and reassembly techniques.

The factory owner's manual explains how everything on the car works, from lowering the convertible top and operating the retractable headlights to replacing interior bulbs and checking for blown fuses. It's a bit simplistic for someone restoring a car, but the information is solid and helpful. The shop manual, on the other hand, is much more detailed, a lot larger, and oriented toward the how-to. It's especially helpful in fine-tuning a restored car to get everything back into spec, and back into harmonious operation. It will also prove invaluable when rebuilding certain components, such as the headlamp systems, brakes, etc. Our project car came with an original owner's manual in its glove box, and our library yielded an original shop manual.

The final member of our initial trio of factory sources is the assembly manual. This little number was compiled from factory drawings, schematics and other documents detailing the entire car down to the smallest chunk of body hardware. These books have been reproduced for most years of the Corvette and are a "must" for anyone who is taking one of these cars apart, or putting one back together. John Dragich, of Dragich Auto Literature, Minneapolis, Minn., donated a new reproduction assembly manual to the project, complete with binder and the newly published index.

In addition, there is a factory parts book that lists virtually every part for every Corvette model from 1953 through 1981. It's called the *Chassis and Body Parts Catalog – Chevrolet Corvette 1953-81*. It's a must for identifying and tracking down the correct parts, communicating intelligently with vendors, shopping for the right hardware at swap meets, etc. There are also other parts books available.

Aside from the factory paper, there are many aftermarket assists to help the Corvette restorer. Among these are videos oriented toward restoration. One of the most useful is a video entitled *Body Lift and Chassis Disassembly* by noted Corvette historian, restorer and author Noland Adams. A companion book, *The Body Lift Workbook*, came free with the purchase of the video at about $40. We'll be viewing the tape several times, and using both it and the book as reference marks during disassembly and body removal.

Speaking of Noland Adams, he contributed substantially to the new *Catalog of Corvette ID Numbers 1953-93* compiled by *Cars & Parts* Magazine, and we'll be relying on that publication for various VIN and code deciphering exercises, as well as consultations in the paint chip and upholstery sections, which are produced in full color. These are very true reproductions, just like those found in the coveted dealer's album, but neither source is 100 percent on the money, so paint formulas should be used to determine precise color mixes.

Another source of info are the magazines published that are devoted to this special breed of sports car. The newest member of this group is *Cars & Parts Corvette*, a colorful, feature-oriented magazine that covers the entire Vette scene from 1953 through to the current model year. The premiere issue of the newest offering from *Cars & Parts* is available now, with a second edition due out soon. There are, of course, several

Photos by Ken New

1. *Original factory releases, such as sales brochures, owner's manual, shop manual and parts catalog, are indispensable to any restoration. Due to the car's immense popularity, Corvette manuals are liberally reproduced.*

2. *A new entry in the field of Corvette paperwork is the* Catalog of Corvette ID Numbers 1953-93 *from the publishers of* Cars & Parts Magazine. *This heavily illustrated 255-page manual is a gold mine of information for deciphering VINs, body and trim codes, engine numbers, etc. Special full-color sections depict original Corvette paint colors and upholstery materials and colors.*

3. *Of extra help in any restoration are Noland Adams' book and the Corvette assembly manual. Both are invaluable in disassembling, restoring and reassembling a Corvette. Also of great benefit are original magazine road tests of the year and model being restored. Many of these old road tests are now captured in book form (upper right). Even if they don't help with a resto per se, they make enjoyable reading.*

other Corvette-only publications, such as the oldest independent publication still in existence, *Vette Vues*, and *Corvette Quarterly*, the official Chevrolet magazine that replaced the popular *Corvette News*. The latter magazine was typically sent free to every new Corvette owner for one year after buying a new Vette, and then by subscription. The author has an extensive but incomplete collection of older issues of *Corvette News* and has found them to be extremely valuable sources of information, although there's an obvious bias, being a factory printed medium. The author, who spent a couple of years as the editor of a trio of Chevrolet house organs back in the '70s, is familiar with the controlled circumstances under which such publications are produced and circulated.

Another factory effort that has proved beneficial, and has become the single most collectible paper item among car buffs, is the sales brochure. Distributed free when new at Chevy showroom, and sometimes even mailed to hot prospects, the sales brochure usually shows specs, standard equipment, options, new features, etc., and almost always depicts the car in color, sometimes in actual photos, sometimes in artists' renderings.

There were two main issues in the Corvette-only sales brochure for 1963. The author, who has a fairly complete collection of original Corvette sales literature has both the '63 Corvette pieces. The first, featuring a black split-window coupe on the cover, is unique in that it contains editor's marks and copy deletes that showed up in the revised edition, indicating that the one brochure came from either the Chevrolet advertising department, or the Campbell-Ewald agency that produced the brochure. This

little number, picked up from a Detroit-area auto exec many years ago, is an interesting piece and a bit more collectible than a regular brochure, although not necessarily worth any more.

Next on the agenda in our paper chase is the restoration book written by Noland Adams, an extensive and impressive hardcover edition entitled *The Complete Corvette Restoration & Technical Guide Volume 2 - 1963 through 1967* (a separate book, volume 1, covers 1953 through 1962). These two resto "how-to" books are heavily illustrated and show components in fine detail. Each is about 430 to 450 pages in length.

Also of great help is the Master Judging Manual from the prestigious National Corvette Restorers Society. This two-inch-thick manual details what to look for when judging 1953 through 1972 Corvettes. Anyone restoring a car to NCRS standards must have this manual by his side for the duration of the restoration project. The NCRS publishes a quarterly magazine, *The Corvette Restorer*, another good source of info.

While on the subject of clubs, it should be pointed out that several national organizations exist specifically for the Corvette enthusiast. These include the National Council of Corvette Clubs, National Corvette Owners Assn., Corvette Club of America, Straight Axle Corvette Enthusiasts, etc. A good source of information, as well as help, are fellow Corvette owners. The best way to tap this source is through a local Corvette club, and there are hundreds around the country. Most of the national clubs also have regional or local chapters that provide the same kind of services and camaraderie.

Intended to help in the buying and authenticating of a Corvette is Michael Antonick's *Corvette Black Book*. This pocket-style guide is small in size only, as it contains vital info on all Corvettes from 1953 to the present, including option availability, retail prices and production, engine codes, serial number info, historical sketches, etc. The same author has produced a couple of interesting resto-related volumes, *Secrets of Corvette Detailing* and *Corvette Restoration - State of the Art*. The latter work chronicles the 4,000-hour restoration of a 1965 Corvette owned by David Burroughs, the father of the Bloomington Gold Certification Meet.

Obviously, there's a ton of information and help available for the Corvette restorer, whether amateur or professional. And, as we disassemble our project car and dispatch its various components around the country for restoration, we'll be capitalizing on as many of these sources as possible. While we're not planning a Bloomington Gold or NCRS Top Flight restoration, we do want our baby done right.

4. *There are several national magazines dealing exclusively with the Corvette, including the oldest commercial publication in the field, Vette Vues, and the newest kid on the block, Cars & Parts Corvette. All fill various voids and niches on the Corvette scene. Not shown is the factory publication,* Corvette Quarterly, *which is more of an upscale modern living magazine geared to the owners of current generation Corvettes.*

5. *Clubs are great sources of info, but none is more helpful than the National Corvette Restorers Society, which publishes its own magazine (top left) and newsletter (top right). The club also offers its members a number of Corvette-related books, including its own master judging manual which will definitely prove beneficial in our restoration project. Also, the NCRS spec guide (left) is regarded as an authority on Corvette numbers.*

THE NAME GAME

By Bob Stevens

Naming the car in our first two projects was easy, as both had natural handles that just jumped out at you. The first resto effort involved a 1955 Ford Crown Victoria, so "Vicky" was the obvious choice. The second project focused on a 1957 Chevy Bel Air convertible, painted larkspur blue, so Peggy Sue came immediately to mind. Even the song of the same name seemed appropriate for that project car.

But the '63 Corvette presented a different challenge. Nothing seemed to be exactly right for this two-place sports car with the fiberglass body, the high-performance engine hooked to a four-speed tranny, the light blue exterior finish, dark blue interior, retractable headlights, a split down its rear window and the factory name of Sting Ray. So, we challenged our readers to select a moniker, offering a modest prize for the winner. The response was mind-boggling. More than 1,000 names were proposed by some 250 readers who participated in the mail-in contest.

We heard from a good cross-section of readers. Our home state, Ohio, led the nation, generating 25 entries, just ahead of California's 23. In third place was Texas with 15 entries, followed by Indiana with 14 and Florida with 13. Next was Pennsylvania with 12, and then came three states tied at 11 – Michigan, New York, and Illinois. Then came Canada and New Jersey with 10 each. Some 40 states were represented, plus Puerto Rico, Mexico, and Canada.

Many readers had fond recollections of Corvettes they'd owned, including '63 coupes, and they passed along their nicknames for their cars. Some current Corvette owners, including several who are now restoring their cars, also shared their pet names with us.

It was clear by the volume of mail proposing female names that most car lovers still regard their prized possessions as feminine (not surprising since the vast majority of old car people are male). As one reader in the State of Washington said, "Any car as pretty as a '63 split window must be named a female." Most of the contest respondents shared that sentiment. We received at least one nomination for practically every female name imaginable.

A sample follows: Sue (plus Susie, Suzanne, Runaround Sue, etc.), Ann Marie, Christy, Sally Ann, Cat Balou, Miss Amelia, Sapphire, Elijah Blue, Josie, Claudette, Maggie Mae, Polly, Sally Mae, Angie, Kathleen, Nellie, Lolita, Bonnie (and Bonnie Blue), Mary Lou, Coletta, Lilith, Dianna, Jessica, Nadine, Tilly, Wanda, Donna (and Prima Donna), Samantha, Betty, Emily, Sherry, Matilda, Billy Jean, Samantha, Pearlie, Charlotte, Sandy Kay, Monica, Ellie Mae, Daisy (and Daisy Jane), Gidget, Miss Behave, and Jane.

Male names submitted were few and far between. We thought that such a powerful, masculine car as a Corvette Sting Ray would bring a healthy number of men's names. They were basically confined to this list: Ray, Vinnie, Zorro, Bobbie Blue, Bobbie Ray, Vince, Louie Blue, Billy Blue and Rapid Ray.

There were many that played on the name Sting Ray. They included: Uncle Ray, Stinger, Split Blue, Billy Ray, Stinger Ray, Cool Ray, Blue Stinger, Lickety Split, Slick Split, Splitsville, 63 Sca-doo, Ray Vette (or Rae Vette), Split-Fire, Split-Git, Sky Ray, and Split Decision. One of the more novel suggestions reflected the cars's split personality: "Schizo."

The average respondent to the contest sent in two or three choices, but a number of readers submitted a dozen or more. The record, though was 65 names submitted by a California reader.

Celebrities of all sorts figured prominently in the contest. Among the more notable selections were Vivian Leigh, Elvis, Shelly Fab-Ray, Big Bopper, General Lee (save the thought for when we do a Mopar), Norma Jean (Marilyn Monroe), Bobby Vee, and Brenda Lee.

Several readers created very artsy entries, some complete with flip-up windows revealing their selections. A few even tried their hand at drawing a '63 split window in a manner enhancing their name selection. Unfortunately, none could be reproduced here; some of the caricatures produced were really quite entertaining. One reader from Florida used a poem to promote his suggestion: "Mary Lou and Peggy Sue ... Barbara Ann and Vicky, too." Mary Lou, incidentally, was suggested by a number of entrants.

Several cartoon characters inspired entries. One of the more interesting ones came from California, where a devoted reader used the following to describe his selection of Veronica: "Remember Archie's sultry, raven-haired (highlighted by blue), sex bomb fellow student who always chased after Reggie and his bucks ... how fitting!" The description alone vaulted Veronica into the finals.

A few readers preferred to employ a little Corvette history in naming the *Cars & Parts* project car. "If it wasn't for Harley Earl, there never would have been a Corvette," reasoned one reader who suggested the name Harley for the project car. Several others put forth the name Zora, in obvious reference to Zora Arkus-Duntov, retired chief Corvette engineer. One vote was cast for Mitch, in tribute to the late William Mitchell, chief of design at GM and another for Larry, in honor of Sting Ray stylist Larry Shinoda.

A lot of fun was had with the miscellaneous names, those that were neither celebrity-based or reflective of gender. Some of the more offbeat entries were: Blue Voodoo, Sassy Chassis, Shark Attack, Moody Blues, Fantastic Plastic, Jewel, Blue Lightning, Provette, Bondo, (thanks we needed that), Wild Sapphire, Class Act, Scooter, Blue Boy, Bad Boy, Peaches, Route 66, Apollo, and Blue Magic. A couple of variations of "Blu by U," as in blew by you, were received. One intriguing submission was Bodacious.

A few names were borrowed from popular songs of yesteryear. Among these suggestions were Earth Angel, Cherry (as in Cherry, Cherry Coupe), Blue Moon, Dream Weaver, Surfer Girl, Blue Heaven, Shutdown and many of the previously mentioned girl's names, such as Rhonda, Runaround Sue, Diana, Linda, Maybelline, Donna, Sherry, Cat Ballou, and Crystal (blue persuasion).

An Ohio subscriber thought we should name our project car after boxer Sugar Ray Leonard, because a '63 Sting Ray makes a "sweet" restoration, its second name is Ray, and its 300-horse engine should pack an awesome punch. Also they're both champions.

Coming from a long-time Nevada subscriber was a name associated with a past automotive affair. "One of the few vehicles I had with a moniker was my '63 Impala Super Sport named Marnie. The girls I dated liked the Vettes better, though, and they likely still do. Middle age doesn't change everything."

Granted, most of the finalists are girl's names, as indicated earlier. They include several drawing off or rhyming with the Corvette name, such as Cora Vette, Cory Vette, Rayette, Nanette, Evevette, Vavette, Suzette, Annette, Elizavette, Blue Velvette, Corie Vette, and Yvette. There's a good chance the winner is among this group, but other finalists still in the running include Blue, Blue Angel, Blue Max, Blue Mako, Old Blue, (or Ol' Blue), Blue Fever, Blue Eyes, Blue Velvet, Blue Belle, and Misty Blue.

Or, the eventual winner could come from this group of finalists: C.C. Rider, Thunder, Rhonda, Blue Chip, (as in investment), Mariah, Venus, Veronica, Cecelia, ("you're breaking my heart"), Connie, Jeannie (as in "I dream of"), Mona Lisa, McCoy (as in the real thing), Crystal, Fay Ray, Vanna, Susie Q (or Suzie Q), Mary Kay, Misty, Eve, Bonnie, Silver Bullet, Sybil (split personality), CAndi, and American Pie ("drove my Chevy to the levy but the levy was dry").

The decision, obviously, is not an easy one. But it's very important. We will live with the name for many years, just as we're living with Vicky, Peggy Sue and Barbara Ann. So, It must be something appropriate for a Corvette, adequate for our project, and palatable for everyone. The winner, from our group of finalists, is ... tune in next month for the grand announcement!

LET'S JUST CALL HER ... 'NOT FOR SALE'

By Bob Stevens

1. *The silver blue Vette just didn't look like an Irving, Chester, Lucille or Emily.*

After a few spring shows with our new project car in tow, staff members became so weary of telling excited car shoppers that our silver blue '63 Corvette coupe was "not for sale," that we temporarily dubbed the car "not for sale."

Naming our new project car was almost as much fun as searching for her. Yes, the '63 Corvette coupe project car has assumed a female identity. Readers' suggestions for the name were overwhelmingly in favor of a gal's handle, somewhere along the lines of 25 to 1, or more. Since most vintage car owners, restorers and collectors are men, it's only natural that their "second" passion be treated with the same kind of affection, hence a feminine moniker.

After reviewing hundreds and hundreds of entries, the list of potential candidates was reduced to a dozen or so. They included Suzette, Yvette, Blue Velvet, Annette, Blue Angel, Old Blue (Ol' Blue) Misty, Rhonda, Veronica, Venus, McCoy, Suzie Q, (Susie Q and Suzy Q), Crystal, and Sybil. The last entry, of course, plays on the car's split personality (split rear window). Except for McCoy, all the finalists were women's names, or generic, such as Blue Angel, Old Blue and Blue Velvet.

From that list, we unceremoniously trimmed out all but six: Yvette, Rhonda, Veronica, Crystal, Suzy Q, and Misty. Then the deliberating got going in earnest. Using the process of elimination, Veronica and Crystal were dropped after lengthy thought.

Then it got even tougher. Rhonda was the next name to go south on us, despite such impassioned pleas as: " I associate the '63 Corvette with California and the Beach Boys. I like the song Help Me, Rhonda ... that is the name that will ease the pain of the lost romance," according to Bryce Frey, Annandale, Va. Even more

touching were the words of William L. Shepherd, Toledo, Ohio: "I own a 1985 Corvette, which I enjoy. However, *Cars & Parts*' project cars always come out so spectacular that if by some chance I were to win the '63, I know it would look so fine, and I know it wouldn't take much time, for it to help me, Rhonda, get the '85 out of my heart. If you doubt whether Rhonda is 'the' name, see if you don't spend the rest of the day humming the tune." He was right, we did, but Rhonda was dropped from contention nonetheless.

Next to be axed was Yvette. It was a natural for such a project, but it just didn't have the pizzazz we wanted. Jim Northup, Princeton, N.J., was especially fond of Yvette, although he favored the contraction Y'Vette, as in your Vette. "This is a positive, happy name, and would bring Y'staff, all readers and everyone associated with the restoration into the project on a personal basis. It would make everyone feel that the project car was their car. And, just imagine saying to the lucky winner of the car, 'Here are the keys to Y'Vette!'"

With the choices narrowed down to two, the decision was getting still tougher, yet. Both names, Suzy Q and Misty, were ideal for this particular car and this particular project. If you think Rhonda is a catchy tune, try Suzie Q. ... It'll stay with you like indigestion from bad food, but with a much more pleasant result, of course. And then there's Misty. It has a touch of intrigue to it, no doubt enhanced by the Clint Eastwood movie *Play Misty for Me*. It also seems to be a fitting color for a silver blue car. In fact, several readers suggested both Misty and Misty Blue as names for the car.

Both Suzy Q. and Misty are perfect for the Corvette coupe, but since we can only use one, we decided on ... SUZY Q!

Although a number of readers, about 20, had suggested the name Suzy Q, there could be only one winner, judging by the earliest postmark. Well, we thought there would be only one. Yes, two readers sent their Suzy Q entries in at the same time, with a postmark of Feb. 17, 1994. Both letters traveled some distance getting to *Cars & Parts*' hometown of Sidney, Ohio, as the two winners reside on the left and right coasts. One is a man, one is a woman; one is a subscriber, one is a newsstand buyer; one is from New York, one is from California. Seems pretty evenly "split" to us.

Receiving a copy of the new Corvette Magazine, a '63 Corvette model and a copy of the *Catalog of Corvette ID Numbers 1953-93* are the contest's two winners, David K. Harder, Newark, N.Y., and Connie Watt, Petaluma, Calif. Congratulations to both for selecting the winning name and submitting early-bird responses.

Now, remember back to the song of the same name, and you'll be humming and thinking about Suzy Q. all day, and well into tomorrow. It's a catchy, cute name without being too cute, and it fits the character of our light blue 1963 split-window coupe. Also, its strong graphically, and there is that golden oldie musical connection of an old-time rock 'n roll nature.

Say hello to Suzy Q. the gal with the sparkling personality. As we restore her beautiful features over the next year or so, she'll slowly regain her sexy, spirited and fun-loving nature.

2. *The Vette's split rear window produced all kinds of creative suggestions, ranging from Sybil to schizoid, but we passed on all of them, not wanting to give our special gal a complex.*

Suzy Q Vette Resto

WE FIND A SHOP... AND IT'S OURS

By Bob Stevens

1. *Suzy Q. is backed up to the explosives and flammables building at Amos Press. The project Corvette temporarily displaced the company's lawn tractor.*
2. *Right at home, the project Vette is backed into the building. Hopefully, we will not test the building's explosive-proof construction.*

This time around we'd rather do it ourselves, thank you.

The only major criticism of our first two projects was that we didn't do any of the work ourselves. We farmed everything out to professional shops, something that few hobbyists do in real life.

Most car hobbyists, from what we've seen and heard, do much or all of the disassembly, some of the restoration work and most of the reassembly, "It doesn't take a genius or even a car guy to haul a project to a professional shop and open the checkbook," was the response we heard from some readers over the course of our first two projects. So, we decided that this project would be different ... this one would carry our brand.

We will be handling the first few stages of the project ourselves, including the disassembly of the car, removal of the engine and transmission, pulling the body, stripping the chassis, hauling the engine and tranny to the appropriate shop, carting the body to a restoration facility and delivering the frame to yet another shop. This will enable us to experience the project on a first-hand basis, just like the majority of our readers.

We may even attempt some of the more difficult chores ourselves as we work our way through the project. Several of the professional shops that will be working on the car during the next year have already indicated that we could perform some of the actual

restoration tasks ourselves, with their guidance and supervision, of course. As you can see from the following stories, the project is well underway. The car has taken up temporary residence at Amos Press, which owns *Cars & Parts*, as well as a number of other hobby publications, a daily newspaper, several suburban weekly newspapers and other properties. The maintenance department for the company has a large facility, behind which is a smaller building about the size of a two-story, two-car garage. This sturdy structure is called the explosives and flammables building because it was specially constructed to contain a fire and withstand an explosion of non-nuclear velocity. It's where all the explosive and flammable products used by the company are safely secured. Now it's also home to Suzy Q.

While we're disassembling the car, we'll be reporting on every maneuver,

both in text and photos, and hopefully suggesting a few tips along the way. Then we'll let the professionals take over for the body work, the engine rebuild, the painting, the interior refurbishment, the instrument rebuilding, the tranny overhaul, installation of the new brake and fuel lines, etc.

Although we won't be restoring the car ourselves per se, we'll certainly be much more involved in this project than we have been in past efforts. We've never been afraid to get our hands dirty, we've just never had the opportunity to become personally involved in a company project of this type. We're therefore looking forward to this project with a keener interest than we have past efforts.

Follow along as we guide Suzy Q. along the road to a complete restoration ... structurally, functionally and cosmetically.

SUZY Q

Vette Resto

BUILDING A BODY DOLLY

By Eric Brockman

Once the Corvette body is off the frame, there has to be something to put the body on – preferably something substantial to maintain the structural integrity of the body, with mount points matching those of the frame, and mobile enough to facilitate moving the body around during restoration.

The guide we're using in the disassembly process, *The Body Lift Workbook*, by Corvette authority Noland Adams, includes detailed instructions for a homemade body dolly similar to the ones used by Chevrolet to move Corvette bodies during the manufacturing process.

With a copy of the bill of materials in hand, we took a quick trip to the local lumber yard and hardware store to pick up all the materials. There were no hard to get materials or fasteners on the list. Back at the shop, we were able to construct our own body dolly in an afternoon using common hand tools from our stock at home.

We were fortunate to have the use of a table saw and band saw but the cuts could have been made with common hand saws. Other tools included a 1/2-inch drill with a phillips-head screw driver, a couple of wrenches, a socket set and a carpenter's square.

The book provides dimensions for cutting the various pieces, and detailed drawings of how to put all those pieces together, plus info on which fasteners to use at each location. Although we adhered closely to the measurements recommended by Adams, we didn't follow the list of fasteners to the letter and substituted wood-screws for nails. We wouldn't want the dolly to collapse and damage its precious cargo or injure someone.

Space precludes a detailed blow-by-blow account of constructing the body dolly, but for more information on obtaining the workbook, write to Noland Adams Enterprises, Inc., 527 State St., Newburgh, IN 47630. 📷

Photos by Eric Brockman and Dean Shipley

1. Our finished dolly is ready to receive the Corvette body as soon as we've finished disassembly. With a few common tools, we were able to assemble it in an afternoon.

2. A trip to the local scrap yard netted a set of casters for $7. They might not look like much, but they're good enough to get the job done.

3. Cutting the 4x4s on the table saw required a couple of swipes though the saw.

4. Lag screws were used to fasten the major components together. Noland Adams' plans waste no materials. Only a handful of scrap wood remained from five 2x4x8s and one 4x4x8 once our dolly was completed.

Suzy Q
Vette Resto

BODY DISASSEMBLY

PART 1

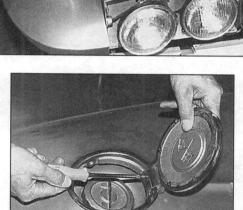

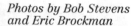

Photos by Bob Stevens
and Eric Brockman

1. Assisting us, as we faced the seemingly formidable task of disassembling our Corvette, were books such as (from the left) the factory shop manual, assembly manual, chassis and body parts catalog, and owner's manual.

By Eric Brockman

W e heard the cries from some of our readers about how we were missing the mark with our projects by turning them over, in their entirety, to professional restoration shops. Many of you said you did much of the work yourselves, and didn't have the finances to let a restoration shop handle the entire project.

After consideration of many, many alternatives, we decided to take some of the advice to heart and turn a few wrenches ourselves. The main portions of the restoration – paint and body work, chassis restoration, engine rebuilding – will be handled by several different restoration facilities, but it was decided we would take a crack at disassembling the car ourselves as well as doing a fair share of the reassembly.

Our parent company, Amos Press, provided us with space

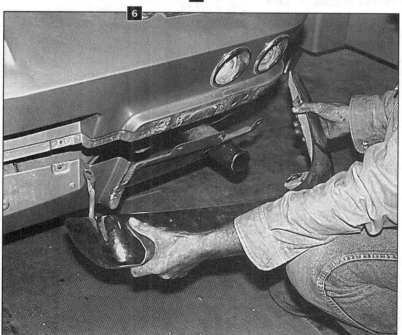

2. We started with a screwdriver, removing the gas filler lid and its accompanying trim ring.

3. To begin the process of removing the rear bumpers, we first removed the license plate trim piece.

4. Technically, we probably should have removed the bumpers before unbolting the valance panel, but those are the sorts of "learning mistakes" that are often made in a restoration.

7. *With the rear bumpers removed, the valance panel came right off.*

8. *The panel showed signs of repairs that were not very well done, and were beginning to crack again.*

9. *We worked our way to the front of the car, where the next pieces to go were the front bumpers. Each side utilizes brackets that are not interchangeable from side to side.*

10. *The rocker moldings also had to be removed. They are held in place by several screws and a retaining strip behind the top edge of the trim piece.*

5. *Bolts on either end of the panel have to be accessed from underneath the car. We discovered that the bolt mounting tab on the right side of the valance panel had been broken.*

6. *Removal of the rear bumpers is difficult, due to limited access to the backside of the bumper bolts. Unbolting the valance panel prior to removal of the bumper aided access to the bumper bolts somewhat.*

in the company maintenance garage to begin the task. Aiding us in the disassembly process was Noland Adams' excellent video, *Body Lift and Chassis Disassembly*, and its accompanying workbook, which detailed the steps necessary to lift the body from the frame. His book also provided instructions for making a dolly to set the body on after lifting it from the chassis (see the accompanying story in this issue for details on construction of the body dolly).

The first steps toward getting the body and frames separated involved removal of a number of key components on the exterior of the car and under the hood. Noland Adams' *The Body Lift Workbook* provided a detailed, step-by-step checklist for the disassembly process.

For us, the obvious starting place was the bumpers, front and rear, followed by the hood. With the hood out of the way, we were able to more easily access the

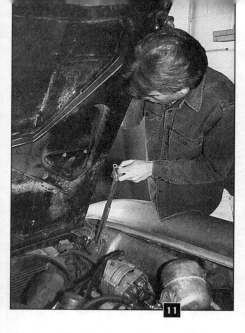

11. *Once the hood was disconnected from the hinges, the hood prop was also removed.*

12. *The author (left) and Art Director Ken New then carefully lifted the hood and brought it forward off the car.*

13. *The hood hinge bolts were temporarily put back into their respective holes in the hood, until we had an opportunity to properly bag and label them.*

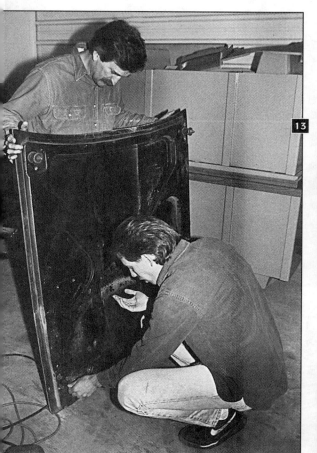

engine compartment to begin making the appropriate disconnections there. As we progressed along, we carefully bagged and labeled all parts that were removed from the car.

With editorial deadlines against us, time didn't permit us to get to the interior of the car or finish making the appropriate disconnec-

tions underneath the car. But with only a few more hours of work, we'll be ready to tackle the body mounts and then pull the body off the frame.

We're still getting our feet wet, and progress is a little slow at this point, but we are making progress. And learning a whole lot about Corvettes in the process.

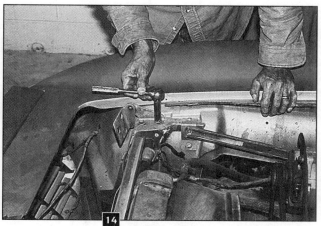

14-15. *The hood hinges and hood prop were then removed from the car, labeled, and stored.*

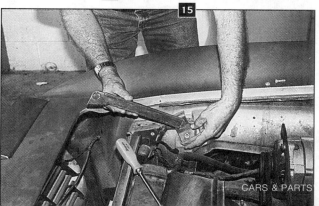

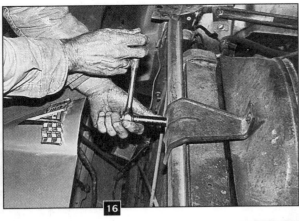

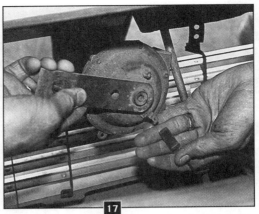

16. *With the hood hardware out of the way, we turned our attention to under-hood disassembly. The fan shroud support bracket was the first item to go.*

17. *The horns were removed and the wiring disconnected. Nearly as important as bagging and labeling parts is labeling wiring that is disconnected.*

18. *We then disconnected the horn wiring at the horn solenoid.*

19. *With the horn solenoid removed, the voltage regulator could then be disconnected and removed.*

20-22. *After draining the cooling system, the surge tank was removed by disconnecting the overflow line to the radiator (photo 21) and the heater hoses (photo 22). The heater hoses refused to come off at the firewall, so they had to be cut.*

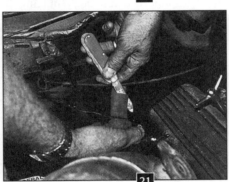

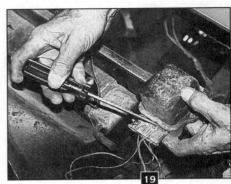

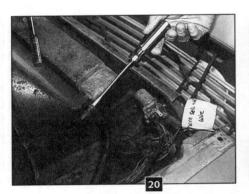

23-24. *Removing the grille wasn't essential for lifting the body off the frame, but it would have to be done sooner or later. It's removal revealed broken grille mounting tabs that will have to be repaired. See arrow.*

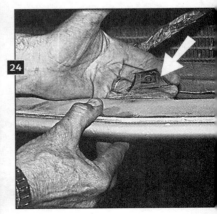

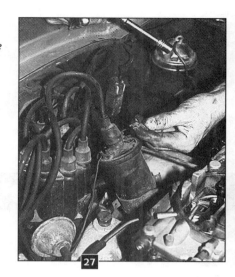

25. *Having disconnected the battery for safety reasons before beginning disassembly, we elected to totally remove it at this point. With the battery out, we disconnected the wiring to the starter.*

26. *Continuing to disconnect the wiring harness, we removed the alternator.*

27. *The wiring to the coil was also removed. We then took off the coil, plug wires, and distributor cap.*

28. *This tangled mess of wires and tags was once the car's wiring harness.*

29. *We turned our attention back to the radiator, removing the upper radiator hose and thermostat housing.*

30. *After that, the fan was unbolted and removed. Next month, we'll remove the radiator and continue disassembly of the car, including removal of the engine and transmission, lifting the body, etc.*

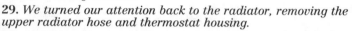

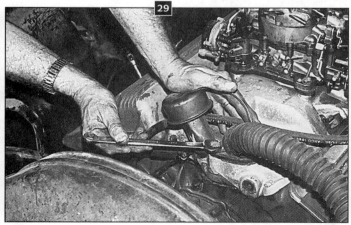

Suzy Q
Vette Resto
BODY DISASSEMBLY
PART 2

By Eric Brockman

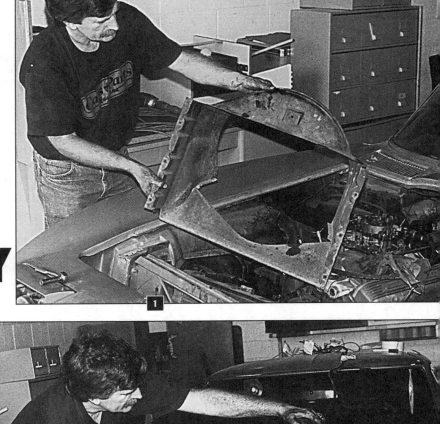

When we ended last month, Suzy Q was slowly but surely coming apart. In this installment, we'll finish the disassembly process, remove the body bolts, and prepare to lift the body from the chassis.

After removing the radiator and disconnecting the steering column, we moved underneath the car and disconnected the emergency brake, various ground straps and the antenna. The interior came out of the car, and we elected to remove the doors. Most restorers don't recommend removing the doors from mid-year coupes, but the passenger-side door did not close properly and would have had to come off eventually for repairs and adjustments.

As we moved to the body bolts, there was some concern as to how frozen in place the bolts would be after all these years. Much to our delight, only one mounting bolt proved stubborn – and all it took to get it out was a little patience. The rest came out with little or no difficulty.

Once again, Noland Adams' *The Body Lift Workbook* was a valuable resource, containing diagrams showing the location of each body mounting point. With the initial disassembly completed, we rolled the stripped shell out of the garage and drafted all available *Cars & Parts* staffers to help us lift the body from the chassis.

Everything went smoothly, which was quite pleasing, considering we are rookies when it comes to disassembling a Corvette. We might have made a couple of mistakes, but that's how you learn. And we have definitely learned a lot about Corvettes in a few short days. 📷

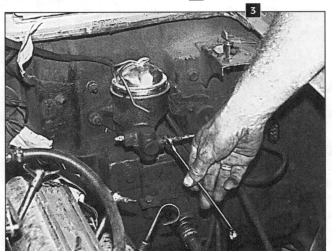

Photos by the author

1-2. *Continuing with the disassembly process, the fan shroud and radiator were unbolted, and each was removed.*

3. *The brake line to the master cylinder was removed.*

4. *The steering column doesn't have to be completely removed in the body-lift process. The bolts are removed at the joint shown, and the shaft separates into two pieces.*

5. *The clutch linkage was disconnected from the pivot arm, and the clutch return spring also was disconnected.*

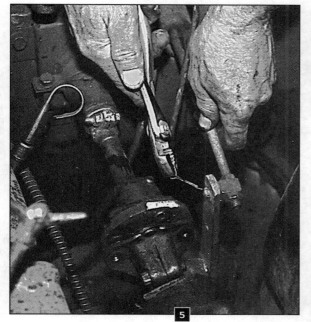

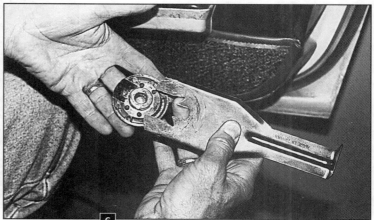

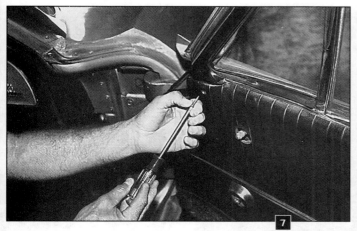

6-8. *Moving back to the interior, the door lock handles, along with the window and vent cranks were removed. Then the door panel retaining screws were removed, and the door panels taken off.*

9. *With the door panels off, we elected to remove the doors, since the passenger side door did not close properly.*

10-11. *A number of shims were in place between the door and the hinges on each side. Be sure to make a note of the type and number of shims at each location.*

12. *With the door unbolted from the hinges, it was removed. This will also make for less weight to lift when the body is removed from the chassis.*

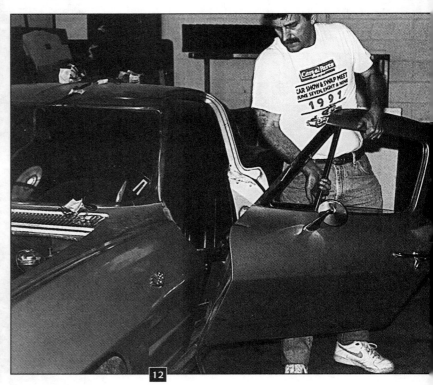

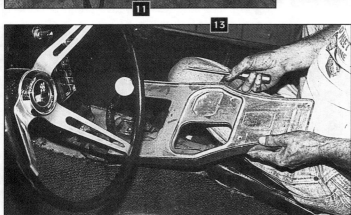

Most restorers don't recommend removing the doors on a coupe...

13. *Next to go were the shift boot and the shifter trim panel.*

14. *With the doors off the car, removing the seats was a snap.*

15. *The rocker panel trim piece was removed from each side of the car.*

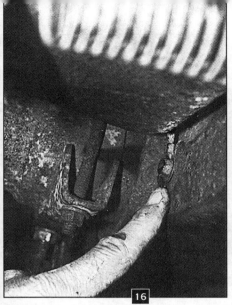

16. *Small details to watch for underneath the car include ground straps such at this one, attached to the frame cross member.*

17. *With a pair of pliers, the emergency brake return spring was disconnected.*

18. *For easier access to the gas tank wiring harness, we removed the spare tire carrier first, then disconnected the wiring.*

19. *We were then ready to move on to the body bolts – our hours of work were nearing completion. The body mount bolts are easy to locate with the exception of two that are located behind access panels in the front portion of the rear wheel wells.*

20-21. *The rest of the body bolts are fairly straightforward propositions.*

22. *The outer body bolts are ready to be bagged and stored. In addition to these bolts, our coupe also had two centrally located body mount bolts that were accessed via the passenger compartment.*

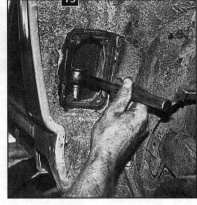

Suzy Q

Vette Resto

REMOVING THE BODY

By Eric Brockman

Disassembly was completed, and now came the moment of truth - lifting the body from the chassis. Even with fiberglass, a complete car body is a heavy item, making lifting the body the most difficult and dangerous portion of the disassembly process.

Once again, we referred back to Noland Adams' *The Body Lift Workbook* for recommended body-lift techniques. Gathering every free hand in the office, we utilized the "buddy" method, which required 11 people. In this method, four people are placed along each side of the Corvette (for a total of eight people actually lifting the body), one person acts a team leader, one rolls the chassis out from under the lifted body, and one rolls the body dolly under the chassis.

As with the disassembly process, lifting the body went fairly smoothly. A pair or exhaust hangers bolted to the floor pan had escaped our attention during disassembly, but once they were unbolted, the body came off with no problems.

The body and dolly were wheeled back into the garage, awaiting delivery to the body shop. The chassis was taken to the engine rebuilder, for removal of engine and transmission. The frame now awaits its turn for a trip to the restoration shop.

Photos by Eric Brockman
and Bob Stevens

1. *Oops! On the first attempted lift, the rear of the body hung up on something.*

Upon inspection, it was discovered we had missed two exhaust hangers that had been bolted into the floor pan of the car.

2. *One, two, three, heave! With four people per side lifting, the body separated from the frame with little difficulty. The body is heavy, so make sure everybody is lifting at the same time.*

3. *With the offending exhaust hangers removed, the body was lifted and the chassis rolled forward. Remember to put the transmission in neutral before beginning the lift procedure.*

4. *The body was then gently placed on our body dolly. The dimensions provided by Noland Adams' book fit to a "T."*

5. *With the lifting process finished, the body and dolly were pulled back into the garage until we were ready to start the body work.*

6. *The frame, meanwhile, was loaded onto a trailer. Its first stop was Comer & Culp Engines, where the engine and transmission were pulled.*

7. *Each body mount point on the frame contained a number of shims. The number of shims at each point was recorded, the shims bagged and the locations noted on the bags.*

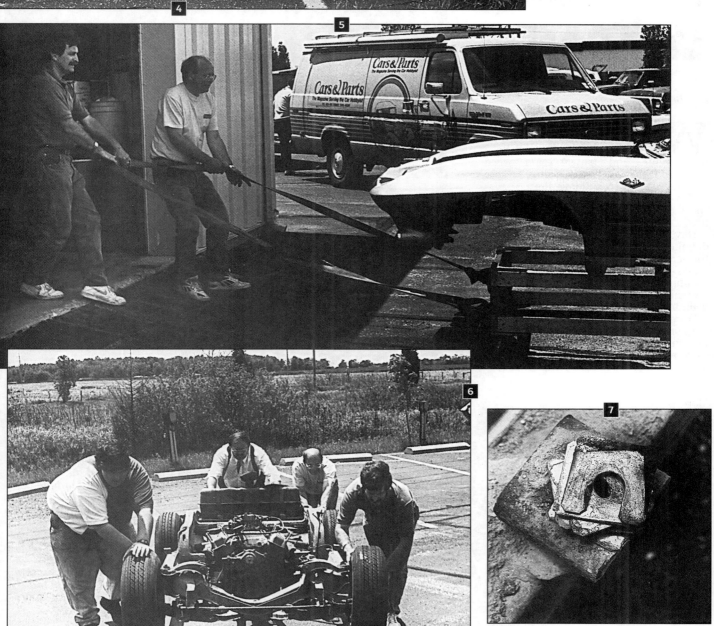

![Suzy Q logo]
Vette Resto

PULLING THE ENGINE & TRANS

Eric Brockman

With the body finally off the frame, our next stop was Comer & Culp Engines of Sidney, Ohio, where the engine and transmission were removed from the chassis. Comer & Culp Engines will be rebuilding the 327 V-8 and taking the four-speed tranny apart for inspection.

Having the body off the car definitely made the removal of the engine and transmission much easier. With the aid of an air impact wrench, it took only a few minutes to have the power train free from the chassis.

Once out of the car, the transmission, bellhousing, clutch and pressure plate, and flywheel were removed from the engine. Mechanically, Suzy Q seemed pretty sound, but the engine will still receive a complete rebuild. More than likely, the transmission will only receive an inspection, new seals and new fluid. If any problems turn up in the inspection, then additional work on the transmission will be undertaken.

We're finally starting to pick up the pace on the project. Last month Suzy Q. was more-or-less a complete car. Now she's a pile of parts scattered in several directions. Now begins the process of renewing all the parts that have been removed, and the slow journey toward reassembly into a gorgeous, like-new Corvette.

Photos by the author

1. *Upon arrival at Comer & Culp Engines, the chassis was unloaded from the trailer, and the driveshaft was first removed from the transmission.*

2. *With no body in the way, getting the exhaust pipes removed from the manifolds was much easier.*

3. *An air impact wrench made quick work of the motor mounts, and the engine was ready to be lifted.*

4. *Glenn Culp (left) raises the engine and transmission, while Earl Comer (right) makes certain everything is clearing the frame and front suspension.*

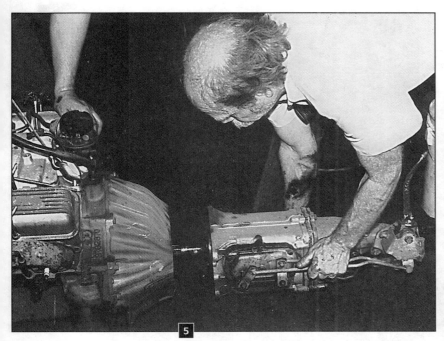

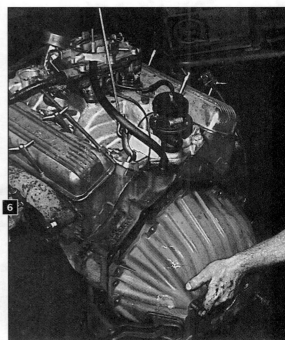

5-6. *Culp first removed the transmission, then unbolted the bellhousing.*

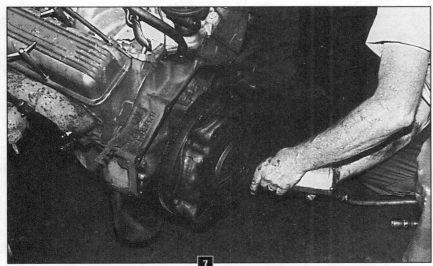

7-8. *With the bellhousing out of the way, the pressure plate and flywheel were removed.*

9. *The clutch and transmission are now just a pile of parts. In the course of a single day, Suzy Q. went from being a complete car to completely disassembled. Now the real restoration work can begin.*

Suzy Q Vette Resto

FINAL DISASSEMBLY

PART 1

By Eric Brockman

Once the body and chassis were separated, our disassembly work wasn't quite over yet. Many components on the body and chassis still had to be removed before each could be sent out for restoration.

Working in the confines of our enclosed trailer, we tackled the chassis first. Major items such as the suspension, coil springs, etc., were left for the professionals at the restoration shop who have the proper tools to deal with those items. But small pieces, such as the fuel and brake lines, exhaust system, and gas tank, were removed by us and stored for future use or reference.

All the brake and fuel lines will be replaced, but we kept the old ones for reference purposes when the new items arrive. We made certain to carefully note the routing of these lines, and sections that had special insulation attached. The exhaust will be replaced, so a hack saw made for easy removal of the old system. The gas tank, however, appears to be in decent shape and will be thoroughly cleaned and reused.

Back in our garage bay, we took to the task of removing the trim and various mechanical components still on the body of the car. In next month's installment, the glass and the

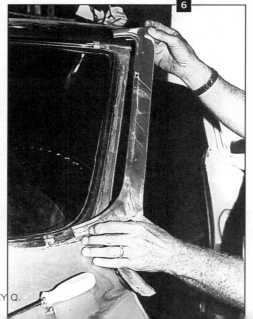

Photos by the Author

1. Since the entire exhaust system will be replaced, we elected to take the "hacksaw approach" to removal of the old exhaust. The routing of the exhaust through the frame crossmember pretty much necessitated this method.

2. The gas tank straps were unbolted, the fuel line disconnected, and the tank was removed.

3. The fuel line is clamped to the frame at several points along its length. These clamps were unbolted, and the fuel line was removed.

4. Similarly, the brake lines were disconnected from the frame at several clamps and junction blocks with a line wrench, and removed from the chassis.

5. On mid-year Vettes, the battery tray is bolted to the passenger side frame rail. It too was unbolted and removed.

6. Turning our attention back to the body, the window trim was removed in preparation for removal of the glass. Work slowly and patiently when removing the window trim, or you'll end up with damaged pieces that could be difficult or expensive to replace.

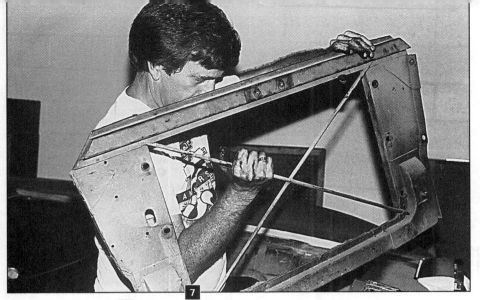

remainder of the interior will be extracted.

The main mechanical components to deal with were the steering column, master cylinder, heater blower motor, and the headlights buckets and motors. The latter proved to be the most challenging items by far. As with the chassis some items were left for the restoration shop to remove.

The body and chassis are now nearly ready for stripping, repair work, and refinishing. As this is written, much of that work is in progress. The frame, prior to any stripping, appears to be solid and in very good condition. The body, however, held some surprises when stripping was completed just prior to press time for this issue. We will show you the details next month.

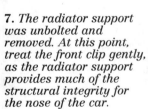

7. *The radiator support was unbolted and removed. At this point, treat the front clip gently, as the radiator support provides much of the structural integrity for the nose of the car.*

8-9. *The most troublesome items to remove at this stage were the headlight buckets, their motors and the respective hardware. This is where shop manuals and assembly manuals prove especially helpful. The holes inside the headlight buckets (photo 8) are there for a reason: access to the bolts securing part of the assembly to the nose of the car.*

10. *A few quick turns of the ratchet, and the master cylinder was removed from the car.*

11. *The blower motor and its housing were unbolted and removed.*

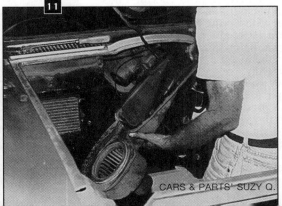

Suzy Q.

Vette Resto

THE ENGINE DOCTORS

By Bob Stevens

Suzy Q.'s heart was beating strong when we parked her for the last time before disassembling her for restoration. But while it ran fine, we knew it would need a complete rebuild to complement the rest of the ground-up, body-off restoration. To ensure that the aging high-performance mill was returned to perfect working order, the small-block Chevy V-8 was carted off to Comer & Culp Engines, a local professional shop.

Owned and operated by Earl Comer and Glenn Culp, the business has been in Sidney, Ohio, at its current location since 1982, when it was relocated to Sidney from Spencerville, Ohio. But the two engine specialists have experience going back long before that ... all the way back to the nifty fifties, in fact.

Culp, who is 52, started his career in 1956 at the tender age of 14, when he joined a Ford dealership as an apprentice mechanic. Comer, 44, launched his career when he landed a job at an auto parts store in 1973. The partners have accumulated 59 years of experience in the auto repair and parts businesses.

Culp opened his engine shop in 1969, and he and Comer began racing together in 1973. They became business partners in 1982. The business, then, is observing its 25th year of operation in 1994, and part of that celebration will be the overhaul of Suzy Q.'s 300-hp 327 engine.

Actually, reworking the small-block Chevy will be a routine assignment for Comer & Culp, as this shop has rebuilt some pretty exotic collector car engines over the years. Although 75 percent of the firm's business comes from late model car, truck, and tractor engines, including diesels, the other 25 percent is devoted to vintage power plants.

Current and recent projects include a Cobra Jet 429 out of a '70 Ford Torino Cobra, Bentley 25-30 six-cylinder 3.5-litre engine out of the '20's, Chevy 409 V-8 with a beefy 429 crank that is being stroked to 452 cubes for installation in a '50's Chevy pick-up truck, '68 Lamborghini LM-400 double overhead cam V-12, '27 Whippet four-banger, 400-cid '67 GTO engine, '69 Mopar 340 V-8 for a '69 Dodge Dart, '38 Packard V-12, '37 Chevy 216-cid inline six, '65 Dodge Coronet Hemi 426, and a '69 MG four-cylinder engine. Now, Suzy Q.'s 327 V-8 has been added to the shop's busy schedule.

There's also another special project underway ... the reconstruction of a 1964 Comet. Comer and Culp are both a couple of old hot rodders, and have owned a variety of super-hot drag cars over the years. The shop, in fact, still sponsors a race car and does a lot of work on competition mills, including boat as well as car engines. The recently acquired Comet will be built into a drag car, but one that will resemble an old factory stocker, an AFX Ford drag car. It will be powered by a Ford 351 Windsor V-8 with Cleveland 351-style heads.

One of the shop's most noteworthy projects was the 283-cid Chevy V-8 that powers Peggy Sue, *Cars & Parts'* '57 Bel Air Convertible project car. That engine went together with amazing precision, and its performance was that of a factory-new engine.

Obviously, Suzy Q.'s heart has been placed in competent hands. The mechanical doctors at Comer & Culp Engines will, in good time, revive the "heartbeat of America" once again. 🔧

About the shop

Located in *Cars & Parts'* hometown at 1604 Wapakoneta Ave., Sidney, Ohio 45365, Comer & Culp Engines is open from 9 a.m. to 5 p.m. daily, and on Saturday by appointment. The phone number is 513-492-9879, and answering the phone will be either Glenn Culp or Earl Comer, the two partners, as there are no employees.

Photos by the author

1. *Glenn Culp (left) and Earl Comer pose under the sign of their shop, Comer & Culp Engines. The Sidney, Ohio business will be rebuilding Suzy Q.s' 300-hp 327 high-performance engine.*

2. *Earl Comer operates a crankshaft grinder while regrinding the humongous crank for a Packard V-12 engine.*

3. *Comer & Culp has raced Dearborn products in the past. Its '64 Comet will be built as an AFX replica, but with a 351 Windsor engine.*

Vette Resto

ENGINE TEARDOWN REVEALS PAST REBUILDS

By Bob Stevens

When we test drove Suzy Q., we realized immediately that the engine was in sound condition. It started quickly, idled smoothly and quietly, didn't smoke, and accelerated with authority. We suspected, in fact, that it had been rebuilt to some degree, and not that long ago. Our suspicions were confirmed shortly after we tore into the engine.

The two partners at the local engine shop where we'd taken the 300-hp 327 Chevy small-block for the overhaul disassembled the engine with the kind of efficiency that only a lot of experience and the right equipment can produce. Glenn Culp and Earl Comer, of Comer & Culp Engines, Sidney, Ohio, both checked the condition of various components as Culp removed them from the engine.

The first things removed were the starter motor and the oil dipstick. No big deal there, except that the starter is incorrect for the application. The number, which should be 1107242, is 1109056, which indicates a much later starter, probably post-'72. That's not at all unusual for a 31-year-old car. We'll search for a correct one.

Stored on a metal cradle, the motor was mounted on an engine stand for further disassembly. The next item on the agenda was the fuel pump. It wasn't original and will be replaced. The same fate will apply to the distributor, which should have carried the number 1111024, but instead displayed 1111069, which means it's off a 365-hp engine of 1964 or '65. The winged high-rising

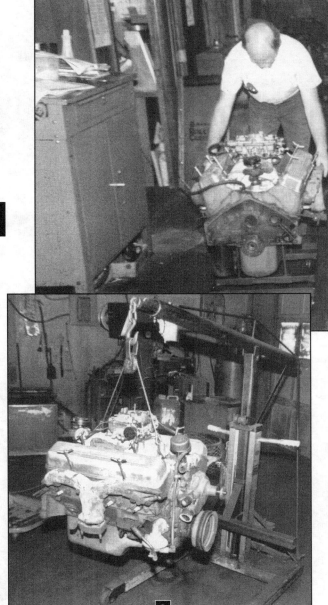

Photos by the author

1. *Glenn Culp wheels Suzy Q.'s engine to the rear of his shop for disassembly. The engine had been stored on a portable stand since delivery to the machine shop.*

2. *A portable hoist is used to lift the engine off the storage cradle.*

3. *Culp bolts the Chevy 327 to an engine stand, which will enable him to turn the engine in about any direction he wants during disassembly.*

4. *The distributor came out without a hitch, and it appears to be in pretty good shape, although we won't be able to use it.*

5. *The band around the distributor's neck is numbered 1111069, which is correct for the 365-hp Corvette motor of late 1964 and all of 1965. The correct distributor for Suzy Q. with her 300-horse 327 would carry the number 1111024.*

6. *The aftermarket custom valve cover bolts with the T-handles were quickly removed, and then off came the valve covers, which are incorrect for the 300-horse motor of 1963 and will be replaced with the proper ones.*

7. *The ridged valve covers carry Chevy number 3767493.*

8. *After loosening a few bolts, the big Carter AFB four-barrel was lifted free. The carb, model number 3318, is a service unit produced by Carter for use by another manufacturer. It does not show a Corvette application per se, but it was mounted on a Corvette intake manifold. The correct carb would be a Carter 3461S.*

valve cover bolts were loosened so the valve covers could be taken off. They are the ribbed kind, incorrect for the 300-horse motor, which should have painted valve covers with decals. We'll swap for the correct ones.

The carburetor and intake manifold are both in fine, working condition, and they were removed as a single unit. The Carter AFB four-barrel is a later model unit, and the aluminum intake manifold is for a 365-hp motor in 1964, or a 350 or 365-horse engine in the '65 model year. Both, of course, are 327 V-8s. The correct intake for the 300-hp 327 of 1963 is a cast iron unit carrying the casting number 3799349 (or 3844459 on very

late models). Since Suzy Q. was assembled in the final week or so of production, the latter number would be most appropriate, but we could slip by with the earlier one if it works out that way. Either one would carry a Carter AFB four-barrel model 3461S.

Then the engine disassemblers turned their attention to the water pump, which will be replaced by a new unit since it's of later manufacture, and the exhaust manifolds, which are correct for the

engine and will be cleaned, blasted, sprayed, and remounted. An air-operated wrench was used to remove these parts, and most other components, internal and external, from the engine. As parts were freed from the engine, all old gaskets and gasket residue were removed.

The spark plugs were then yanked. AC R45S plugs, they were gapped at .060 inch, which is way too wide for a point-ignition engine. Something around .035 inch would have been more palatable. They also showed signs of fouling from too rich of a fuel mixture. They'll be replaced with new plugs of the correct type.

Next came the heads, which are correctly numbered for the 300-horse motor. The rockers were removed, one by one, and the push rods were extracted. The rockers were showing some wear, and the push rods had evidence that they had been used in the engine going both ways. All of the head pieces are in fairly good shape, and mostly reusable, but new parts will be used. In removing the heads, it was discovered that a bolt boss on one head had been busted and was being held in place by a washer. It can be repaired, as can a second similar piece of damage.

Glenn Culp then removed, in succession, the pulley, two engine mounts affixed to the block, the vibration dampener (harmonic balancer) using a special puller, timing chain cover and the valve lifters. The lifters were determined to be hydraulic, which was correct for the 300-hp engine, while the 365-horse motor featured mechanical (solid) lifters. The lifters were in pretty sad shape and would not have lasted much longer; they'll be replaced this time, which they apparently weren't when the engine was initially rebuilt.

Next on the list were the oil filter canister and its cartridge element, and then the oil filter adapter plate. Then off came the oil pan, which necessitated removing 18 oil pan bolts. The oil and anti-freeze had already been drained from the engine, of course, and disposed of properly. The oil pump was then removed with a single bolt, and the dipstick tube was taken out, with the help of a couple of hammer blows. The timing chain and gear were then removed, along with the camshaft, which showed only normal wear. A new cam will be installed anyway.

The engine had definitely been apart, both top and bottom ends, and possibly more than once. A feeler gauge was used to check rod end play, and it was excessive on the first journal. The rods were .030 inch undersize. All new rod bearings will be used. The main bearings were then unbolted and the crankshaft removed. New mains will be used, but the crank will be reground ... again. The crankshaft number is 2680.

All eight freeze plugs were then removed. There were two on each side of the block, two in the front, and two in the back. A hammer and chisel and vise grips were used, and all the plugs were trashed.

Every major engine component was treated to a thorough cleaning in the Storm Vulcan Jet Clean cabinet. This included the block, heads, crankshaft, oil pan, timing chain cover, etc. Smaller pieces are placed in wire mesh buckets. The cleaner sprays the parts with water at 180 degrees or hotter at a pressure of 55 to 60 psi. An industrial-strength soap is used also. Each cleaning cycle takes about 25 minutes. The cabinet door is then opened and the part or parts are rinsed with clean, cold tap water, then blown dry with compressed air. The system works quite well, removing all grease, grime, sealants, etc.

Coming up next was the removal of the three oil galley plugs on one end of the block. A special device featuring an anvil that slides up and down a shaft with a

9

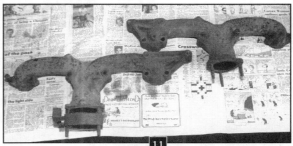

11

12

13

10

9. *Just to make sure that we weren't dealing with an incorrect engine, we double-checked the engine block, and there was the correct 300-hp casting number, 3782870.*

10. *Some quick wrenching and the water pump was removed. It was stamped with the number 3782608 and a casting date of June 28, 1967. Obviously, it was a replacement unit. We'll try to locate a correctly dated pump, but may end up rebuilding and reusing this unit, which was functioning perfectly at the time of disassembly.*

11. *The codes for the exhaust manifolds were spot on for the 300-hp engine: left, 3797901; right, 3797902. They'll be cleaned, blasted, cleaned again and then sprayed with an appropriate coating.*

12. *The spark plugs were partially fouled, and indicated a too-rich fuel mixture.*

13. *In removing the heads, it was discovered that a boss off one of the heads had been busted in an earlier rebuild and the pieces were held in place via a washer. Later, another busted boss was uncovered. Both of the breaks will be repaired.*

pistol-grip handle on one end and a large, penetrating screw on the other was used. The anvil slides up and down with the screw-end in the down position. This drives the screw into the plug, and then the emphasis in sliding the anvil is placed in the up direction to extract the plug.

The oil breather tube was then removed in pieces, along with its anchoring grommet. The tube, for some reason, had been intentionally cut. Culp then used a cam bearing removal tool to, you guessed it, remove the cam bearings. They were in okay condition, but that's academic as they'll be pitched and

replaced by new bearings anyway. Five of them are featured in this engine.

Finally, an air-operated drill was utilized to remove the oil galley plugs on the other end of the block. This method also worked quite well, although metal shavings were produced and deposited all over the engine block. But then another visit to the cleaning cabinet would take care of all that in short order.

With the engine totally disassembled, the various components can now be readied for machining work. And there's a lot of that ahead before Suzy Q.'s heart of gold is beating once again. 📷

14. *Culp lifts one of the heads off the block. Both heads, carrying number 3782461, are correct for the 1963 Corvette 300-horse engine.*

15. *The casting date for the heads, as seen here, is F223, which indicates June 22, 1963.*

16. *It was a bit stubborn and had to be tapped with a hammer, but the timing chain cover finally surrendered.*

17. *Removal of the oil pan was as easy as backing out the mounting bolts.*

18. *After removing just one bolt, the oil pump came free.*

19. *The timing chain and gear were then liberated.*

20. *Culp slips the camshaft out of the block. The cam was in pretty good shape, but starting to show signs of wear, albeit normal wear. A new one will be used.*

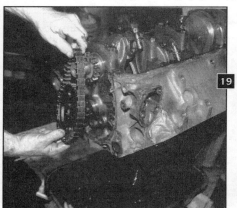

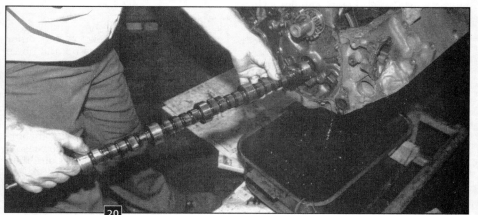

21. *All new rod bearings will be used, of course.*

22. *Culp (left) and his partner, Earl Comer, examine one of the piston and rod assemblies. The rods were found to be .030-inch undersize.*

23. *Armed with his trusty air wrench, Culp attacks the main bearing bolts.*

24. *With all the main bearing bolts loosened and the caps removed. the crankshaft is yanked. No major stress cracks or other problems were discovered in the examination of the crank, but it will be checked further and, of course, reground.*

25. *Close-up of a main bearing shows the polished condition that is created when the bearing moves around in the block. Also shown is the sizing used in the last rebuild, .030 inch.*

26. *Up-close photo shows the crankshaft's casting number, 2680.*

27. *Stripped of all its components, internal and external, the 327 V-8 block is ready for a trip through the cleaning cabinet. The steam cabinet, which uses a combination of very hot water and industrial soap, will remove all grease, dirt and oil buildup, so the engine rebuilders can better assess its condition.*

28. *After some 25 minutes in the cabinet, the engine block was rinsed with cold tap water, then blown dry with compressed air.*

29. *The crankshaft was then treated to a thorough cleansing. The heads also spent time in the Jet Clean cabinet.*

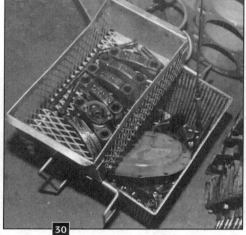

30. *Assorted other engine parts, including main and rod bearing caps, oil dipstick, timing chain cover, etc., were blasted with a steady stream of 180-degree water at 55-60 psi in the Storm Vulcan cleaning cabinet. The washing cycle is very effective and produces super clean parts, but all major parts must still be sandblasted, acid-dipped, glass-beaded or otherwise stripped before they are machined, painted, plated, etc.*

31. *A special device (not shown here) was used to remove the trio of oil galley plugs.*

32. *The breather tube had been cut off for some unknown reason. Also shown here is the grommet for the tube.*

33. *Culp uses a special cam bearing removal tool to knock the cam bearings out of the block.*

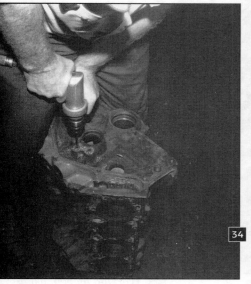

34. *A power drill is employed to remove the oil galley plugs on the other end of the block.*

35. *The block is stripped, cleaned and ready for shipment to the chemical stripping plant for an acid bath. The code G17 is the block's casting date, July 17, 1963. This coincides with the* car's assembly date, which was at the very tail end of July 1963.

36. *There are five cam bearings in the 327 V-8. All of them will be replaced with new stock.*

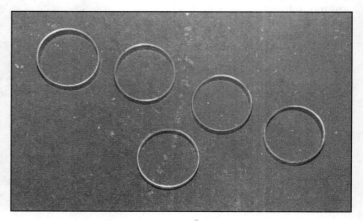

Vette Resto

REMOVING A BOLT BROKEN IN BLOCK

By Ken New

Frustration and breaking a bolt off in a casting go hand in hand to irritate the daylights out of the collector car do-it-yourselfer. Although not familar with a method to rectify the problem, most collectors are very familiar with the law of probability of breaking bolts off in engine blocks. The law goes something like this: the bolt that is going to break, will break just as the job is being wrapped up and the part left in the block is hardly visible.

Fortunately for most old car do-it-yourselfers who attempt restoration work, the necessity to get the job done by Monday morning so the car can be used to get to work is not a problem. Unfortunately, the broken bolt will not go away and it'll wait until the DIY gets around to it.

What's a feller to do? Fortunately, we have wandered onto an interesting answer to the not-so-uncommon problem. Earl Comer, Comer & Culp Engines, Sidney, Ohio, removed the stub of a broken bolt using some procedures we'd never seen before. Of course, Comer has the double advantage of experience and some professional (read expensive) equipment often not found in even the well-equipped hobbyist garage. Nonetheless, the broken bolt problem has a solution. See the accompanying illustrations.

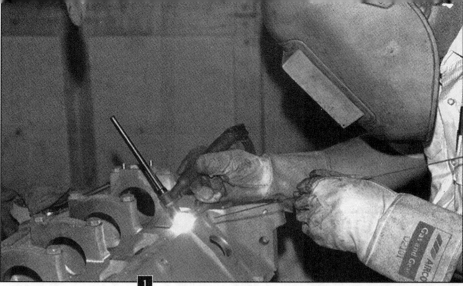

Photos by the author

1. *Earl Comer welds a cap screw nut to what remained of a broken-off oil pan nut. Comer prefers a MIG welder for its versatility.*

2. *A common stainless steel washer was placed under the nut to prevent it from welding to the block. Stainless melts at a higher temperature. Notice it didn't turn black with carbon like the nut did.*

3. *Working quickly while the nut and stub were still hot, Comer extracted the broken stub with ease.*

4. *"No sweat," says Comer as he points to the bolt hole. The threads were unharmed by the procedure. A tap will be run down the hole (as well as every threaded hole in the block) to redress the threads and remove any debris that may have gotten inside during Suzy Q.'s 30-plus years, then the hole will be blown clean with compressed air.*

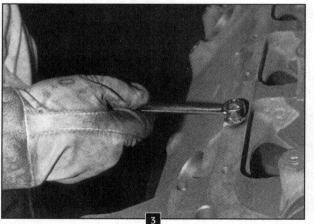

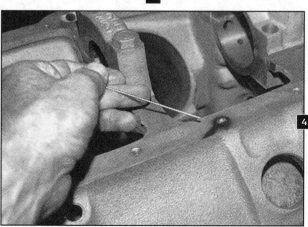

Suzy Q.
Vette Resto

ALIGN BORING

By Dean Shipley

The internal combustion engine qualifies as an incredible piece of machinery. As such, the engine's parts must be machined as perfectly as man can make them. The crankshaft bears a great deal of stress in its job of transmitting the engine's horsepower to the transmission. In its lifetime, the crank spins millions of times in response to the pistons' downward thrust, following the explosions in the combustion chambers.

So as the crank spins those millions of times, it needs a perfectly round environment in which to spin. This is accomplished through align boring.

The task of machining the main bearing housing bores back to a perfect state of round was given to Parsons Hi Performance Engine Service in Dayton, Ohio. Any reader who has been out to the drag strip any time in the last 30 years may recall the name of Garland Parsons, the shop's owner. Parsons has won several national drag racing championships and is nearly always a contender when he shows up at drag racing meets. Working with Parsons is Colin Myers, an experienced, skilled machinist who took great care in align boring Suzy Q.'s 327 cubic-inch block.

"It's important to have the crankshaft housing correctly aligned," he said. "Because all other machining operations will 'key' on the crankshaft." It's definitely a "turn" for the better.

Myers thoroughly cleaned all the parts before actually launching into the align boring process itself.

During the process, Myers champfered the hard edges to alleviate any tendency for an extremely sharp edge to break off and cause damage.

Photos by the author

1. *Inside these walls are built some of the best high-performance engines in the Midwest. The shop is located in Dayton, Ohio.*

2. *Colin Myers, a skilled machinist with 22 years in the business, loads Suzy Q.'s 327 V-8 engine block into the align honing machine. Once installed in it, the engine's bearing caps and bolts were then removed and washed in a solvent to remove any loose debris that could cause future problems.*

3. *Myers runs a tap through the main cap bolt holes to expel any debris. The holes were also scrubbed with solvent and a small wire brush.*

4

5

4. *Myers is seen here inserting the align hone, or honing bar. It is equipped with three stones, that when rotated, perform the cutting duties needed to bring the bores into alignment.*

5. *Thrust cap number five gets "a close shave" in the Sunnen cap grinder. Each cap was shaved .005 of an inch, making the diameter of the bore smaller than it should be. This would allow the align hone to take off enough metal to make the diameter the correct size again. The caps were then bolted into place with 65 lbs.-ft. of torque before the honing bar was put in place.*

6. *Myers measures the inside diameter of each bore to make sure the caps are in line.*

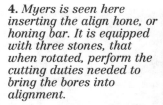

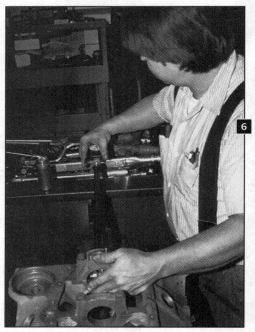

6

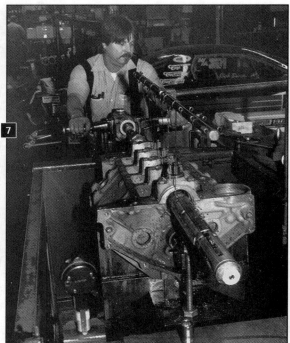

7

7. *Myers gives a hefty push-pull action on the bar through the bores. During this process, the block was rotated 180 degrees to ensure the bores remain the same and to even out the wear on the honing stones.*

8. *Myers checks the bore diameter after several passes. It's lookin' pretty good.*

8

About the shop

Parsons Hi Performance Engine Service is located at 711 Hall Ave., Dayton, Ohio 45404. It is close to the Keowee St. exit from Interstate 75. The phone number is 513-228-7278. The hours are: 8 a.m. to 5 p.m., Monday through Friday, and 9 a.m to noon on Saturday.

9

9. *Whatta buncha perfect bores! In this case, that's what we were shooting for. But don't take 'em to any parties.*

![Suzy Q logo]

Vette Resto

REBORING THE CYLINDER BLOCK

By Ken New

Suzy Q.'s 327 wasn't noticeably tired before it was broken down. No visible wisps of smoke were escaping past the rings and we didn't hear any abnormal peckings or thumpings that warned of failing engine parts. In fact, the *Cars & Parts* staff was quite pleased with how Suzy Q. could scoot along with seemingly little effort. But when the engine was broken down, serious shortcomings were uncovered that caused us to reassess our previously optimistic conclusions.

Although the engine appeared to run fine, failure of one or more of the major components was just a matter of time. In measuring the cylinder walls of Suzy Q.'s mill, they were found to be "out of the ball park" when compared to factory specs. They were out of spec in the range from .004"-.005" in one inside cylinder, to as much as .010" in one of the "corner" cylinders.

Therefore Suzy Q.'s V-8 definitely needed her cylinders rebored, the topic we'll address in this article.

While reboring cylinders to oversize is considered a routine engine rebuilding procedure, it is one that should not be taken lightly. If the cylinders are out-of-round and not straight, proper sealing of the piston rings is not possible. In fact, the fit of piston and rings is so critical experts recommend that pistons are most efficient when they snug up to the cylinders wall to within .001".

Common oversize pistons and rings sizes for domestic engines are .030",

.040" and .060" with .020" and .050" being less common sizes. Glenn Culp, Comer & Culp Engines, Sidney, Ohio, advised us that proper machining to restore roundness and straightness in a "restoration engine" takes away no more metal than is necessary to round out the cylinders. While the customary overbore for many of the assembly

5. *Once the fixtures are locked into sync on the Rottler boring machine, the boring bar will be perpendicular to the block's deck surface and to the main bearing saddles which were machined earlier.*

Photos by the author

1. *First order of business for Glenn Culp, the machinist who performed the precision boring of Suzy Q.'s block, was to make visual and tactile checks for metal burrs or debris embedded on the block's pan rail surfaces. A small chunk of welding slag was found and removed near one of the oil pan bolts.*

2-3. *Since the block sits on its pan rails when in the boring machine, Culp sanded away any abnormality in the surface that would cause an out-of-square condition.*

4. *Culp gently clamped the bare block into a large V-block which correctly aligns the block with the stroke of the boring bar. Then Culp measured each cylinder a second time to ensure that oversizing the bores to .030" would clean up all of the cylinders.*

6

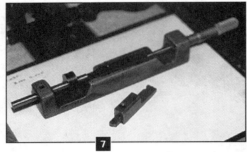

7

8. *Addressing the boring bar to the cylinders with precision was possible via an air float-air clamping system that hovers over the surface until Culp locks it into place.*

9. *Culp points to four fingers which project equally from the bar to center the carbide cutting tool in the cylinder. The cutting tip is shown just above the deck surface at this point.*

6. *A precision dial indicator revealed that Suzy Q's cylinders, while oversize from wear, weren't really that much out of round. The average out-of-round condition varied around minus .0015 to .002 thousands. One of the worst cylinders measured minus .004".*

7. *Culp explained that the cylinder bore will be cut at 4.026" which is .004" under the desired 4.030" dimension. Cutting .004" undersize is necessary since the surface produced by the boring bar is too rough for the setting of rings. The finish honing operation that follows will remove an additional .004" and bring the bores to exactly 4.030".*

8

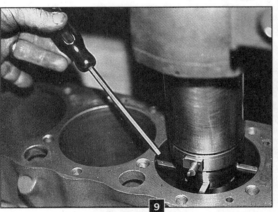

9

10

11

line rebuilders is .060" to ensure cleanup of the bore, Culp thought that was taking too much too soon. (Culp uses the term "restoration engine" to describe a segment of the shop's business which deals with engines destined for use in restored cars versus another segment which deals with race engine requirements).

Culp's initial measurements of the cylinders brought him to the conclusion that the bores would clean up at .030", the most common overbore (also the most commonly available oversize piston rings). It also maximizes cylinder wall thickness and permits rebores in the future.

Since the stock bore of Suzy Q.'s cylinders is 4.0", the boring operation will increase the bore size to 4.025"-4.026" with final honing taking the bores to exactly 4.030".

Now, follow along and study the pictures and captions closely as one of the best engine men in the business squares up his boring machine and advances our quest to restore our engine's heartbeat to full strength.

10. *It took only a couple of minutes for the cutting tool to shave the length of the bore and true each cylinder. Note the brightness of the finished cylinder at right versus those that haven't been bored yet.*

11. *A faint whisker of metal was untouched in the rear passenger-side cylinder even after a .026" swipe by the cutting tip. The difference is so slight it can't be felt by touch and the finish honing to .030" will remove it. The cylinder surface is too coarse at this point for piston rings to set properly.*

12. *With all eight cylinders machined, this part of the rebuilding operation is complete. Here Culp hoisted the block from the boring bar machine and readied it for the honing operation that will follow.*

12

Vette Resto

DECKING THE BLOCK

By Dean Shipley

Solid metal moves. So says Glenn Culp of Comer & Culp engines of Sidney, Ohio. "People don't believe metal moves around," Culp said. Supporting that statement were the head gasket surfaces, or decks, of Suzy Q.'s engine block. They "waved" at ya.

No, not exactly like poorly bondo-ed body panels; it's much more subtle than that. The movement of the metal, or warpage, may be only a few thousandths of an inch. But just a slight variation from perfectly flat decks can cause problems with sealing between the block, the head gaskets and cylinder heads. It's a very "tightly wrapped sandwich," those three, and it has to hold together in some high stress, high heat situations.

Engine operation under those conditions should be nearly perfect. That means mating surfaces should be perfectly flat.

To solve that problem, the surfaces of both components are machined to return them to their perfectly "flat" state when they were fresh from the factory. We observed the process of decking the block or making those head gasket surfaces perfectly flat.

The block was loaded into yet another expensive milling machine. With the block in place, machine operator Glenn Culp adjusted it so it would be perfectly level as it coursed its way through the process.

A spinning ten-segment carborundum stone gradually ground away the irregularities of the head gasket surfaces. It made repeated passes until the surface showed no evidence of high or low spots.

The process was done on both surfaces. The passenger side surface showed evidence of a little more stress than the driver side. The amount of material removed from the block went to a depth of .008 inch.

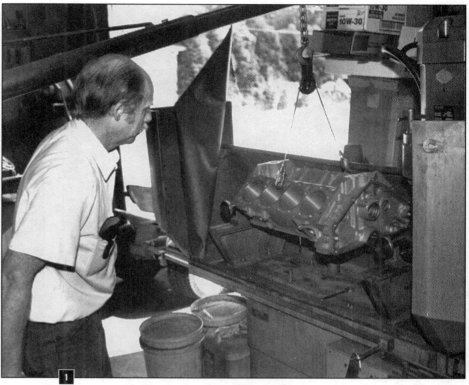

Photos by the author

1. *Glenn Culp loaded the 327 V-8 engine block into the Storm-Vulcan milling machine in preparation for the process known as decking the block.*

2-3. *With the block in the machine, Culp adjusted it so the block was level. It's very important for the final outcome.*

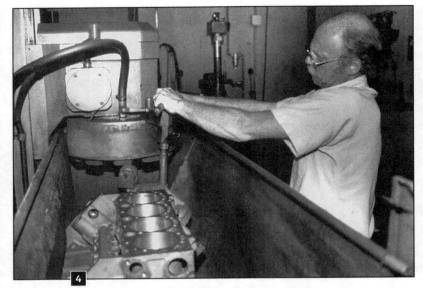

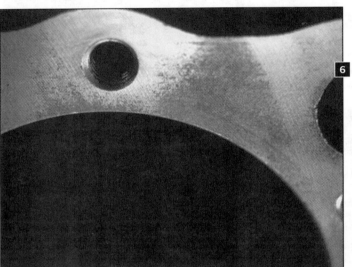

4. *A 10-segment carborundum wheel did the actual grinding of the metal. Here Culp was "dressing" the stones to make them sharp for the grinding process.*

5. *Shown here is the block with the passenger side passing under the cutting stones in a wash of a water soluble lubricant.*

6. *A close-up look revealed the cutting needed to continue. The shiny areas are those already ground by the stone. The flat-colored areas indicated the stone had not yet cut deep enough to remove the imperfection.*

7-8. *In photos seven and eight, the decks have been laid straight. Only a few more steps remain to make Suzy Q.'s block actually better than it was when new.*

Suzy Q Vette Resto

HONING THE BLOCK

By Ken New

Honing the cylinders is like the icing on the cake when applied to the boring of the engine cylinders, detailed in an earlier article. While the boring operation waged the major battle to restore integrity to the worn cylinders, honing accomplished two steps in the rebuild process. It took Suzy Q.'s cylinder barrels to exactly 4.030" oversize and prepared the cylinders to accept the 30-over pistons that will be installed in the engine reassembly.

Glen Culp, Comer & Culp Engines, Sidney, Ohio, said the surface finish inside the cylinders is a critical issue that should never be taken lightly. Culp explained the material used in the piston ring will determine what kind of finish is placed on the cylinder wall. For example, if a chrome or cast iron piston ring is used, the finish on the cylinder wall will be rather "rough." That roughness, if you will, allows oil to be trapped in the minute areas to lubricate the walls properly.

If a molybdenum (moly) piston ring is used, the surface of the wall will be much smoother than in the chrome or cast iron application. Culp selected moly rings and prepared the cylinder walls accordingly.

The extreme care used to prepare the finish on the cylinder walls will ensure longer engine life. The honing operation removed the .005" of cylinder wall metal left after the boring operation and left a crosshatched finish which will retain a film of lubricating oil once the engine is up and running.

Culp's honing procedures are illustrated in the accompanying photos and captions. The related honing of the valve lifter bores is explained as well.

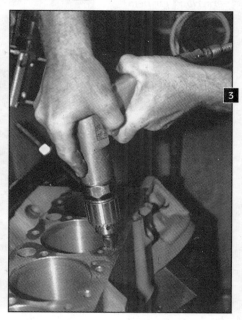

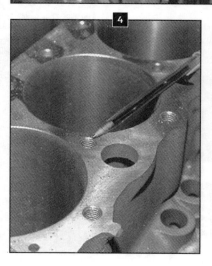

Photos by the author

1. *Glenn Culp dropped Suzy Q.'s block into the honing machine to remove the additional .005" of material necessary to bring the cylinders to .030" oversize.*

2. *After squaring the block to the honing bar, Culp chamfered the tops of the cylinder walls approximately 1/32" with a flower pot-shaped stone to eliminate sharp edges* that could cut hands. Plus the bevels make piston ring installation easier during engine assembly. The grind angle and width are not critical under normal conditions.

3-4. *Culp chamfered the tops of the head bolt bores so the threads can be pulled tightly against the cylinder heads when torqued during final engine assembly. The debris in the bores was then blown out.*

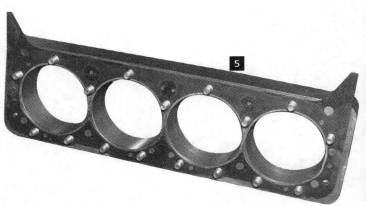

5. *This torque plate complete with head gasket was bolted to the block to simulate actual stress in the block once the engine is running. This is a step taken to fine tune the honing process.*

6. *Following the tightening sequence perscribed for head bolts, Culp applied an initial torque of 40 lbs./ft. A second trip around the tightening sequence brought the torque to 65 lb./ft., Chevy's recommended torque spec for the 327 engine. One bolt broke under the stress, leaving the threaded portion in the block casting. Culp said, "Chevy blocks are notorious for weak threads."*

7. *The holes in a torque plate are approximately .100" larger than the cylinder bores. Culp moved the honing stone fixture aside and double-checked the diameters of the cold bores to see how much metal must be removed.*

8. *As the honing commenced, lubricating oil (see white tube) was piped onto the grinding stone to wash away the minute pieces of metal removed from the cylinder walls. A 150-grit stone was chosen to begin the operation. Successive stones used were 220 and 320 grit. Proper*

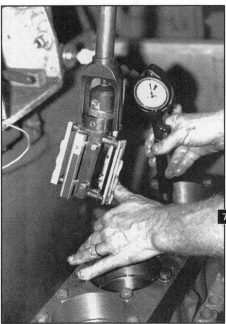

cylinder wall surface is crosshatched and sufficently abrasive to seat the rings. Honed finishes of the various ring metals (chrome, moly, etc.) are different. Dial gauge checks were taken periodically to zero in on .030" since proper ring seal is of upmost importance. The microscopic surface of the cylinders will hold a thin coat of oil and aid lubrication.

9. *Culp ran a honing brush through the cylinders to ensure no upsets in the surface of the walls remained.*

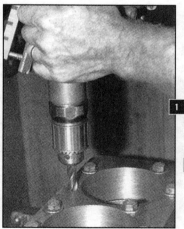

10-11. *A smaller honing brush was used to ensure the valve lifters fit freely, as well.*

12. *A thing of beauty! Suzy Q.'s block is finished and ready for assembly. Isn't it purty?*

(Note: the following photos illustrate the repair of a broken bolt that occured during the honing process (see photo 6). It is presented here so as not to distract from the continuity of the honing story.

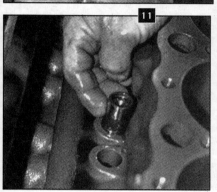

1. *Culp decided to drill-out the broken bolt with the torque plate in place. A hole slightly oversize of the original thread was drilled so a helicoil could be installed to replace the damaged threads.*

2. *A helicoil is shown here. Requiring only minimal oversizing of the original hole, the use of helicoils (made of stainless steel) is a fix endorsed throughout the rebuilding industry. Interestingly, helicoils are considered 50-percent stronger than the original threads in the casting. A helicoil is normally 1/16" larger in diameter than the original hole and has the same thread pitch as the original thread.*

3. *A helicoil tap was run down the bore to cut threads for the installation of the helicoil.*

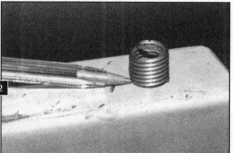

4 *The hole was blown clean. Using a special installation tool which locked into a tang on the coil (the bright section just above the deck surface) was screwed into the bore one turn below the deck surface. Designed with a weak spot, the tang was broken off easily, then the coil was stacked into place with a punch.*

Suzy Q.
Vette Resto

GRINDING THE CRANK

By Dean Shipley

1

By now you know Suzy Q.'s engine had been the motivating force in a *sports* car. It wasn't pampered. She was "rode hard," but not necessarily "put away wet." But hey, after 30 years of use, *most any* engine will show wear. Glenn Culp, of Comer & Culp engines, said the crank in Suzy Q.'s 327 V-8 not only showed normal wear but also evidence of previous grinding. But that's no sin. Grinding the crank is a necessary operation in a complete engine rebuild.

You wouldn't think a shaft of metal such as a crankshaft would "move around" in its environment, but it does. We're not talking feet and inches here, but just minute fractions of the latter. Over the years, it moves around as it spins those hundreds of thousands of revolutions per minute actually floating, if you will, on a film of oil about one thousandths of an inch thin. However, when the oil becomes dirty, those dirt particles rub like sandpaper on the metal parts. Likewise, excessive heat, as in engine overheating, can cause damage. During these situations, wear can take place. When the journals wear and get "out of round," it adversely affects other engine parts.

So the crank and rod journal surfaces are brought back to a true state of roundness that they were given when first made. This is done by taking off enough material from the journal surfaces so they become perfectly round again.

The crank was cleaned by means of media blasting. The crank was then loaded in a lathe-like machine, a Storm Vulcan RG-200. (Don't go out and try to buy one for your home shop unless you have around $70,000 to spend). The crank was leveled and secured in the machine. A grinding wheel, which will do the actual work, is selected by the operator. There are different grits for differ-

Photos by the author
1. *After it was removed from the engine block, the crankshaft was media blasted to clean it. Some residue remained on the main and rod journals,* which were about to be ground at Comer & Culp engines. Here, Earl Comer used a belt sander to remove the remaining media residue from rod and main journals. He said the residue can clog the grinding wheel in the crankshaft grinder, the Storm-Vulcan RG-200 machine.

2

2-3. *With the crank secured in the Machine, Comer chamfered the oil holes with a small stone bit. Chamfering removes sharp edges, where cracks could possibly form. A chamfered edge spreads the stress over a wider area, according to Comer.*

ent jobs. The necessary measurements were taken and the machine set up. Each main bearing journal was ground with the crank in the initial position. For the rod journals, the crank is re-positioned in the machine.

Measurements of the crank journals were taken periodically throughout the process. Suzy Q.'s crank was ground .040" under (the original diameter) on both the main and the rod journals.

After the process was completed, the crankshaft was marked. It was stamped with "CC," for the shop that did the work, and in Suzy Q.'s case, .040 for the rod journals and .040 for the main journals. That way, if the crankshaft needs to be ground at sometime in the future, the machinist will have a starting point of reference.

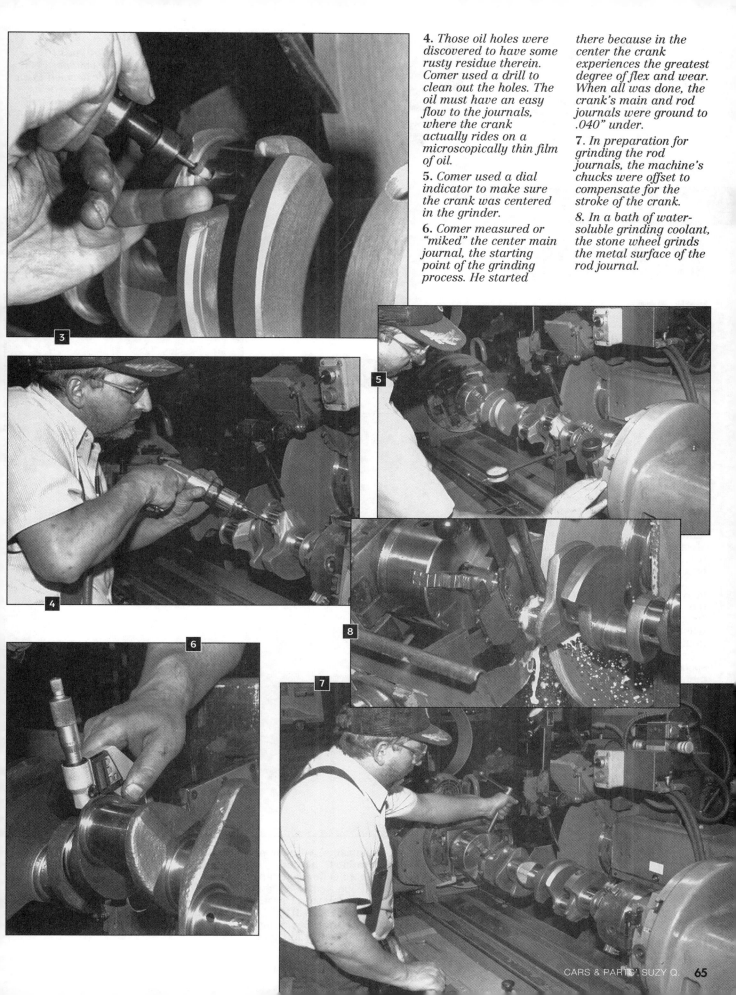

4. *Those oil holes were discovered to have some rusty residue therein. Comer used a drill to clean out the holes. The oil must have an easy flow to the journals, where the crank actually rides on a microscopically thin film of oil.*

5. *Comer used a dial indicator to make sure the crank was centered in the grinder.*

6. *Comer measured or "miked" the center main journal, the starting point of the grinding process. He started*

there because in the center the crank experiences the greatest degree of flex and wear. When all was done, the crank's main and rod journals were ground to .040" under.

7. *In preparation for grinding the rod journals, the machine's chucks were offset to compensate for the stroke of the crank.*

8. *In a bath of water-soluble grinding coolant, the stone wheel grinds the metal surface of the rod journal.*

Suzy Q

Vette Resto

RESIZING THE CONNECTING RODS

By Ken New

Connecting rods live in a very hostile envirnoment. With every stroke of the engine, they are stressed, stretched, squeezed, subjected to intense heat and even improper lubrication at times. Despite the heavy load, con rods are survivors in most applications and failure is not a common problem. Almost always, a failure in the rod area can be traced to a broken bolt or bearing that bit the dust.

Although Suzy Q.'s rods showed signs of wear and abuse, nothing more than the typical symptoms associated with "egg-shaping of the big ends" were found when Earl Comer, Comer & Culp Engines, Sidney, Ohio, inspected them. To restore Suzy Q.'s con rods to factory specs, Comer removed some .003" of metal from the parting faces of both the rods and caps to deliver an out-of-round condition in the bores of the big ends. Then, he precision machined the bores to perfect circles which matched the manufacturer's original specifications.

The resizing of Suzy Q.'s connecting rods followed a standard path prescribed for reconditioning stock production rods from a street-driven motor. All machining was directed at restoration of the big ends of the con rods. If our intentions were to prepare Suzy Q. as a viable threat in a stock class (requiring stock rods, etc.) at the drags, we would have considered spending more time and money to synchronize the figures relating to the small ends and those of the center-to-center dimensions from the small ends to the big ends. But according to Earl Comer, the master machinist who performed this block of work on Suzy Q.'s engine renewal, "That's overkill. A

Photos by the author

1. The set of connecting rods from Suzy Q.'s engine are common production run. Comer deemed them suitable for resizing. Despite being stressed, overheated, and stretched, they had been amazingly resilient. No cracks of flaws were found.

2. The rods and caps were correspondingly punched with a number of dots to identify them when disassembled. Note the dots at the end of the rod, near the tip of the pen. Some units carry markings or numbers from the factory while others (Chevy, for example) are not always well identified.

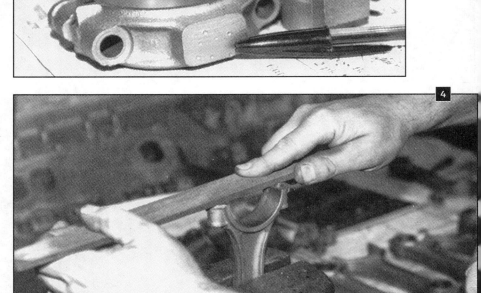

motor can be blueprinted without performing those operations," he said. "The small ends of the connecting rods are a press fit type, and the center-to-center measurements of a stock set of production rods will vary as much as .010". "We finished up with Suzy Q.'s rod varying no more than .004" from center to center," he added.

What you see illustrated here represents the precision machining Comer & Culp performs to resize eight rod assemblies for a street motor. The charge is $104. An additional charge of $65 will buy the high-torque replacement bolts Comer installed.

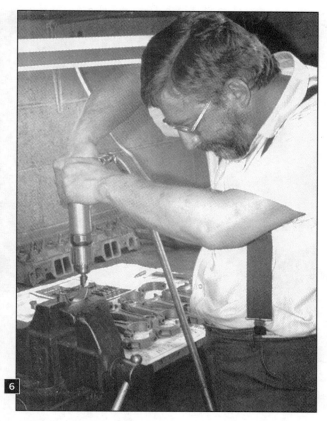

3. *Comer pointed to the scarred condition inside this rod cap and said it was a dead giveaway that "the rod and cap had been spun hard, and (unfortunately) reassembled in this condition" by one of Suzy Q.'s past acquaintances. Note that the bolt hole at right is chamfered (that's good) while the left one isn't (that's bad).*

4. *The first operation is to deburr the parting faces on both the rods and caps.*

5. *The edges along the inside of the parting faces were beveled to remove sharp edges that might interfer with "crushing" of the insert bearings once the engine is reassembled.*

6. *Chamfering the bolt holes insures that the parting faces will be in perfect contact. If this is not done, the threads will pull slightly above the parting faces when the rods are torqued into place and perfect contact will not be possible.*

7. *Under close inspection, you can see that the rod cap at front is chamfered at the right end while the one at rear is not. Note that the holes at left of both caps are counterbored eliminating the need to chamfer them.*

8. *Comer & Culp's shop is well equipped to handle precision reconditioning of rods. This primo Tobin-Arp rod and cap machine is a standard in the industry.*

9-10. *Comer shaved some .003" of metal from the parting faces of all rods and caps to purposely reconfigure the big end bores out-of-round and to correct any misaligment that was present. Almost always the removal of .003" of metal is enough to clean up the faces. The maximum that Comer would consider grinding away before using a replacement rod and cap would be .010"-.015."*

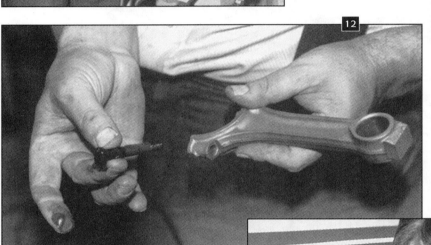

11. *All rods and caps were blown clean, then a very thin layer of heavy-duty moly grease was applied to the parting faces.*

12. *Another dab of moly grease was rubbed on the new replacement rod bolts and they were pressed into the snug-fitting bores of the rods. Failure of con rods, although rare, usually occurs in the fasteners. Suzy Q.'s stock rod bolts were discarded in favor of Manley 8740 moly bolts (#42181), premium replacements that are 50-percent stronger than the stock parts.*

13. *A special rod and cap vise was employed to insure that the rods and caps were in alignment when bolted together.*

14. *The initial torque was 40 lbs.-ft. for the moly-greased high-torque bolts. A torque of 65 lbs.-ft. will be administered during final assembly.*

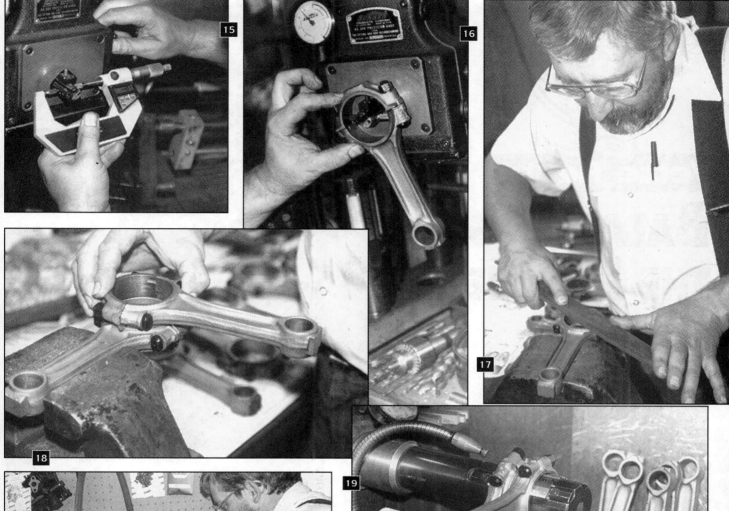

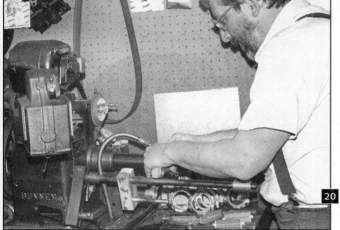

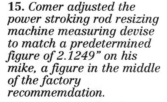

15. *Comer adjusted the power stroking rod resizing machine measuring devise to match a predetermined figure of 2.1249" on his mike, a figure in the middle of the factory recommemdation.*

16. *Before he started to grind each unit, he checked its out-of-round condition. This one was .003" out of spec on one side, .010" at the other side and .004" from top to bottom.*

17-18. *Prior to starting the resizing operation, Comer gingerly deburred the side faces since they will run against one another or* *against the crank as illustrated by Comer in photo No. 18. Removing too much metal increases side clearance and undesirable oil throw-off.*

19. *Connecting rods are placed on the mandrel two at a time to speed up the work, plus it helps prevent the bores from becoming bellmouthed or tapered.*

20-21. *Stroking the rod assemblies back and forth, Comer carefully removed metal to return the bores to the original manufacturer specifications.*

Suzy Q

Vette Resto

BALANCING THE ENGINE

By Dean Shipley

Balancing an automobile engine is a routine procedure in its assembly at the factory. The short block components, the pistons, connecting rods, harmonic balancer, flywheel and crankshaft, are balanced to prevent undo stress on the engine while it's in operation. An engine that is not balanced will wear out the bearings much sooner that it should. The balancing that occurs in the factory is satisfactory and within acceptable tolerances.

But because the engines are on an assembly line, the balancing they receive is not as close as it could be. Achieving a more delicate balance is a labor intensive procedure that is not cost effective for an assembly line operation.

But in a custom engine shop, such as Comer & Culp Engines of Sidney, Ohio, a closer, more delicate balance can be achieved. With the pistons and rods each weighing within less than a gram of each other, the stress on the bearings, when they are in operation, is minimized. When the stress is minimized, so is the potential for wear. If the engine is properly cared for hereafter, it can, more than likely, run forever.

Glenn Culp performed the balancing tasks on Suzy Q.'s 327 V-8. Each component was weighed. He said aftermarket piston makers, in general, have become much better in their product's quality control, and weights don't vary as widely as in the past. He weighed the eight pistons and found the lightest piston of the eight. Then the other seven had material removed so they weighed within a half a gram of the lightest. A similar procedure was performed for the rods.

The crank assembly was also balanced in its own way. The photos seen here illustrate the many steps taken to make sure the 327 in Suzy Q. will purr well into the next century.

Photos by Dean Shipley and Bob Stevens

1. *Glenn Culp weighs the eight pistons to learn which one is the lightest; in this case, it was 768 grams. Each piston's weight will then be brought to within a half a gram of the lightest. There was a three and a half gram spread from the lightest to the heaviest.*

2. *One method to remove weight is to drill out material from the cast piston's underside. Culp selected a 3/8th-inch "flat-tipped drill bit" to remove excess weight.*

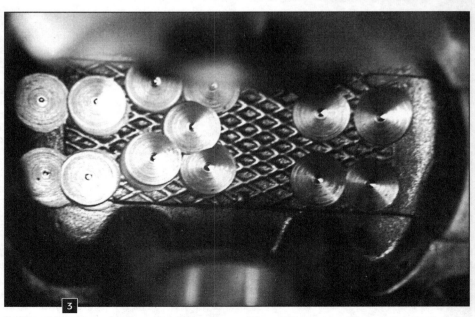

3. *The drill bit tracks reveal weight removed from this piston. The most removed from one piston was 3.5g.*

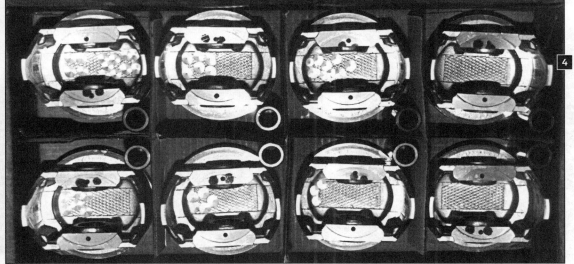

4. *All eight pistons are now in balance and in the box. Six of seven pistons needed adjustment to weigh close to the lightest piston. One was close enough to require no adjustment.*

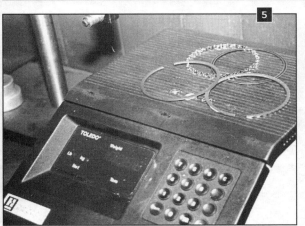

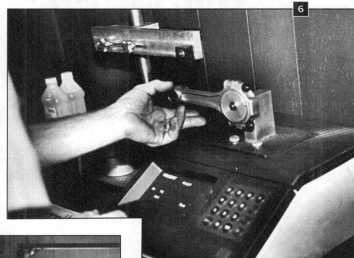

5. *The piston rings are weighed as well, but nothing is done to them. Little variance is detected in their weight.*

6. *Culp weighs the larger end of the connecting rod. The smaller end is placed in a support so only the larger end's weight is recorded. The lightest is found, then the seven remaining are adjusted to match it. Both ends of the rod are balanced.*

7-8. *Culp grinds excess weight from the rod. The larger ends varied by as much as 11 grams.*

9

10

11

9. *The rod on the right shows evidence of metal removed to make it match the weight of the rod on the left, which has not been ground.*

10. *A weight card is completed for every engine the shop balances. Each component's weight is recorded. A total of 1,904 grams was reached.*

11. *That amount of weight is then loaded onto four "tree fixtures," one for each of the* rod bearing journals.

12. *The four fixtures are poised for positioning on the crankshaft rod journals.*

13. *The harmonic balancer is prepared for remounting to the crankshaft. Culp taps the holes to remove debris. The balancer is cleaned and balanced itself.*

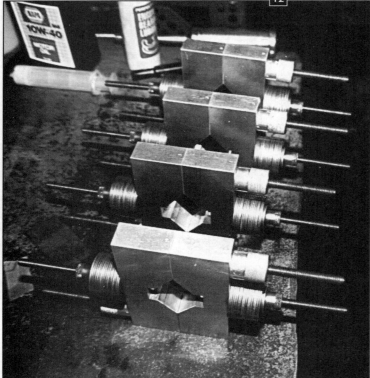

12

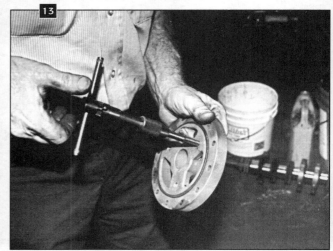

13

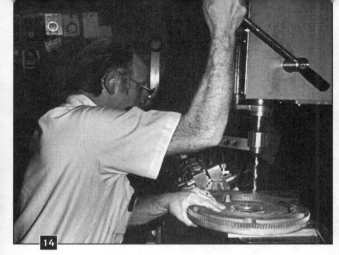

14. *Before mounting the flywheel on the assembly, Culp balances it, removing metal by drilling it out. He noted the flywheel appeared to have been balanced in a previous engine overhaul.*

15. *The harmonic balancer is bolted to the crankshaft.*

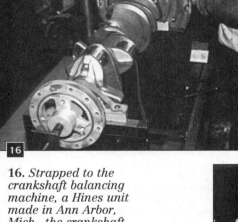

16. *Strapped to the crankshaft balancing machine, a Hines unit made in Ann Arbor, Mich., the crankshaft assembly is ready made for a balancing spin.*

17. *The fixtures are mounted one by one to the crankshaft. They simulate the weight of the rod, piston, etc.*

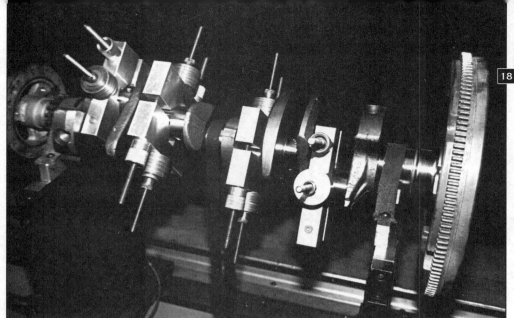

18. *The machine spins the crankshaft assembly at approximately 500 rpm. At this point, its sensors are hard at work to determine the imbalances in the crankshaft.*

19. *The machine tells Culp, seemingly miraculously, where the imbalances are, how much material is to be removed, at what point it's to be removed and at what angle it's to be removed.*

20. *Per the machine's guidelines, Culp drills out material from the crank's counterweights.*

21. *The drill debris is removed by a shop vac.*

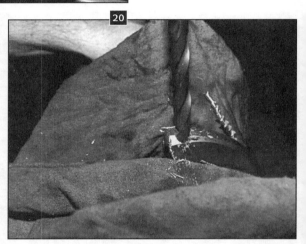

Suzy Q.
Vette Resto

INSTALLING CAM BEARINGS

By Bob Stevens

Installing the cam bearings is a routine procedure, as long as high quality, precision-fit bearings are used and they are inserted with a cam bearing installation tool.

At Comer & Culp Engines, Sidney, Ohio, all five of the cam bearings were knocked into place without protest or problem. First, Glenn Culp lubricated each bearing saddle with motor oil, then carefully inspected each bearing before driving it into place with the cam bearing installation tool, a long steel rod designed specifically for the process. Each Clevite bearing is numbered relative to its position in the block.

Photos by the author

1. A pack of fresh Clevite cam bearings was supplied by AE Clevite Engine Parts, Ann Arbor, Mich. Nothing but the best for Suzy Q.'s hot 300-hp 327 V-8. There are five cam bearings in this installation. Glenn Culp, Comer & Culp Engines, Sidney, Ohio, checks the numbering on a Clevite bearing. Each bearing carries a number relative to its position in the block.

2. The block is placed on the floor, bottomside up, and the cam bearing saddles are lubricated with standard motor oil. Each bearing is also lubricated. The long tool alongside the block is the cam bearing installer.

3. With a gentle tap from a hammer, the special cam bearing installation tool drives the five bearings into place, one bearing at a time, starting with the fifth one and working forward. A shorter version of the cam bearing installation tool is used to secure the last bearing because of its close proximity to the end of the block.

4. With all five bearings installed, Culp eases the cam itself into place and turns it by hand to check for clearances. Everything checks out fine.

Each bearing was coated with lubricant before insertion into the block. This eases installation and also prepares the bearings for engine startup, protecting both the bearings and the camshaft. After three of the bearings were installed, Culp inserted the camshaft to check for clearance, a procedure he repeated after all five bearings were in place.

When Suzy Q.'s engine is fired to life after a year-long silence, the all-new cam will be spinning in properly spec'd and installed bearings. What more could a valve-popper want?

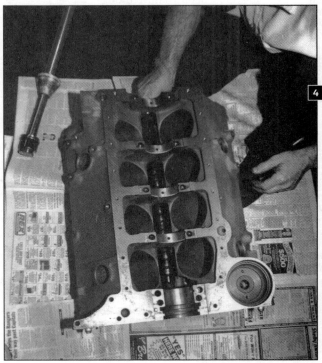

SUZY Q
Vette Resto

INSTALLING FREEZE PLUGS

By Bob Stevens

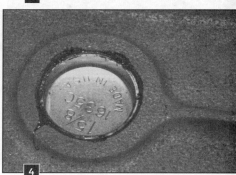

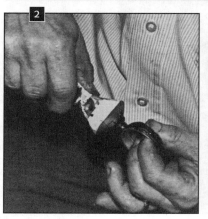

Any engine rebuild requires that a new set of freeze plugs be installed in a freshly machined block. Suzy Q.'s 327 V-8 deserved the best, and it got it, including a new set of freeze plugs inserted into the bare block by Glenn Culp, a partner in Comer & Culp Engines, Sidney, Ohio. It was a quick, clean installation, and one that will serve for many, many years.

A set of Elgin plugs specifically made for the Chevy small block was used. The old freeze plugs had been removed long ago, of course, before the engine block was machined.

A hammer and a driver for the plug were employed to drive the plugs home. But before that, each plug was coated in Permatex Form-A-Gasket to ensure a good seal. The job was completed quickly, easily and with perfect results.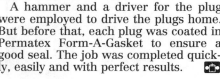

Photos by the author

1. A new set of freeze plugs, also called expansion plugs, was used to refit the cleaned and machined 327 engine block belonging to Suzy Q.

2. Permatex gasket material is applied to a freeze plug. The gooey substance works like a charm in seating freeze plugs, and was applied to the oil galley plugs as well.

3. A little tap with a hammer seats a freeze plug into the block.

4. Some gasket material seeps around the perimeter of an installed plug. Once the plug is inserted into the block, it is peened around the edges to prevent its movement.

5. Oil galley plugs are installed with a hex wrench providing the motivation.

6. With all its freeze and oil galley plugs installed, the 327 V-8 block is ready for the next step in reassembly ... the installation of cam bearings.

Suzy Q

Vette Resto

HEAD BOLT BOSS REPAIR

By Dean Shipley

1. *David Kronauge, the son of owner Fred Kronauge, performed the welding functions on Suzy Q.'s cylinder head.*

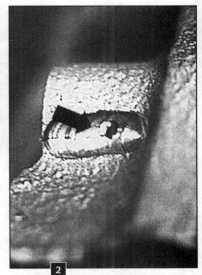

2. *After magnafluxing this boss, Kronauge drilled out a portion to reveal the crack from the inside. A hole also existed.*

Just like a human being's head, when at work, an internal combustion engine head is under a lot of pressure to perform. The head or heads, as in the case of a V-8 engine, often times perform well for years and nothing happens. But sometimes under pressure the engine head (as well as the human being's) can crack.

One of Suzy Q.'s heads did just that. With the heating during operation and cooling of the cast iron when the engine is not running, the metal's molecules expand and contract and metal fatigue takes place. Add to that, the stress applied by 75 ft.-lbs. of torque placed on the bolts holding the head in place.

But we're here to tell you, it's *not* serious. Two of the threaded bosses, through which the head bolts are inserted to fasten them to the engine block, were damaged. One had metal completely broken away, while another had a less-serious crack. Both required attention, however, which they received from American Engine & Welding of Dayton, Ohio.

American Engine & Welding has been making such repairs, and many more complicated and specialized, for 20 years. The owner, Fred Kronauge, has experience that goes far beyond two decades. He has capably trained his technicians, his son David Kronauge, Dave Angus and Jim Swisher.

Together they stay extremely busy fixing, in some cases, the seemingly unfixable and sometimes the irreplaceable.

Because Suzy Q.'s head would be difficult to replace (it's off a matching numbers engine from a Corvette), repair was the route to take. Had it been the head from a newer engine, and much easier to

3. *One of the repairs to be made was mending the broken boss. Metal fatigue and continuous pressure by the bolt broke it.*

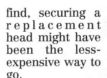

find, securing a replacement head might have been the less-expensive way to go.

The repair on the two bosses took several hours. One had to be magnafluxed to reveal the location of the crack. It was similar to fixing a tooth with a cavity. Part of the metal was drilled away. Then new metal, in the form of nickel rod, was added to repair it. Then excess material was filed away and made to resemble the boss of pre-crack days.

On the other boss, David Kronauge welded nickel rod to build up the area that had been broken off. Nickel bonds very well with cast iron and will be strong enough for that application. The newly formed area was then filed and smoothed.

Though Suzy Q.'s head did not require it, American Engine and Welding also performs a process called heat welding

or cast fusion. It is performed on parts that are irreplaceable, such as the cylinder head for a four-cylinder 1917 Monroe automobile. The part is heated to 1,200 degrees Fahrenheit, then it is welded with cast iron rod. The freshly welded part is then cooled very slowly and then shot peened to relieve stress.

About the Shop

American Engine and Welding is located at 600 West Third Street, Dayton, OH 45407, phone 513-228-3001. The shop offers pre-heat cast iron welding service and other comprehensive machine shop services. Their hours are 8 a.m. to 5 p.m., Monday through Friday, 8 a.m. to noon on Saturday.

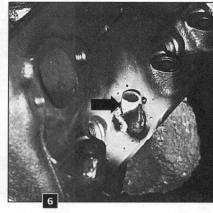

4. *Carbon rods were inserted in the boss holes to prevent welding material from collecting therein. It will not adhere to the carbon.*

5-6. *A cornea-searing flash indicates the weld is taking place, in photo 5. Kronauge slowly and methodically built up the area.*

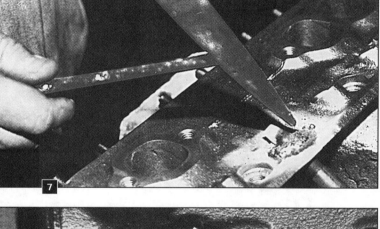

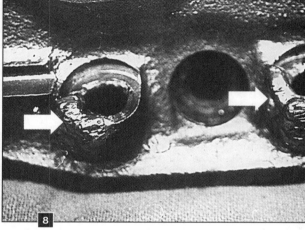

7. At several points during the process, the weld was peened. Peening removes slag and relieves stress in the weld. This process reduces the risks of the weld cracking.

8. The bosses have been thoroughly welded.

9. Die grinders fitted with a stone and a disc are used to remove the excess welding material.

10. The repaired bosses are looking more and more like an original, far right.

11-12. The ridged areas of the bolt at left are the culprit in breakage which has been illustrated here. Too much pressure is exerted in a small area of the boss. To relieve and spread out the pressure, a special heat-treated washer, front, can be used. Or, as seen in photo 12, a bolt with a built in washer can also be used.

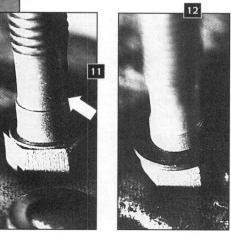

Vette Resto

INSTALLING VALVE GUIDE INSERTS

By Eric Brockman

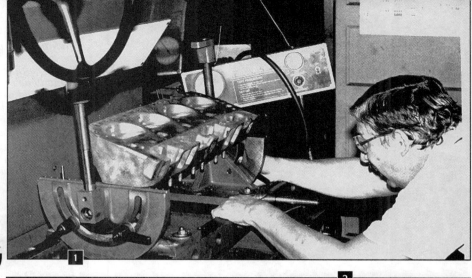

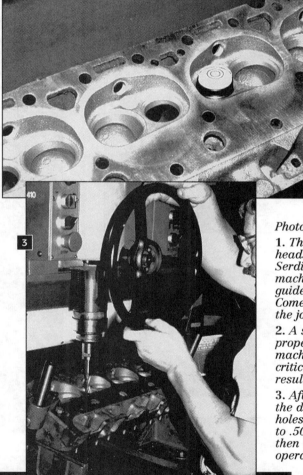

As an engine gets older and the miles begin to roll up, it starts to consume increasing amounts of oil. The heads provide one potential source of oil consumption: the valve guides.

Valve guide wear is a normal part of an engine's aging process. The constant motion of the valve stem eventually takes its toll on the surrounding metal of the guide hole. As the guides wear, more and more oil is allowed through the gap between the valve stem and the head. That oil finds its way into the cylinders, where it is burned. This, obviously, is not a desirable state of affairs. As part of the engine rebuild process, Suzy Q.'s heads were given a fresh set of valve guides. The entire process is neither long nor complicated, but it requires precision machine work. Setup takes nearly as long as the actual process.

Comer & Culp Engines, of Sidney, Ohio, handled the work. The valve guides were drilled oversize on a Serdi valve guide and seat machine, and replacement inserts were installed. The new guide inserts were then machined to the proper length. Follow along, as the heads are made "oil tight." 📷

Photos by the author

1. *The cleaned and disassembled heads were positioned on the Serdi valve guide and seat machine in preparation for valve guide replacement. Earl Comer, of Comer & Culp Engines, handled the job.*

2. *A small level was used to properly align the heads on the machine. Proper alignment is critical in order to get the desired results.*

3. *After using a guide bit to align the drill with the valve guide holes, Comer drilled the holes out to .500". Two bits, a core drill and then a reamer, were used for the operation.*

4. *The three valve guide holes on the left have been drilled oversize, while the three on the right are still the stock size.*

5. *After removing the metal shavings from the drilling procedure, the holes were cleaned with a wire brush. Engine bearing lubricant was applied to make installation of the new guides easier.*

6. *Initially, the new valve guide inserts were started into place with a hammer and guide driver.*

7. *Using an air hammer and guide driver, the valve guides were inserted the rest of the way.*

8-9. *The excess metal was then machined away (photo 8), leaving a finished product (photo 9).*

10-11. *The heads were then turned over on the machine, and the previous operation was performed topside.*

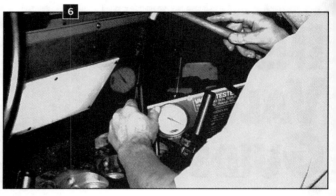

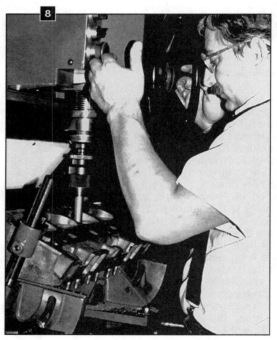

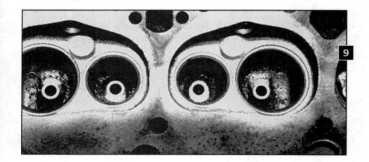

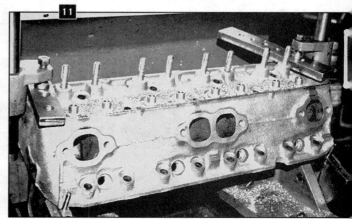

Suzy Q.
Vette Resto

REBUILDING THE HEADS

By Eric Brockman

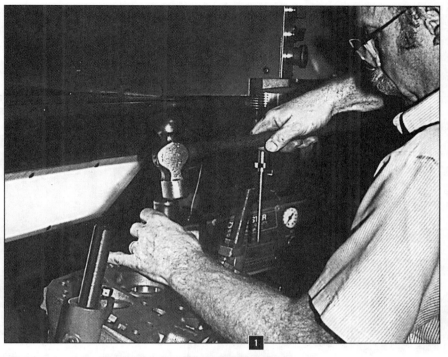

Slowly but surely, Suzy Q.'s mechanical heart is coming back to life. In this segment, machine work on the engine's heads will be completed, and the units readied for the decking operation.

Suzy Q.'s 327 V-8 engine came from a time when leaded gasoline was the norm. Tetraethyl lead, as it was called, served a dual purpose. It raised the gasoline octane rating and provided a lubricating cushion of sorts between an engine's valves and valve seats.

Lead gas, though still used in some applications, is, for the most part, history as far as most passenger cars are concerned. With unleaded fuel now in her diet, Suzy Q.'s engine had to be rebuilt accordingly. The stock "soft" valve seats needed to be replaced by hardened units that wouldn't need the lubricating effects of lead.

In addition to the issue of valve seat recession from the lack of lead, there was evidence that the valve seats had previously been worked over by someone with ... how shall we put it ... less than skilled hands. The old valve seats, like the valve guides, had to go.

Comer & Culp Engines, Sidney, Ohio, handled the job. Some careful, precision machining is required, but the process isn't all that complicated. Machining and installation of the new valve guide and seat inserts, as well as the machining of the new hardened valve seats were performed on a Serdi valve guide and seat machine.

After careful placement of the cylinder head on the machine's roll-over fixture, the operations were performed, one at a time. First up were the new valve guide inserts. The valve guides were drilled oversize, and then new inserts were driven into place. Each end of the inserts was then machined to the proper specs.

With the cylinder head properly repo-

Photos by the author, unless otherwise noted

1. *After aligning the cylinder head on the Serdi valve guide and seat machine, Glenn Culp drilled out the valve guide holes. First, the drill was aligned with a pilot bit, then the guides were drilled out with a core drill, followed by a reamer (shown).*

2. *With the guide holes drilled .500-inch oversize, Culp started the new valve guide inserts into place with a hammer and guide driver.*

3. *Using an air hammer, Culp drove the valve guide inserts the rest of the way into position.*

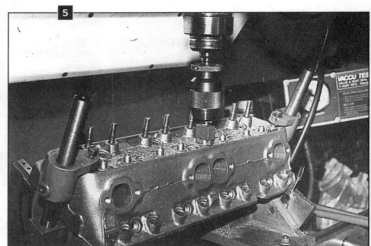

4-6. *The inserts were then cut down to the proper height (photos 4-5), and the inside diameter of each was chamfered (photo 6).*

7. *The cylinder head was turned over in the machine. After properly aligning the head, Culp cut down the port side of the valve guide inserts to the proper height. He also chamfered the port side of the guides, and then test-fitted the valves to make certain the stems wouldn't bind in the new guides.*

8. *With the installation of the valve guide inserts finished, Culp set up the machine to cut away the old valve seats. Here he used a gauge to check the runout in the pilot for the cutter.*

9. *With the cutter set to the depth of the new insert seat, Culp cut away the old valve seat.*

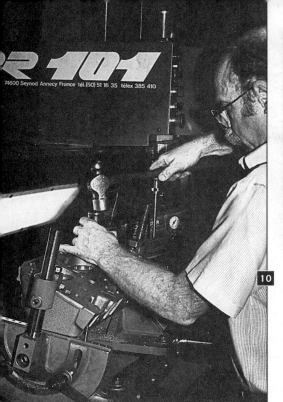

10. *The new valve seat inserts were driven into place with a hammer.*

11. *In this photo, the valve seat on the left is the new insert, and the one on the right is the old valve seat.*

sitioned on the machine, it was set up for the valve seat replacement operation. A cutter removed enough material to allow the hardened valve seat inserts to be hammered into place.

Using a small, hand-held grinder, the new valve seat inserts were "blended" into the surrounding metal of the ports and combustion chambers. The combustion chambers were polished at this time, to help eliminate any potential "hot spots" during engine operation.

12. *Using a hand-held grinder, Culp smoothed out the rough edges around the new valve seat inserts and blended the metal in with the surrounding material in the combustion chamber and port.*

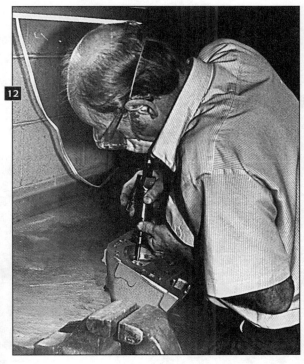

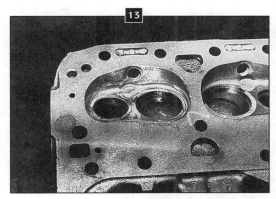

Then it was back to the Serdi valve guide and seat machine, to machine the new valve seats to the proper specifications. Each valve seat was cut to .020-inch under the outside diameter of its respective valve. For our 327, 1.94-inch intake and 1.50-inch exhaust valves were used.

During the cutting process on each seat, a small amount of "bluing" was applied to a valve and it was inserted into the head to check how well it seated. This compound left a telltale mark on the valve seat, revealing any deficiencies in the cut. After making the appropriate cuts on each valve seat, a valve was inserted and the port vacuum-checked to make certain the valve seated properly.

13. *In addition, Culp polished the combustion chambers to help eliminate any potential "hot spots" that could lead to detonation during operation.*

14. *Next, the head went back on the Serdi valve guide and seat machine. Now the new valve seats were cut to accept the valves. The cutter was set for .020-inch under the outside diameter of the respective valves. The diameters of the valves were 1.94 inches for the intake and 1.50 inches for the exhaust.*

15. *The seats were cut at three angles, 30 degrees on the outside of the ring, 45 degrees in the middle (where the combustion is sealed), and 60 degrees on the inside. (photo by Ken New)*

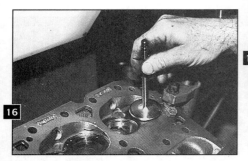

16. *After the first cut, a little "bluing" was put on the valve, and it was inserted into the seat. An even circle left on the seat by this special compound indicates the valve is seating properly in the cut.*

17. *After the cuts were finished, a valve was inserted in each seat and the port was vacuum tested to make it certain it sealed properly.*

18. *With the cuts completed, the heads were ready to be decked and cleaned (covered elsewhere in this issue). Assembling the prepped heads was the next step.*

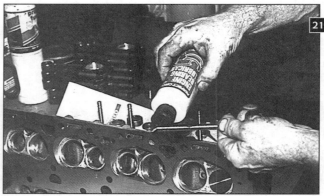

19-20. *Before beginning reassembly, Culp ran the valves, one at a time, through the valve grinding machine to make certain the specs were the same for each one. (photo 20 by Ken New)*

21. *Each valve stem received an application of engine bearing lubricant prior to being inserted into the cylinder head.*

22. *Each valve spring was compressed to its assembled height, in order to make certain it would exert the proper pressure when assembled. The dial gauge indicated the pressure.*

![Suzy Q Vette Resto]

DECKING THE HEADS

By Ken New

Continuing our quest to give Suzy Q.'s V-8 the potential of another 100,000 miles of service life required decking the cylinder heads. Decking shaves a thin layer of metal from the heads' faces that mate with the cylinder block. Decking ensures proper head gasket sealing, a prerequisite of continuing good performance.

Decking the heads eliminates warpage, that can be caused by uneven engine cooling, as well as the malformations caused by the improper escape of hot engine gases, which occurs when a head gasket blows. Other benefits decking provides include: the removal of damage resulting from improperly tightened head bolts, the removal of gouges and dents left by non-professional fixes, and the erasing of corrosion around water passage openings.

The fact that Suzy Q.'s heads were out of spec was no surprise. Figures compiled by professional rebuilders indicate that nearly 50 percent of all heads that are brought to their shops for routine service require a decking operation to return them to factory specs.

In the course of routine maintenance, many mechanics prescribe decking of the heads. Engine blocks, although subject to the same problems that distort deck surfaces, are far less likely to be sent to the machine shop for service.

Earl Comer, a partner in Comer & Culp Engines, Sidney, Ohio, performed the decking operations to restore Suzy Q.'s cylinder heads. He then gave them a hot bath to prepare them for final reassembly.

Before installation of the valves, each valve received a grind to double check specs and help ensure a proper seal. Each valve spring was also checked at its assembled height to make certain the springs pressure was correct.

Then a valve was inserted into the

Photos by the author

1-2. Earl Comer, Comer & Culp Engines, muscled Suzy Q.'s heads into the Storm Vulcan grinder, then leveled them horizontally and vertically. Fixtures on the machine allow for perfect alignment.

3. With each pass of the grinding wheel, some .004" of metal is removed. Normally, a couple of passes will clean up the cylinder head decks. Within reason, there's no limit as to how much metal can be removed from a head, however each swipe of the grinding wheel reduces the combustion chamber volume and increases the compression ratio. A .004" cut will reduce the chamber volume approximately one cubic centimeter. The liquid spray is an environmentally-friendly fluid that delivers the metal shavings to a recovery tank.

4-5. *After two swipes of the wheel, Comer could still see signs of distortion where the area around the water jacket openings had sunk. He pointed to shadows of metal still untouched by the grinder. One more swipe did the trick.*

6. *Comer placed one of the heads in the hot-wash booth for a "bath."*

7. *Immediately after the hot bath, Comer hosed down the head thoroughly inside and out with fresh water to remove any debris that may have gotten lodged during the operation.*

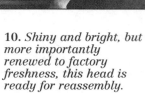

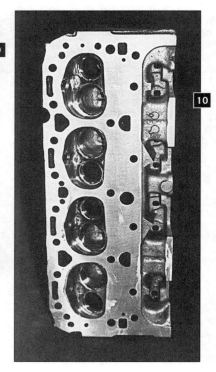

8. *Following the rinse, Comer dried the heads inside and out with compressed air.*

9. *Comer finished the job by spraying a liberal coat of silicone spray over the head.*

10. *Shiny and bright, but more importantly renewed to factory freshness, this head is ready for reassembly.*

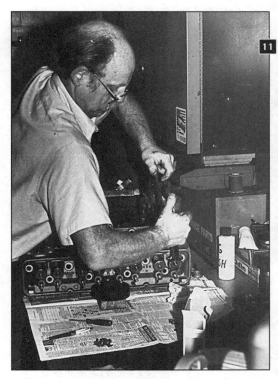

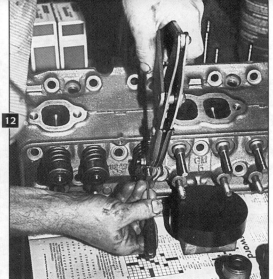

11. *A special valve spring compressor was utilized to compress each valve spring enough to allow installation of the seals and keepers.*

12. *With the valve spring compressed, Culp used a small screwdriver to carefully push the rubber seal into place.*

head and the valve spring was placed in position. Using a special tool, the valve spring was compressed, allowing the seal and keeper to be installed. This procedure was repeated until all the valves and valve springs were installed. A tap on each spring assembly with a hammer made certain everything seated properly.

The heads are now ready to be bolted on the engine when the time comes.

13. *The keeper was then installed by hand, and the spring compressor was released.*

14. *Once all the valves and valve springs were installed, a light tap on each with a hammer helped to make certain each assembly seated properly.*

15. *Suzy Q.'s heads, assembled and ready to go once the short block is reassembled.*

Suzy Q!
Vette Resto

RESURFACING THE FLYWHEEL

By Eric Brockman

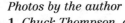

After 30-plus years of clutch-riding drivers, and probably more than a few power shifts along the way, Suzy Q.'s flywheel showed its age. But the wear was by no means terminal.

To ensure proper clutch operation once Suzy Q. is completed, we took the flywheel to Kiamy's Auto Supply, located at 308 Ash Street (phone 513-773-4242) in nearby Piqua, Ohio. Chuck Thompson, the resident machinist, resurfaced it. The process involved removing metal from the side of the flywheel that mates with the clutch disc, in order to eliminate uneven wear or warpage from the years of use.

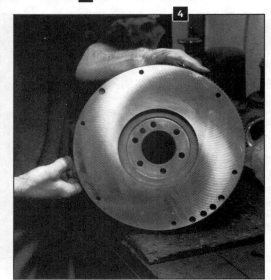

Photos by the author

1. Chuck Thompson, of Kiamy's Auto Supply, first cleaned up the flywheel with brake cleaner and then a grinder disc on an electric drill.

2. Thompson then prepared the resurfacing machine. A fitting was placed on the machine to properly center the flywheel. The flywheel was then put in place and secured on the machine.

3. Thompson adjusted the machine's cutter to remove the required amount of metal from the flywheel's surface. Five-thousandths (.005) of an inch was removed. At various stages in the process, Thompson stopped the machine to make certain that the cutting operation was proceeding evenly.

4. After coming off the machine, the flywheel received another cleaning, to remove any residue from the cutting operation.

Suzy Q Vette Resto

DECKING THE EXHAUST MANIFOLDS

By Bob Stevens

The myriad of preliminary procedures and intricate details involved in the rebuilding of an engine is seemingly endless at times. For instance, to ensure a smooth and proper fit between the engine block and the exhaust manifolds, the latter were decked. It was a routine decking process, such as that used on other components, and the results were very satisfactory.

Comer & Culp Engines, Sidney, Ohio, performed the routine procedure in a matter of minutes, although it took numerous passes under the grinding stones to shave the manifolds into spec. At the helm of the unique decking machine was Glenn Culp.

Each pass of the manifolds under the grinding stones removed approximately one-half of a thousandth (.0005) of an inch of metal. The machine shaved the same amount off each time, on each pass, both ways, as the manifolds (one at a time) passed under the cutters and then back through again.

Culp used sight, feel and instruments to check progress. A bubble balance measured the effectiveness of repeated shavings. Overall, a couple of dozen passes were made on each manifold. The machine, a 5.5-hp Scledum RT 17Y, contains 10 grinding stones, which rotate at about 730 rpm.

After they were decked to spec, the exhaust manifolds were cleaned, dried and sprayed with silicone to protect them from corrosion. The next step will be to coat them with a proper dressing.

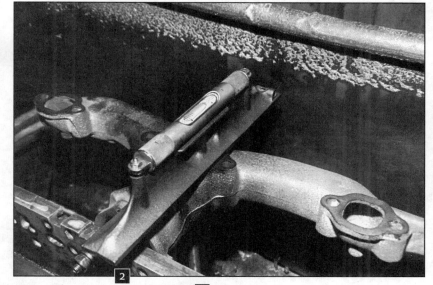

Photos by the author

1. *Glenn Culp, Comer & Culp Engines, Sidney, Ohio, checks the alignment on his shop's decking machine before activating it to shave an exhaust manifold from Suzy Q.'s V-8 engine. The manifolds had already been cleaned and sandblasted.*

2. *A bubble balance checks the levelness of the center collector on one of the exhaust manifolds. The bubble balance was used repeatedly ... before, during and after the decking procedure.*

3. *Culp passes the manifold under the cutters to check for alignment, clearance, etc. It's a precision operation, of course, so everything must be just right for the best results.*

4. *The machine, lubricated with a special solution, does its number on a manifold. It's an amazing machine to watch operate. Actually, the cutting head remains stationary while the manifold (or engine block, head, etc.) passes underneath, all the way through and then back again, with material shaved on each pass.*

5. *Culp closely monitors progress as the manifold passes beneath the cutting stones, receiving a "close shave" every* time. *The protective vinyl curtain helps keep the water spray in and hands out while the machinery is in motion.*

6. *Red dye is applied to each of the three collectors on the inboard side of the manifold. The dye will help visually track the evenness of the decking operation. The dye disappeared on the left collector first, then the middle, and finally on the right end. It took a couple of dozen passes to bring each manifold into spec.*

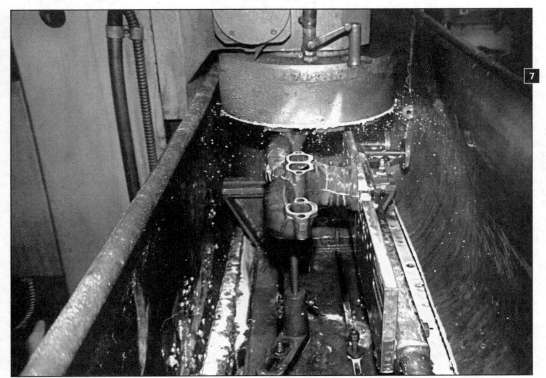

7. *The 220-volt, 5.5-hp decking machine trims away another .0005 inch of metal. That's how much was removed on each pass. Periodically, the machine was halted and the manifold was examined. A bubble balance reflected levelness. Sight and feel were also used to check progress.*

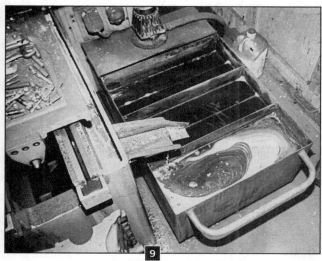

8. *There are 10 grinding stones in the decking machine's cutting head. They rotate at 730 rpm.*

9. *The water-based lubricant is recycled.*

10. *Culp keeps his eye on the bubble as he checks the final product for levelness.*

11. *After a quick rinse in the Jet Clean Cabinet removed residue from the decking operation, Culp dried the castings with pressurized air. A coating of spray silicone on the manifolds will protect them while they're being stored awaiting application of a special dressing. Lacquer thinner will be used to remove the silicone before applying the high-temp dressing.*

12. *Sandblasted, cleaned, dried, decked and cleaned again, the pair of exhaust manifolds is ready to go to work, once a protective coating of finish dressing has been applied.*

COATING THE EXHAUST MANIFOLDS

By Eric Brockman

Under the hood of a restored car, the exhaust manifolds can be like the Grinch that stole Christmas when you show your car.

If left unprotected, the heat of the engine's exhaust gases soon cause the manifolds to rust and detract from an otherwise immaculate engine compartment. But finding a paint or coating that can withstand the intense heat the exhaust manifolds endure can be difficult.

For the restoration of Suzy Q.'s exhaust manifolds, Virginia Vettes (110 Maid Marion Place, Williamsburg, Va. 23185; 804-229-0011), a supplier of Corvette parts and accessories, came to the rescue. The company supplied us with a container of "Hot Stuff," a special exhaust manifold dressing it markets.

Described as a "space-age blend of stainless steel and ceramic," the coating gives the appearance of raw cast iron and is capable of withstanding temperatures of 2,400 degrees Fahrenheit.

Each Hot Stuff kit includes a container of the gooey coating, a mixing stick, and a set of instructions. Application is a snap, with the directions calling for application with either a rag or toothbrush. Our manifolds had been thoroughly bead-blasted and cleaned, but according to Virginia Vettes, such extensive preparation is not necessary. All that is needed is to wire brush any loose rust and grease from the manifold.

After the Hot Stuff is applied, allow it to air dry for two hours, then run the engine for 10 minutes to heat-cure it. Clean up with soap and water. Now Suzy Q. will never have to exhale through rusty, unsightly manifolds again.

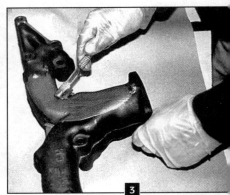

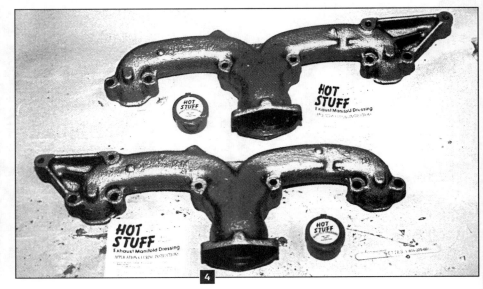

Vette Resto

ENGINE REASSEMBLY

PART 1

By Dean Shipley

After the various engine parts have been replaced, balanced and/or polished to satisfaction, the engine can be reassembled. This is an important procedure that should not be taken lightly. Numerous pitfalls await the unsuspecting do-it-yourselfer if he/she is not wise to the nuances of reassembling a V-8 engine. Missed details not performed in the reassembly have a way of returning to haunt the hobbyist in the form of a broken engine. We did not want such a scenario, so we let the pros at Comer & Culp Engines perform the reassembly.

The procedure begins with "the bottom end" and works upward. We will illustrate the steps that essentially complete the short block assembly. Another segment of the reassembly will be covered in our next issue.

Comer and Culp worked methodically and efficiently through each step as if they'd done it a hundred times. (Chances are good it's been a few more than that. You're invited to follow along as Suzy Q's 327 V-8 engine is reassembled by the experts. Only the best for "our girl."

Photos by Eric Brockman and Dean Shipley

1. *Earl Comer gives the crank journals one last quick buffing with a "nearly worn out" aluminum oxide sanding belt. This creates a polishing effect, but does not remove material. After polishing, the crankshaft was cleaned and dried prior to installation.*

2. *After the block had been washed and dried to remove all possible machining residue, the main bearing halves that go in the block are set in place.*

3. *Glenn Culp lowers the balanced crank into place.*

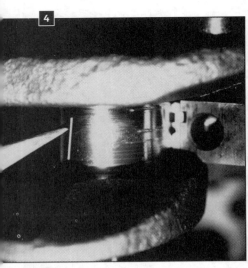

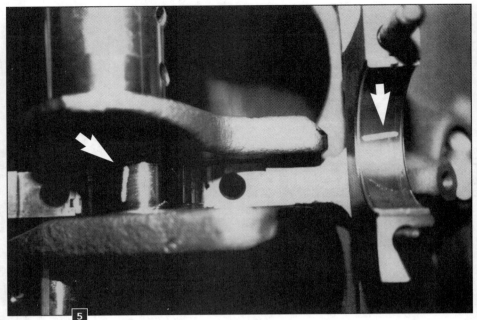

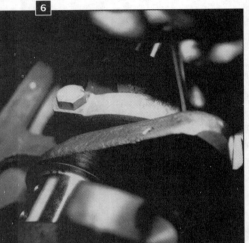

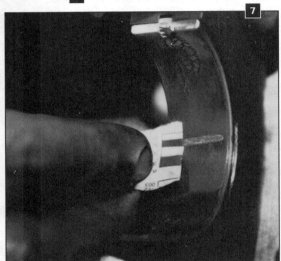

4-7. *Culp places a Plastigauge clearance indicator on the crank journal (No.4). The crank journal cap is then bolted into place and torqued down to specifications, 65 lbs-ft (No. 6). This flattens the piece of plastic placed on the journal and makes a mark on it and the cap (No.5). Culp then measures the mark and determines the clearance to be .00175", which is acceptable (No. 7). This is done to just one since all were ground to the same specifications. The remaining caps were then installed. The crank spun easily in place. The camshaft lobes and bearings (not pictured) were then lubricated and the cam slid into place.*

8,9. *The crankshaft gear is put in place, (No.8) and the timing chain and cam gear are pressed into place.*

10. *The crankshaft gear was placed in the "O" key way. Note the "O", which has the letters "CE" just above it, are lined up with the mark on the cam gear. Two other options are available: The "A" top right, can be aligned with the mark to advance the camshaft, or the "O," to the left in the 8 o'clock position, can be aligned to retard the camshaft.*

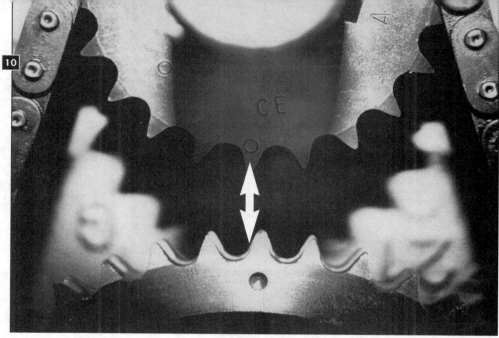

11. *Culp uses a torch to heat the head of the connecting rod to approximately 600 degrees F. (the metal turns light blue in color) At that heat, the hole has expanded enough to allow the piston wrist pin to be inserted and hold the piston in place.*

12. *Eight pistons with rods await the next step.*

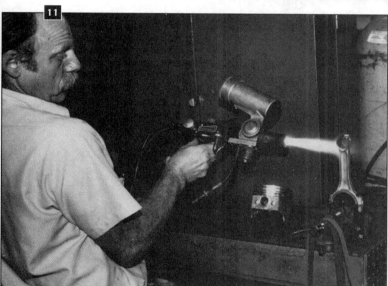

13. *Each piston receives three rings: an oil ring and two compression rings.*

14. *"It's a clean machine." Culp wipes down the cylinders with a cleaner to remove any unwanted residue that may have fallen in the cylinders during the crank installation.*

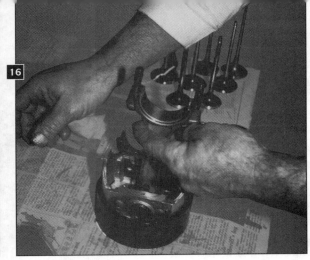

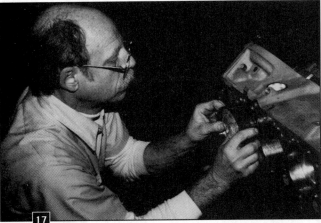

15. *A ring compresser holds the piston rings in prior to the piston's insertion in the cylinder.*

16. *The rod bearing material is set in place. It's notched so it can only go in one way.*

17. *Culp loads the piston into the cylinder.*

18. *In a view from the opposite end, one sees the rod cap bolts sheathed in rubber, to protect the crank from unwanted scratches from the bolt tips.*

19. *The cap receives its bearing material.*

20. *The cap is slipped over the rod bearing journal and mated to the rod.*

21

22

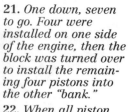

21. *One down, seven to go. Four were installed on one side of the engine, then the block was turned over to install the remaining four pistons into the other "bank."*

22. *When all piston rods were attached to the crankshaft, each cap bolt was rechecked to make sure it had been torqued to the proper tension.*

23. *Culp sets the oil pump in place and aligns the pickup properly. He marks the alignment.*

24. *With the pump held in the vise, he pressure fits the pickup into the pump.*

25. *The dip stick holder is tapped into place.*

26. *The gasket is set in place.*

27. *The plumbing for the oil filter is installed.*

28. *One bank of the completed short block.*

23

24

25

26

27

28

Suzy Q

Vette Resto

ENGINE ASSEMBLY

PART 2

By Dean Shipley

Last month our intrepid engine assemblers, Earl Comer and Glenn Culp, put the short block together. This month, we'll pick it up right about where they left off.

In watching them work, they make the assembly of the 327 cubic-inch Chevrolet appear to be routine and almost simple. One part of their routine that is noteworthy is their attention to cleanliness. They make sure all parts are thoroughly cleaned before assembly.

Again, the internal combustion engine is a precision designed and manufactured piece of machinery that deserves to be assembled by professionals who know the intricacies of this work. These pros offer a guarantee, so if something goes wrong after it's together and running, they'll fix it. We are confident no ills will befall this engine, so long as it is well maintained.

You're invited to follow along as Suzy Q.'s engine continues to be reassembled.

Photos by
Eric Brockman
and Dean Shipley

1. *Picking up where we left off last month, the timing chain cover has been fitted with a gasket, then bolted to the front of the engine.*

2. *Adhesive is applied to the engine's underside to hold the oil pan gasket in its proper place.*

3. *Once the gaskets are in their proper position, the pan, which has a coat of epoxy primer, is set and bolted into place. Care is taken not to overtighten the bolts. Putting too much load on them can cause failure and breakage. And they're no fun to extract from the block.*

4. *The fuel pump plate is bolted to the engine's front corner.*

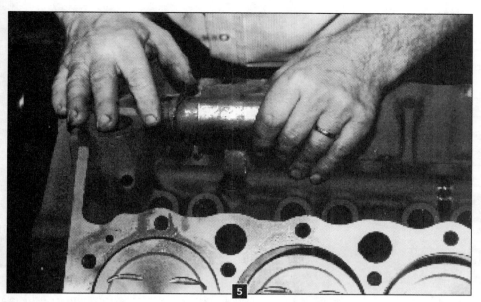

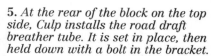

5. *At the rear of the block on the top side, Culp installs the road draft breather tube. It is set in place, then held down with a bolt in the bracket.*

6. *Culp points to wear on the shaft of the harmonic balancer. To correct the problem, a sleeve was pressed into place over the worn area.*

7. *The harmonic balancer is installed with a tool made specifically for its installation. While holding the shaft in place with the left hand, Culp turns the wrench on the threaded shaft to press the balancer in place. The belt pulley is bolted to the harmonic balancer. It was torqued to 45 ft.-lbs.*

8. *The block gets a head.*

9. *The head bolts are tightened in stages and in a pattern. Starting in the center of the cylinder head and working outward in a circular or "criss-cross" pattern, the bolts are tightened to 25 ft-lbs., 45 ft.-lbs. and then 65 ft.-lbs. Culp goes over all of them one more time to verify that the load on each bolt is to spec.*

10. *Using camshaft bearing lube, Earl Comer lubricates the hydraulic lifters.*

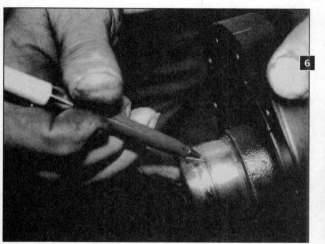

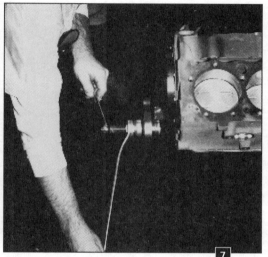

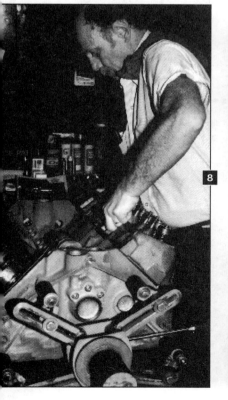

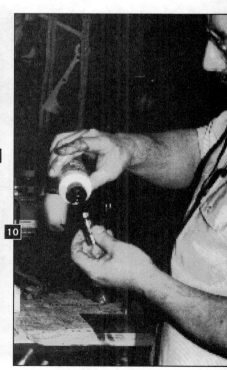

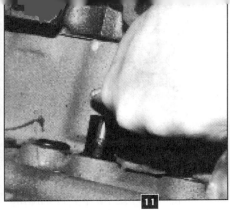

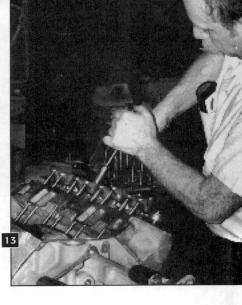

11. The lifters are set into place.

12. With the pushrods and rocker arms in position, the nuts are turned into place.

13. Culp twists down the adjusting nuts on the valves to preload the lifters to .020 of an inch.

14. The installation of the heads has been completed.

15. Using duct tape, Comer seals off the various engine orifices in preparation for the engine's coating with epoxy primer. He trimmed the tape carefully around the exhaust manifold holes, so the final job looked very neat.

16. To prepare the engine for priming, Comer sprays the block with a paint thinner to remove any oily residue.

17. *Comer sprays on the epoxy primer, which is extremely toxic. In his mask are hazardous duty filters. Using the throw-away style mask as protection from the fumes is not recommended.*

18. *The picture shows two of the four intake manifold gaskets installed.*

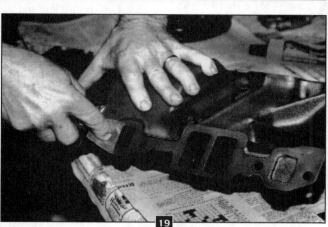

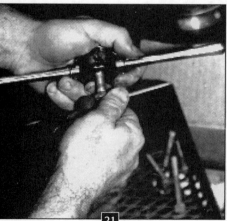

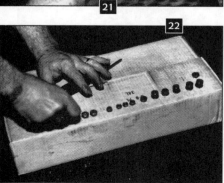

19. *Culp scrapes the intake manifold surfaces that are to be mated to the block. Cleanliness is the key to a good seal.*

20. *The intake manifold is set in place.*

21. *The bolts used to fasten the manifold were tumbled clean, then run through a tap to ensure the integrity of the threads.*

22. *Culp inserts the bolts into a box, so that just the heads are visible. After cleaning, they were primed to be ready for painting. This ensures no paint spray finds its way into the bolts' threads.*

23. *The intake manifold is bolted on. Again, Culp starts in the center and works out to the edges, criss-crossing as he goes.*

24. The water pump is bolted in place. It's so much easier to put on when the engine's out of the car.

25. Culp plugs the manifold orifices with paper towels to keep out any spray paint that may enter during painting.

26. The engine receives two coats of Chevy orange paint. The pulley and harmonic balancer were removed to be painted black. They were then reinstalled.

27. The surfaces of the exhaust manifolds, to be bolted to the engine, are scraped clean.

28. The engine motor mounts are installed.

29. Culp slips a bolt through the exhaust manifold, its gasket and into the engine block.

30. *Culp uses a fuel pump rod tool to hold that pesky rod in an up position in preparation for the fuel pump installation. The rod must be held up so the arm of the fuel pump can be properly installed.*

31. *The fuel pump is installed.*

32. *We're getting close. The engine receives fresh oil in preparation for priming the oiling system.*

33. *Using a drill fitted with a mechanism to activate the oil pump, Culp primes the oiling system. This makes sure all the parts are well oiled and the oil pressure is sufficient. The dial reads just over 60 lbs. of pressure.*

34. *By turning the crankshaft, Culp rotates the engine to bring the number one piston to top dead center on the compression stroke. A whistling device has been screwed into the number one spark plug hole to sound off when the piston reaches the desired position.*

35. *With distributor cap in hand, Culp marks the distributor to indicate the correct position of the rotor. This step essentially completed the engine reassembly, as far as it could be done, while in the capable hands of Earl Comer and Glenn Culp.*

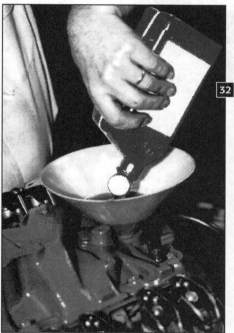

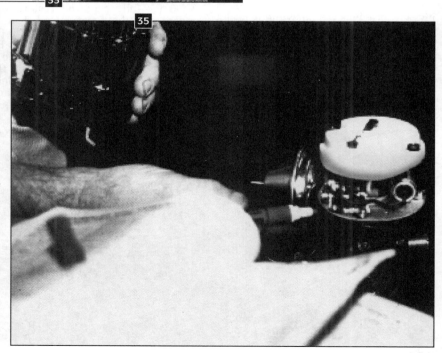

Suzy Q

Vette Resto

ANTIQUE AUTO: PEGGY SUE TO SUZY Q.

By Bob Stevens

After the extraordinary job the Antique Auto Shop did on our last project car, the '57 Chevy Bel Air convertible, Peggy Sue, we simply had to find a way to involve the Kentucky restoration shop in our latest project. The firm's owner, Terry Kesselring, provided just such an opportunity by suggesting that his shop handle the frame disassembly, restoration and reassembly. We graciously, and without hesitation, accepted Kesselring's invitation.

Given the high quality of the work performed on Peggy Sue, we had no misgivings at all about returning to the Antique Auto Shop for any kind of work. As evidenced by the swift, thorough and professional disassembly of the chassis, as

detailed in this issue, we made the right decision.

The shop was founded more than 18 years ago by Fred and Ray Vagedes, two brothers who have been car collectors for many decades. They retired in 1989 when they sold the thriving and growing auto restoration business to Kesselring. They recently came out of retirement, albeit briefly, to produce an excellent video series on antique car restoration. The six-part series covers everything from planning a restoration, performing body work and rebuilding drivelines to painting and woodgraining.

Kesselring, who took the helm of the business in November of 1989, has maintained the shop's solid tradition of producing show-winning examples of everything from antiques and classics to postwar special interest vehicles.

Some of the cars in the Antique Auto Shop for full or partial restorations in recent months have included a 1931 Duesenberg Murphy roadster, '57 Chevy Bel Air sport coupe, '37 Rolls-Royce Gurney Nutting drophead coupe, '82 Corvette Collector Edition, '25 Dodge sedan, '62 MGA convertible, '51 Mercury coupe, '63 Ford XL hardtop, '39 Packard Super Eight convertible coupe, one-

owner '77 Corvette T-top coupe, '65 GTO hardtop, '71 Oldsmobile 4-4-2 convertible, two '54 and one '53 Jaguar XK-120 roadsters, '52 Pontiac Catalina two-door hardtop, '71 Jaguar XKE V-12 coupe, '29 Packard roadster, and several woodies, such as a '46 Olds and '41 and '46 Ford station wagons. Several recently completed restorations have won national awards. Obviously, a tremendous variety of collector cars can be found at the Antique Auto Shop at any one time.

The shop specializes in complete, body-off, ground up restorations, producing high quality automobiles in concours condition. However, scaled down restorations are also offered, as well as partial restorations, mechanical work, paint jobs, routine tune-ups etc. Overall, about 100 vehicles pass through the shop each year, with approximately five complete restorations handled in the same time frame. As a sideline, the company also manufactures one-piece window frames for vintage cars.

The shop employs 11 professionals, including nine full-time and two part-time, and subcontracts numerous services from chrome plating to chemical dipping. The company also locates obsolete parts all over the hemisphere. It's a full-service operation that specializes in stock restorations, but will adapt its many capabilities to the customer's specific needs and desires.

In our case, that amounts to a stripped, dipped chassis that is correctly refinished to stock configuration and show condition. 📷

Suzy Q. Vette Resto

DISASSEMBLY OF REAR SUSPENSION

By Ken New

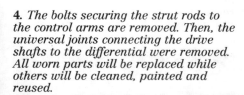

Breaking up Suzy Q.'s chassis into singular parts has been an arduous task. There were hundreds of parts to identify and tag, wear conditions both obvious and unseen, to examine and note and a "a ton" of dirt, rust and grime in which to wallow. Though as unaccustomed as we might have been to the dirty disassembly task, for Richard Snyder, the amiable mechanic at the Antique Auto Shop, chassis disassembly was all in a day's work.

Only the independent rear end and its bolt-on components were intact when we joined Snyder to record the final segment of the disassembly of Suzy Q.'s chassis.

A strong selling point to the potential Corvette buyer of the '63 Corvette Sting Ray was the new independent rear end. Replacing the conventional straight axle design offered on previous-year 'Vettes, independently suspended drive axles delivered better handling characteristics. The Sting Ray exceeded its predecessors in handling on tight curves and road hugging on uneven driving surfaces. Join us as we follow Snyder through the final segment of Suzy Q.'s chassis disassembly.

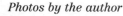

Photos by the author

1. With the "pumpkin" supported by a floor jack, Suzy Q.'s independent three-link type rear end appears to need nothing more than a clean up and new rubber bushings to restore it. However, we will go the extra step and have an expert inspect the gears thoroughly and repair any ailing parts found. We had detected no offending noises or signs of ailments prior to its removal the chassis.

2. Continuing the stem-to-stern chassis teardown, Richard Snyder, a master mechanic at Antique Auto, Elsmere, Ky., loosened the bolts that held the rear leaf spring in place.

3. Most of the potentially dangerous sprung weight in the springs was relieved once the unit was removed from the car, however Snyder recruited an extra pair of hands in Jerry Davis, a retired railroad auditor who works part time at Antique Auto.

4. The bolts securing the strut rods to the control arms are removed. Then, the universal joints connecting the drive shafts to the differential were removed. All worn parts will be replaced while others will be cleaned, painted and reused.

5. *Shop foreman, John Bastian and Snyder discuss the condition of Suzy Q.'s rear end. Moments later the second strut was removed.*

6. *Snyder removed the strut rod bracket which houses the camber adjustment cam at its ends. It also supports the rear end. Virtually no wear was detected during inspection. Camber adjustment was noted before the bolts were loosened.*

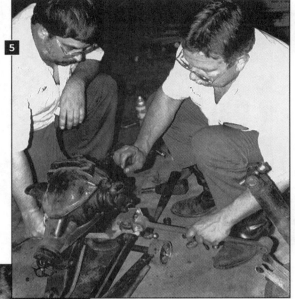

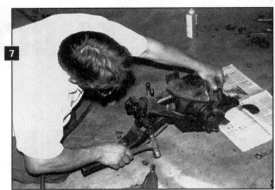

7. *Sometime in the past the front carrier support had been "jerry-rigged" with good intentions but with poor results. Crude workmanship was obvious in welding alongside the bolt holes.*

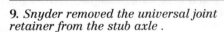

8. *An axleshaft is removed from the trailing torque control arms which are box-like in design for extra strength. The universal joints at both ends will be replaced with new parts. The wheel hub assemblies will be disassembled next.*

9. *Snyder removed the universal joint retainer from the stub axle .*

10. *The torque arm was separated from the backing plate to gain access to the stub axle.*

11-13. *To drive the wheel bearing from the stub axle, Snyder used the shop's hydraulic press after carefully positioning it to align with the press ram.*

Suzy Q
Vette Resto

FINAL CHASSIS TEARDOWN

By Bob Stevens

Upon inspecting the frame that has carried Suzy Q. for more than 30 years, the staff at the Antique Auto Shop, Elsmere, Ky., pronounced it very solid. In fact, they called it one of the best they'd seen. They were eager to see how easily the chassis came apart, and what a detailed inspection would produce. So were we.

And we were all pleasantly surprised at what we did find when the air-powered wrench started loosening bolts, and frame pieces began falling away from the chassis. At the operating end of the air wrench was Richard Snyder, a veteran technician with the Antique Auto Shop, who resides in nearby Burlington, Ky. It was obvious from his approach to the project that he'd done this many times.

As the chassis came apart, it became evident that the car was indeed, a solid Southern car with very little, if any, serious rust damage in its history. The frame and all its appendages were intact and very solid.

Initially, we were under the impression that the frame would be dipped in a special commercial chemical solution with all of its key parts in place, but the Antique Auto Shop said "no way," because many smaller parts will trap rust and create problems later on if they're not completely removed prior to dipping or blasting. All the small frame outriggers, shims and other pieces were removed. Some of the parts will be dipped, while others will be sandblasted.

Although it wasn't necessary, as the chassis disassembly was fairly routine, a shop manual and assembly manual were referred to periodically just to make sure the correct parts were present.

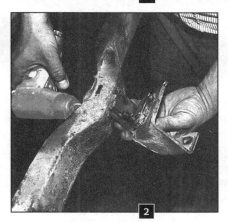

Photos by Bob Stevens and Ken New

1. *Shortly after arriving at the Antique Auto Shop, Elsmere, Ky., final disassembly began on the classy chassis that had supported Suzy Q. all these years. Doing the honors was veteran craftsman Richard Snyder, who is seen here removing a body brace.*

2. *As the frame outrigger falls free, a full set of shims is revealed. All such pieces were bagged and tagged with their exact location, so that after blasting they can be re-inserted in precisely the same spot.*

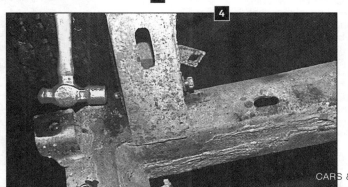

3. *Snyder uses an air gun to remove a shock absorber mounting bolt. The air-powered wrench makes quick work of chassis disassembly.*

4. *A hammer taps a stubborn bolt free.*

5. *All of the shims were in remarkably good condition, indicating that this frame, and the car it was married to for the past 30 years, did indeed, hail from the relatively dry climate of the deep South (Alabama and Florida).*

6. *Even with air-powered tools, a little penetrating oil is needed now and then to free up rusted bolts.*

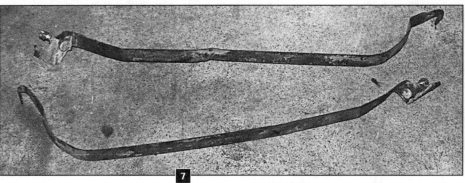

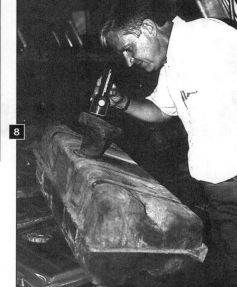

7. *The gas tank straps loosened easily, and appear to be in good shape. They're certainly reusable.*

8. *Inspecting the inside of Suzy Q.'s gas tank is Terry Kesselring, owner of the Antique Auto Shop.*

The tank will be cleaned, inside and out, and reused.

9. *Most of the frame bolts were in amazingly good condition. All could be reused with no real problem.*

10. *Snyder (left) uses a floor jack to lift the frame in preparation for removal of the rear end, while fellow Antique Auto Shop technician Mark Cleek steadies the unit and watches for possible problems.*

Assisted by hammers, screwdrivers, conventional wrenches, and penetrating oil, Snyder and his air-powered wrench quickly removed the body brackets, rear suspension and rear end. All shims, and there were dozens of them scattered around the frame, were bagged and marked for their precise location, number of shims in each group, etc., to aid in reassembly. To further insure that the shims aren't mixed up, they'll be sandblasted by hand, one set at a time.

Actually, all of the parts were removed with very little frustration. No bolts were broken, no shims were lost and no damage was done to the frame. Since all bolts were given a quick shot of penetrating oil before they were wrenched they loosened quickly and easily. Assisting in yanking the rear end was Marc Cleek, Hebron, Ky., a recent addition to the team at the Antique Auto Shop.

Once the first phase of the final disassembly was completed, which included removal of the gas tank, the frame was inspected thoroughly and found to be quite righteous. There's little doubt that the car spent its first life in the deep South as initially believed, and there appears to have been no frame damage due to an accident, even though we know the body has been hit at least once, and maybe two or three times. The suspected collisions were apparently not severe enough to reach the main frame.

Also, there was no evidence of rust damage, although there was certainly a coating of surface rust on the frame, but that's normal. Overall, the frame was declared extremely solid, correct and original. The final test will come when the unit is dipped in a heavy duty chemical derusting solution at American Metal Cleaning in Cincinnati, Ohio. The process bares all ... good, bad or otherwise.

After rolling the remnants of the chassis outside, we began our search for the all-important frame stamping. With a wire brush, we scrubbed the left rear (driver's side) frame kickup and removed a healthy buildup of scale and grime; in the process, we uncovered the car's serial number, S120317, stamped into the frame. It's right on the top of the frame and still very visible to the naked eye. Even though we had no reason to doubt that the car was still riding on its original frame, it's always a relief to confirm it.

With Suzy Q.'s chassis now heading into the last stages of disassembly, it appears that few surprises have been harbored in the car's substructure, which will prove a real plus to the restoration and reassembly of the chassis.

11. *After the rear end was slipped free, the chassis was rolled outside for temporary storage until disassembly could continue.*

12. *Kesselring examines the driver's side rear kickup in the frame, where the Vette's serial number is stamped.*

13. *The frame number- S120317 - is barely visible, but it's there and it precisely matches the serial number of the car.*

14. *The final phase of chassis disassembly began with a calculated and systematic approach. The rear end had already been detached from the*

frame. Every member of the staff at Antique Auto, Elsmere, Ky., said it was in great shape. Other than the usual coat of grease and dirt, only minor surface rust was present.

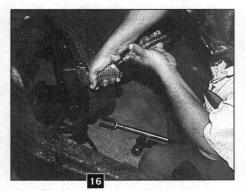

15 **16** **17**

15. *Then Snyder drove a pickle fork between the joints to separate the stubborn pieces.*

16. *Next, nuts securing the steering links were spun free. Air-powered tools quickened the job.*

17. *The shock absorber mounted on the relay and tie rod assembly was removed next.*

18. *Freed from the frame, the steering mechanism, complete with steering gear, is ready for freshening and installation of new joints and bushings.*

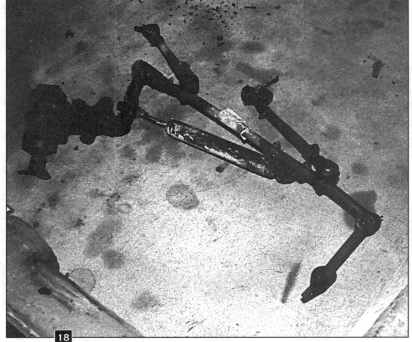

18

19. *The front stabilizer bar came off cleanly. It appears to have been replaced earlier and doesn't need renewal, only a refreshing.*

20. *The two braces that connect the front bumpers to the frame are also replacements, probably put here after a front end collision.*

21. *Moving to the front suspension, Snyder began disassembly by unbolting the steering knuckle and wheel hub assembly. Next he loosened the upper control arm from the steering knuckle by driving a pickle fork between the two parts.*

22. *The front wheel hub housing, including drum and brake shoes, etc., was removed as a unit. Those parts will be broken apart later for renewal.*

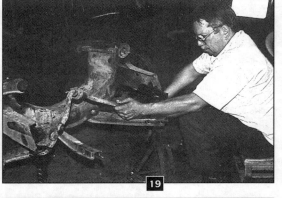

19 **20**

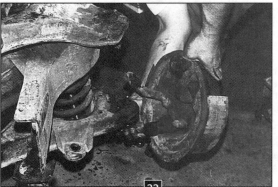

21 **22**

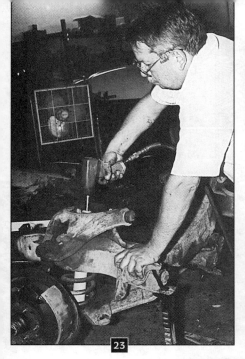

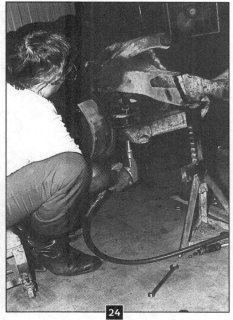

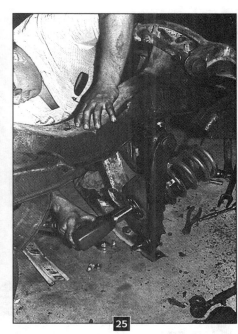

23. *After the securing nuts were wrenched off, the tired shocks were removed and discarded.*

24. *Next a special tool designed specifically to compress coil springs was attached to the upper and lower A-frames. Drawing the coil down is a cinch with this tool. Snyder cautioned that removal of coil springs can be very dangerous and only tools specifically designed for the task should be used.*

25. *Once the fastening bolts securing the A-frames opened up, only the spring compressor held the coil to the lower arm.*

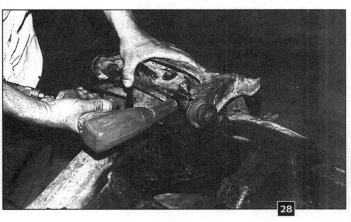

26. *After the pressure on the spring compressor was released, the coil spring was free. The coils will be replaced with new windings.*

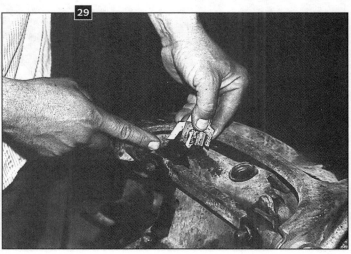

27. *Snyder prefers to reinstall each major component in its original location. To properly identify each part, he stamped an L or R on each component as appropriate.*

28. *The nuts holding the upper A-frames and caster and camber adjustment shims in place are removed.*

29. *Snyder carefully bagged and marked each grouping of shims. When the chassis parts are reassembled, arriving at the proper steering inclination, even though it will not be exactly the same as before disassembly, will be easier since the starting point for fine tuning will be easier to find.*

Suzy Q.
Vette Resto
Chemical Derusting: Suzy Q.'s Rust Is 'Zapped

1-2. *Before the parts left the Antique Auto Shop, they were tagged with identification washers to ensure the parts were returned to the right place. John Bastian of the Antique Auto Shop shows the i.d. washer wired to this part and every other loose part.*

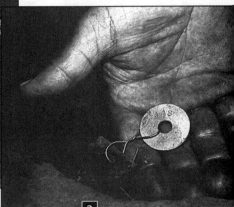

By Dean Shipley

Cleanliness, they say, is next to godliness. If that is indeed the case, Suzy Q. will be one "heavenly" ride when she's done. By then she will have had every square inch of her metal surfaces as clean as humanly possible. In the case of steel components, that means removing every minuscule bit of grease and rust that had accumulated in her 31 year lifetime.

Because they had done such a fine job cleaning and derusting Peggy Sue, our '57 Chevy resto project. *Cars & Parts*

elected to take Suzy Q.'s metal components to the men of American Metal Cleaning in Cincinnati, Ohio. *C&P* knew AMC had the means to make the dirtiest, filthiest metal become as clean and bright as the day it was cast or stamped. It is achieved with a goodly amount of time and metal cleaning techniques not generally available to the home restorer.

American Metal Cleaning is, no joke, an "industrial strength" metal cleaning/derusting business. Its 6,000 sq. ft. building (big but "shrinking" according to manager Mark Kormelink) houses the right equipment needed to handle some large cleaning jobs sent in by its clients.

The company primarily serves a commercial/industrial clientele, who have need of AMC's services on a continual basis. For example, a large grocery chain had contracted with AMC to strip off the paint from hundreds of feet of shelving in preparation for repainting. Another client, a painting firm, sends AMC its painting fixtures to be stripped of the paint buildup that occurs while it is painting lighting fixtures, etc.

AMC can also strip paint from, and derust, metal automotive components. But AMC does it as a supplement to its commercial accounts, according to Kormelink. Its accounts include Proctor

3. *Since American Metal Cleaning on Northland Road, Cincinnati, Ohio, had done such a fine job with Peggy Sue's rusty parts, Cars & Parts had no problem using the firm's services again for Suzy Q.*

4. *Upon arrival at AMC, the smaller parts were placed on a pallet to await a time to go into the process.*

5-6. *The time had come. The frame and a large basket, holding the smaller parts, are lowered into the degreasing tank. It holds an alkaline solution that is heated to 180 degrees. The tow motor lowers the parts into the tank.*

7. *After 8 to 10 hours in the degreaser, much of the foreign material has fallen to the bottom of the tank or loosened. A hot water power wash of the parts prepares them for their dip in the "electrically charged tank" for derusting.*

8. *The part has been degreased and washed and is now ready to join the other metal parts in the derusting tank. It is an electrolytically active tank. The parts are submerged in a basket ad attached to an electrode that supplies a low voltage, high ampere current. The alkaline liquid is charged with the opposite polarity. The electrolysis removes the rust completely - over time.*

& Gamble, General Electric, and Cincinnati Milacron. The smaller automotive work is performed in between the larger jobs.

But the job they do is, in our opinion, well worth the wait, should a hobbyist decide to employ the modern chemical cleaning/derusting system.

AMC dispatches the undesirable coatings on metal surfaces basically two ways. One is by heat. Though it was not used on any of Suzy Q.'s parts, AMC has a large oven in which it stacks painted shelves, for instance. When the oven is as crammed full as possible, the doors are swung shut and the thermostat turned up. Up, up to 800 degrees Fahrenheit, at which temperature anything on the metal's surface literally incinerates. When the doors swing open again all the metal parts have on them is a coating of ash. Manager Mark Kormelink said heat is a very good means for cleaning metal parts.

Suzy Q.'s metal parts, her frame, suspension components, engine block, etc., were cleaned and derusted another way, however.

The cleaning/derusting process AMC uses is essentially a two-step procedure. The first is a degreasing process; the sec-

ond the derusting. For the parts to be effectively derusted, they must first be cleaned and degreased completely, according to Kormelink.

"The parts have to be 100 percent clean before going in the deruster." Kormelink said. AMC achieves perfect cleanliness through chemistry.

A diluted alkaline solution of caustic soda in water simmers at 180 degrees Fahrenheit in a large tank. Into this tank the metal parts are submerged, preferably over night. "It's not a hurry-up process, not one that can be short cut." said Kormelink. He also points out that

this solution attacks only the materials coating the metal's surfaces. It does not attack or eat away the metal itself as an acid cleaning process does.

Suzy Q.'s metal parts were loaded in via a tow motor and submerged overnight. The combination of the chemicals, heat and time gradually but completely loosened, if not lifted off, nearly every variety of "stuff" that has adhered itself to the parts' surfaces.

That which remains on the surfaces, as well as the chemical residue from the caustic solution itself, must be washed away. That is done by way of high-pressure, hot water washing. All parts are thoroughly washed to rinse away every sign of chemical and/or dirty residue. Nothing withstands the jet of water blasting out with a pressure of 2,000 psi.

9.

Once pronounced clean, the parts proceed to the derusting process. It also takes place in a multi-thousand gallon tank, but the process differs. The parts are suspended on bus bars in a diluted alkaline solution. Then the "juice" is turned on. The parts receive an electric charge, direct current of up to 1,520 amperes at three volts. The "soup" receives the opposite polarity electric charge of the same strength. With the power on, an electrolytic cleaning action is engaged. "It's a reversal of electroplating," says James Taylor, owner.

Each cycle is approximately four hours. The parts receive as many cycles as needed to completely electrolytically scrub away the rust. Suzy Q.'s parts had minimal rust, so her parts received the minimum treatment.

With the parts completely purged of rust, they are washed again to remove any chemical residue. After washing, a light, water-soluble coating of a rust inhibitor is applied to keep them free of rust. It must be washed off prior to priming and painting.

So you may be thinking to yourself, hmm, great process. What does it cost?

Taylor prefers you call him for a price on whatever part you may want to have degreased and derusted. It can vary depending on the condition of the part. The more rust on the part the longer the process takes, thus the more it will cost.

9. *Suzy Q's parts, as well as others from other smaller jobs, had been batched together to get the most out of a "dip in the soup." Here Kormelink and employee Randy Woods have taken the parts out of the derusting tank and moved them to the wash area.*

10. *Kormelink washes an A-arm that is looking remarkably clean.*

10.

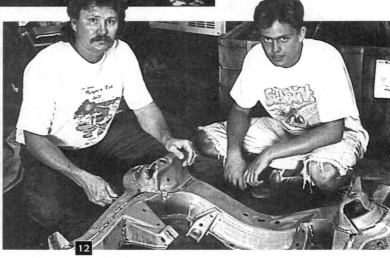

11.

12.

About the business

American Metal Cleaning of Cincinnati offers degreasing, derusting, and powder coating services. It is located at 475 Northland Road, Cincinnati, Ohio 45240; phone 513-825-1171. The owner is James Taylor and the manager is Mark Kormelink. Business hours are: 8 a.m. to 5 p.m., Monday through Friday, 9 a.m. to 1 p.m., Saturday.

13.

11. *Kormelink forces the water jet inside the frame to flush the remaining solution from the metal's surface. It is important to flush all residue from the metal's surface to completely halt the reaction.*

12. *AMC owner James Taylor (left) shows off Suzy Q.'s pristine frame to John Bailey, son of the former owner of AMC. It doesn't get any cleaner than this. It's ready for priming and painting.*

13. *The spindle, which has been derusted, will be coated with a water soluble rust inhibitor to prevent oxidation.*

Suzy Q Vette Resto

PAINTING THE FRAME & CHASSIS PARTS

By Ken New

Suzy Q.'s frame was in great shape when the restoration started. Not a single rust hole or sign of structural damage was found anywhere. There was the usual surface rust, but it was very thin, and there was no pitting. Even the factory black paint, a finish that has never been known for durability, was reasonably sound in places. It was obvious that Suzy Q. had spent her life in a friendly climate where corrosive road chemicals were virtually unknown. We were fortunate that a cosmetic restoration was all that was needed.

Around restoration shops, the term "chassis black" has become synonymous with a cheap and substandard type of paint that auto manufacturers have used for decades to finish frames and chassis parts. It appears they have not been overly concerned with the appearance of the undercarriage and bolted-on parts of cars once they hit the road. With little money or effort spent to ensure the finish applied to undercarriage components be formulated to withstand the rigors of time and road conditions, an original frame in pristine condition is extremely rare. While fully aware of the shortcomings of chassis black, we were still seeking a finish that would duplicate the non-shiny factory-look, but provide some toughness. We were in luck.

Several years ago, Jim Wietholder, head painter at the Antique Auto Shop, Elsmere, Ky., came up with a paint formula that replicates the flat black look of chassis black, but is capable of deliver-

Photos by the author

1. The painters at Antique Auto prefer to perform all paint work with the frame supported upside down on wooden horses. The logic is simple: Since the bottom of the frame is the "showy side" once the body is reattached, painting it upside-down provides easy access for even coverage and it is less likely that the paint will be scraped, etc.

2. The beauty of chemical rust removal can be seen in this close-up photo of the front coil spring area. We had to look hard to find the small chunks of undercoating left inside the spring tower. They were scraped out.

3. Andy Reeves hosed down the frame with straight tap water to rinse away a water-soluble, temporary rust prohibitive coating applied by American Metal Cleaning.

4. All moisture had to be removed. Reeves dried exposed areas of the frame with baby diapers as he looked for rust and grease that had not been removed by the chemical bath. Wiping rough sand-blasted surfaces is not recommended.

5. *Next, air was blown through the inaccessible portions of the boxed frame. The frame was tilted temporarily to allow runoff of standing water.*

6-7. *As an added precaution, Reeves ran a torch along the frame to administer just enough heat to evaporate remaining moisture. Too much heat would have distorted the frame. Reeves could have achieved the same result by placing the frame in hot summer sunshine for a few hours, but the threat of rain prevented it.*

5

6

7

ing the durability associated with modern catalyzed enamels. While the exact proportions and properties of Wietholder's formula are a well-kept secret, at the Antique Auto shop, Wietholder didn't mind telling us that the finish starts with clean metal, the cleaner the better, followed by applications of an etching primer, a high-build primer and the top coat he had formulated to replicate the look of chassis black.

Arriving at the Antique Auto Shop at 8 a.m. to witness the refinishing of the frame, we

8

8. *Spots are indication of places where grease build-up was removed. Even the best chemical cleaning fails to completely remove greasy deposits that are embedded in the pores of the metal. The spots were scrubbed with lacquer thinner to leach-out the grease.*

9

10

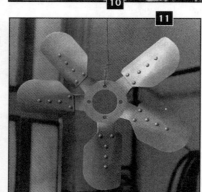

11

9. *Reeves counted 60-plus small chassis parts. All were hosed down with tap water. The necessity of rinsing the parts properly cannot be overemphasized, according to Reeves.*

10-11. *Properly cleaned surfaces will repel water readily. Here the engine fan gets a dousing. Close up of the fan shows the sanitary condition chemical cleaning produces.*

found Andy Reeves, Wietholder's right-hand man, eager to get started. Having arrived at the shop hours earlier, Reeves, with the help of other members of the staff, had positioned the frame upside down on wooden horses to ready it for the day's work. Join us for an informative and enjoyable visit to the paint booth at the Antique Auto Shop to watch as a couple of master painters return the "chassis black" look to Suzy Q.'s frame and chassis parts with space-age paints. At a later date, the insides of the boxed-in portions of the frame will receive a coating of rust inhibitor.

12. *Hanging rinsed parts, such as the rear suspension support, aided drainage. As a safety precaution, forced air and heat were administered as well.*

13. *Small parts, such as the brake backing plates which are of non-layered steel construction, are rinsed and dried.*

14. *We wanted the factory look of GM's chassis black, but not its weak resistance to rust and the effects of road chemicals. Antique Auto's finish painter, Jim Wietholder devised a formula which produces the original flat look of chassis black and the durability of modern catalyzed enamels. Wietholder likes DuPont products for their workability under humid conditions.*

15-16. *Reeves hung the small parts on a wire stretching across the paint spray booth, wiped the parts with a grease and wax remover solution, donned his protective clothing, and then applied two medium coats of activated DuPont Variprime 615 S, a gray-green self-etching primer, at 35-40 psi.*

17. *After 30 minutes of flash-off time, Reeves loaded his gun with DuPont's Prime 'N Seal 2640 S High Hiding Red primer and applied one medium coat. Hiding all gray-green surfaces with red primer ensured that all parts were covered.*

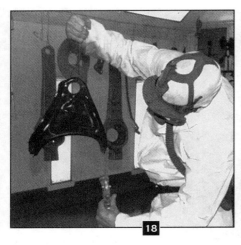

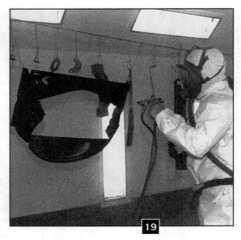

18-20. *After a second 30 minutes of drying time, Reeves applied the finish coat, a combination of various catalyzed DuPont products that produces a GM chassis black look and space-age durability.*

21. *The frame was moved into the spray booth and a new participant joined our program. Jim Wietholder, the inventor of the formula alluded to in previous captions, relieved a tired Andy Reeves who had spent 12-plus hours in and out of the spray booth on our project. Dust blown off the frame was caught in the spray booth's air filtration system.*

22. *With the frame still upside down, Wietholder proceeded to repeat the three-part finish procedure performed earlier by Reeves. Wietholder explained that Prime 'N Seal primer is available in at least five colors and offers excellent adhesion when applied directly to metal. The etching primer step taken on Suzy Q.'s frame and chassis parts was added insurance, he said.*

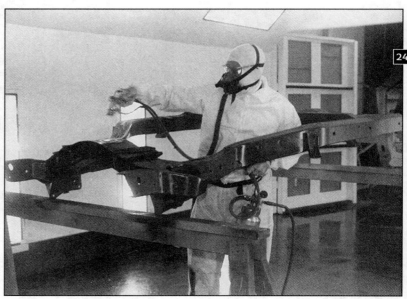

23-24. *Wietholder wiggled in, around and under the frame, working his magic until the frame was a thing of beauty. It is now ready to accept its refurbished parts and replacement pieces, and then the body.*

Vette Resto

SPRINGING TO ACTION

By Dean Shipley

With Suzy Q.'s frame blasted and painted, it's ready to accept the componentry that will make it a rolling chassis again. In this article, we will follow along as Antique Auto Shop technicians Bob Heeger, Tom Eggleston and John Bastian assemble the '63 Corvette Sting Ray's front suspension.

The procedure appears, on the surface, to be a basic bolt-it-on process. For many of the parts that is true. But there were a number of tricks of the trade we learned in the assembly process that restorers may find as interesting as we did.

Naturally, the first order of business is to make sure that all the new parts are on hand to do the job. Some parts, such as fasteners, need to be secured separately as they do not come in the component "kits."

If the restorer plans to reuse the fasteners, etc. that were on the car in the first place, he/she has to decide if they are suitable for reuse. In our case, some reused fasteners needed a little work, such as the retapping of threads, before they could be put back in place.

With all the parts accounted for, they were one by one fastened to the upper and lower control arms. Tom took the upper control arms, while Bob took the lower control arms.

Bushings for the control arms were driven into place. According to shop technicians, a special press is available, but the shop found a hammer and driver to be adequate tools for the job. One bushing was put in place, then the control arm shaft was inserted into it. As the second bushing was put in place, care was taken to allow the shaft end to be in proper position so the bushing could properly engage it.

Bolts holding the bushings in place were not tightened down completely.

1. *Suzy Q.'s frame has been blasted, primed and painted black. It's ready to accept components to make it a chassis again.*

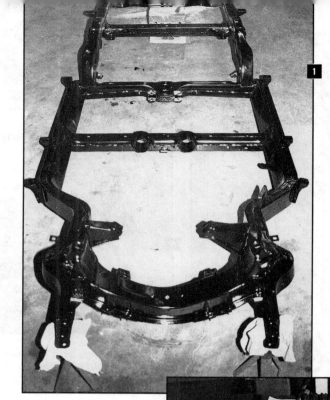

2. *The several hundred parts needed to rebuild the front end are all present and accounted for. Most of the parts were provided by Performance Suspension Technology. Along with the parts, the restorer should have a shop diagram of the front suspension and any photos taken when the component was disassembled.*

3. *Restorer Tom Eggleston puts the second control arm bushing into place. Sometimes the holes into which the bushings fit must be cleaned of paint buildup or other residue. The bushings fit very snugly and are lubricated with lithium lubricant prior to being driven into place. For a driver, Eggleston used a wrench socket that fit the flange of the bushing. The driver was "motivated" by a healthy ball peen hammer.*

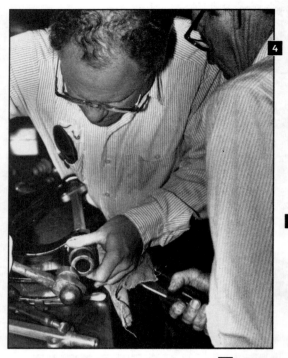

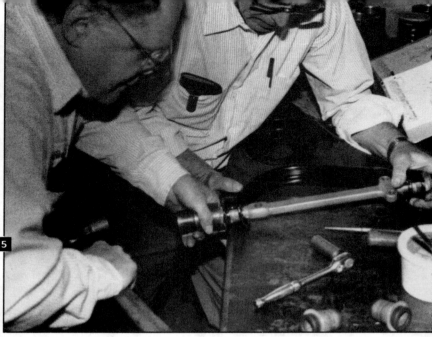

4-5. *Bob Heeger, with hammer, enlists the help of Eggleston to drive the bushings into place on the lower control arms. Because the lower control arm bushings have two holes to pass through, it is twice as difficult to install them. The bushings' flanges must be flush with the surface of the control arm into which they are inserted.*

6. *With the control arm shaft in place within the control arm bushings, Heeger installs, but does not tighten down, the bolts and washers for the bushings. This will allow the suspension to flex with the weight of the engine. The bushing bolts will be tightened later.*

7-8. *Antique Auto Shop restorer Bob Heeger inserts the ball joint into the lower control arm. It and the other ball joints were coated with a clear rust inhibitor prior to installation. Bolts are inserted from the top; nuts are on the bottom. Photo 8 illustrates Eggleston's installation in the upper control arm.*

9. *The ball joint is in place in the lower control arm. The nut on the right is a steering stop bolt that prevents the steering mechanism from rubbing on the lower control arm.*

They will be tightened securely once the engine is in place on the frame. By waiting until the engine is in place, the arms will have adjusted to the additional weight. When the bolts are tightened, the little teeth in the bushings will "bite" into the A-frame and hold it securely in place. If they are tightened down too soon, the added weight of the engine is enough to strip the bushings' teeth loose — not good.

It is also not good to attempt to mount the coil springs without a spring compression tool. The device squeezes the spring so the technician can mount it in place and connect the upper and lower control arms with the spindles. It's a tricky tool to work with, so gather all the patience you can muster and a helper before attempting to rebuild the front suspension.

10. *The lower control arms, with snubbers and bumpers, which merely bolt on, have been completed. The upper arms, not pictured, were completed similarly.*

11-12. *Before the coil springs can be installed, they must be compressed. The compressing tool is hooked around the coils. The threaded rod in the center provides the leverage to compress the spring. It is turned with the impact wrench until the spring compresses to a satisfactory height. Note the difference in photo 12.*

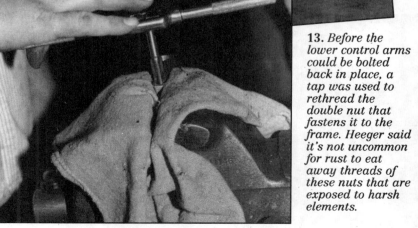

13. *Before the lower control arms could be bolted back in place, a tap was used to rethread the double nut that fastens it to the frame. Heeger said it's not uncommon for rust to eat away threads of these nuts that are exposed to harsh elements.*

14. *The lower control arm is bolted into place.*

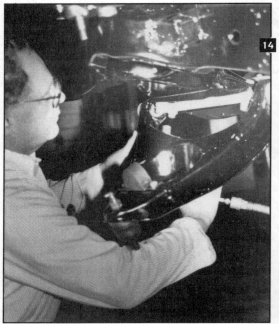

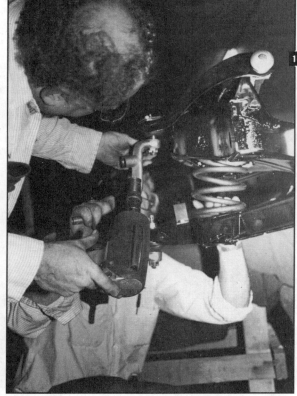

15-16. *With the coil spring in its housing, the control arms are connected by bolting them to the steering knuckle or spindle. Once those nuts are tightened, the spring compressor is loosened and gingerly removed from the coil spring. It is a "bit of a bag" to deal with, but just takes time to remove.*

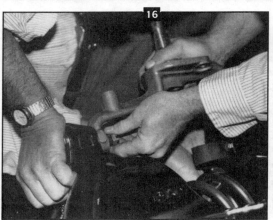

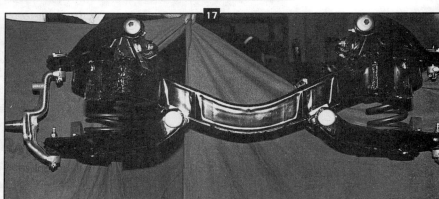

17. *The front suspension assembly is nearly complete. All that remains at this point is to install the shock absorbers and the PST replacement sway bar. It is considerably heavier than the original equipment.*

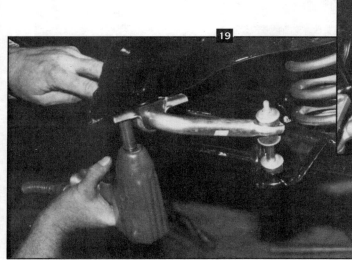

18. *John Bastian installs the bushing assembly around the end of the sway bar.*

19. *Heeger snugs up the bolts that clamp the sway bar to the forward section of the frame.*

Suzy Q.
Vette Resto

REBUILDING THE REAR END

By James B. DeWolfe with Ralph E. Holmquist, Keith E. Morgensai and Raymond L. Carver

1

W hen Suzy Q.'s rear end carrier assembly arrived by FedEx at my home in Marshall, Mich., I noticed immediately that it did not contain a limited slip differential as I had anticipated. When I rotated the input flange, the two output yokes turned in opposite directions, not the sign of a Posi unit. Had Posi gears been aboard, a similar twist of the input shaft would have caused the output shafts to rotate in the same direction. It appears that the open differential had been installed sometime in the past, possibly by a former owner who didn't have enough pocket money to afford the more desirable Posi unit.

After the initial inspection and the help of a strong neighbor boy, the heavy unit was in my car ready for transport across town to the Eaton Proving Ground Differential department where Ralph

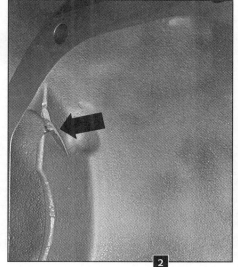

2

Holmquist, Keith Morgensai and Ray Carver had volunteered to assist me with the project. Upon arrival, I gave verbal directions "to disassemble, clean, inspect and replace, if necessary, all external and internal components." I explained that the goal of the project, which the Eaton employees had appropriately labeled "Eaton job code: Suzy Q.", was to rebuild the carrier assembly while maintaining the original 1963 factory integrity.

Advantages of a Positraction

Before we address the disassembly and rebuild of the Eaton Positrac limited-slip differential in detail, an explanation of the advantages of using a limited-slip differential is in order. The basic function of the limited-slip differential is to control or limit wheel spin of a single drive wheel – which can occur from a variety of reasons, i.e. different traction surfaces from one side of the car to the other, or weight transfer of the vehicle during cornering. A limited slip differential will attempt to control or limit wheel spin on the low traction side or the unloaded wheel during cornering, resulting in more torque being applied to the high traction side.

Photos by Ken New unless noted otherwise

1. All of the gentlemen pictured here contributed their expertise to this article. They are staff members of the Eaton Torque Control Products Division, Marshall, Mich. with the exception of Jim DeWolfe who retired from Eaton in 1981. From left to right, Keith Morgensai, Differential Lab Supervisor; Raymond Carver, Senior Lab Technician; Jim DeWolfe, retired; Ralph Holmquist, Chief Engineer, Differentials; Frank DeLong, Eaton newsletter reporter.

2. A visual inspection of the carrier cover revealed a crack in the casing (see arrow) and scars made by the heads of the bolts securing the ring gear. (Photo by Ray Carver)

The Positraction design that became a part of Suzy Q.'s drivetrain is engaged 100 percent of the time, whereas the newer Eaton Locker differential used in Chevrolet and GMC trucks functions much like an open differential until traction is lost by one of the rear wheels, then engine torque is applied to both rear wheels. Unlike the former design, the design of the Eaton Locker differential allows this action only when the vehicle is being driven at very low speeds.

Disassembly and analysis

The disassembly process of Suzy Q.'s unit was started by removing the rear cover casting and draining the fluid. Quickly, it became obvious that untrained hands had worked on the carrier unit sometime in the past. Several undesirable conditions existed, including gouges in the internal face of the carrier case made by contact by the heads of the ring gear bolts. Also, a small casting crack in the area of the vent compartment on the rear cover was found. The case was cleaned and an expert welder on the Eaton staff sealed the crack with a beautiful nickel weld.

The team agreed that all bearings and seals should be replaced due to the amount of contamination found in the drained fluid. The new parts were ordered, as an interesting peculiarity of Suzy Q.'s makeup surfaced.

When '63 vintage parts were ordered, the team discovered the carrier unit was actually a 1964 subassembly. Having followed the restoration articles, I was aware that Suzy Q.'s build date was July 1963. We concluded that the build date was apparently right at the transition point when production of the '64 Corvettes began, and Suzy Q. had received a '64 subassembly. The correct identification of the limited slip unit is GM3863415 and the Eaton number is ED12463-1. Interestingly, the factory option G81, an Eaton Positraction, priced out at $43.05 back in 1963.

The disassembly of the open differential and the build-up of an Eaton limited slip unit generally followed the procedures outlined in Chevy repair manuals of the period. Readers who wish to compare the procedures in the Chevy manual will notice that some special tools designed by members of Eaton's staff were used in some procedures. Due to time constraints, the Eaton staff installed the gears, set the tolerances and performed preliminary work prior to the arrival of *Cars & Parts'* art director, Ken New, who took the accompanying photos.

3. *A welder built-up a nickel weld to repair the damage to the cover.*

4. *Built very late in the 1963 production run (July 1963), Suzy Q. received a 1964-style rear end. The crush sleeves are different as seen in this photo. The '63 is at left, the longer piece is a '64 part.*

General description

The internal components of a 1963 Corvette rear axle carrier are of conventional design. A hypoid gear set is used with an overhung pinion supported on two preloaded tapered roller bearing assemblies. The optional traction improving Eaton Positraction differential assembly is supported on tapered roller bearings. The drive pinion mounting distance adjustments are made through the use of shims, as are the differential bearing preload and backlash adjustments. The Eaton Positraction differential side gears drive two side gear yokes that are retained laterally by snap rings located on the yoke splined end. The yokes are supported on caged needle bearings pressed into the carrier, adjacent to the Eaton Positraction differential bearings. A lip seal pressed in the carrier outboard of the bearings prevents oil leakage and dirt entry. The carrier cover is bolted to the carrier and provides accessibility to the internal parts. The filler plug is located on the right side of the cover near the bolting flange.

Disassembly steps and visual inspection

A visual inspection of the complete external differential carrier case, drive pinion and side gear yokes did not indicate any apparent damage. The disassembly followed GM manual recommendations:

1. The removal of the cover bolts and carrier cover confirmed that a standard GM "open" differential (not an Eaton Positraction) was installed in the carrier. The lubricant was drained, examined and later discarded. The examination showed that it

Tooth Contact Pattern Test

● **Low flank contact:** Correct by decreasing drive pinion shim thickness

● **Heel contact:** Correct by decreasing backlash

● **Correct pattern:** No correction necessary

● **Toe contact:** Correct by increasing backlash

● **High face contact:** Correct by increasing drive pinion shim thickness

was contaminated with metal particles. Further investigation showed that the metal particles were from contact between the ring gear bolt heads and the interior walls of the carrier housing and carrier cover.

2. The side gear yokes were pulled out after removing the differential pinion pin retainer, pinion shaft and side gear yoke snap ring. A visual inspection revealed both the right and left yokes to be in good condition.

3. The side bearing caps were removed after they were marked to insure that they could be identified and returned to their original locations during reassembly. Interchanging them is not recommended.

4. The differential assembly was removed and the side bearing shims were marked for future reference. The standard GM open differential was in good condition. However, the ring gear bolts were damaged from contact with the inner walls of the carrier and carrier cover. The probable cause was improper installation of the open unit.

5. The drive pinion nut, companion flange washer, companion flange and hypoid drive pinion were removed. It appeared that the hypoid drive pinion had been removed and/or replaced, because the original bearing spacer showed attempts at rebuilding by adding homemade shims. The hypoid drive pinion shim measured .020" (this was out of the norm, very low), resulting in a poor contact pattern between the hypoid gear set. Both bearing assemblies were in good condition, although contaminated.

Restoration steps

1. Due to the poor wear pattern of the original gears, a decision was made to replace the original 3.55 ratio hypoid gear set with a new set, GM part 3961420 which matches the original 3.55:1 ratio.

2. New pinion bearing assemblies, GM part 7451155 and GM part 7451281 were installed, along with a new pinion bearing spacer (commonly called a crush sleeve), GM part 3817864. A .030-inch pinion bearing shim was selected based on GM recommended gauging procedures.

3. A new pinion oil seal (GM part 3869910), a companion flange washer (GM3714792), and a pinion nut (GM3752901) were installed along with the original production companion flange. Per GM specifications, torque required to rotate the pinion after proper installation should range between 15-30 in.-lbs. with new bearings and seal, or 5-15 in.-lbs. when used parts are reinstalled. Suzy Q.'s new unit was set up with a rotating torque of 17 in.-lbs.

Checking Ring-to-Pinion Gear Tooth Contact

1. Wipe the oil from the insides of the carrier and carefully clean each tooth of the ring gear.

2. Use gear marking compound 1052351 or equivalent and apply the mixture sparingly to all ring gear teeth, using a medium-stiff brush. When properly used, the area of pinion tooth contact

will be visible when hand load is applied.

3. Tighten bearing cap bolts to the specified torque.

4. Expand the brake shoes until a torque of 40 to 50 lbs.-ft. is required to turn the pinion. A test made without loading the gears will not give a satisfactory pattern. Turn the pinion flange with a wrench so that the ring gear rotates one full revolution, then reverse the rotation so that ring gear rotates one revolution in the opposite direction.

5. Observe the pattern on the ring gear teeth and compare with the accompanying drawings.

Restorers who wish to review other detailed illustrations of gear wear patterns are advised to consult an appropriate repair manual. Due to space limitations, we are unable to show them here. This pertains to the following two sections.

Gear Tooth Nomenclature

The convex side of the ring gear tooth which curves outward is referred to as the "drive" side. The concave side is the "coast" side. The end of the tooth nearest to the center of the ring gear is referred to as the "toe" end. The end of the tooth farthest away from the center is the "heel" end. The toe end of the tooth is smaller than the heel end. The lower half of the gear tooth contact surface is called the "flank," and the upper half is called the "face." It was very important that the tooth contact be tested before the rear axle carrier assembly is disassembled. Variations in the carrier or pinion rear bearing may cause the pinion to be too far away from, or close to, the ring gear. Thus, the tooth contact must be tested and corrected, if necessary, or the gears may be noisy.

Effects of Increasing Load on Tooth Contact Pattern

When the load on the ring and pinion gear is increased, such as when Suzy Q. is accelerated forward from a standstill or from normal drive, the tooth contact will tend to spread out and, under very heavy load, will extend from near the toe to near the heel on the drive side. The entire contact also tends to shift toward the heel under increasingly heavier loads and will become somewhat broader with respect to the tops and bottoms of the teeth. The patterns obtained by this tooth contact pattern test approximate a light load. For this reason, they will extend only about halfway. The important thing to note is that the contact pattern should be centrally located up and down on the face of the ring gear teeth. Insufficiently preloaded drive pinion and differential side bearings will also cause a change in tooth contact pattern under load.

Tooth contact adjustments, Fig. 1

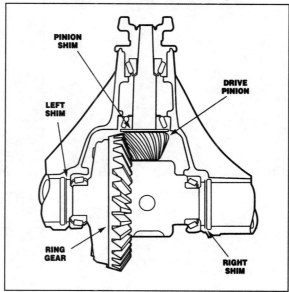

Pinion Depth adjustments, Fig. 2

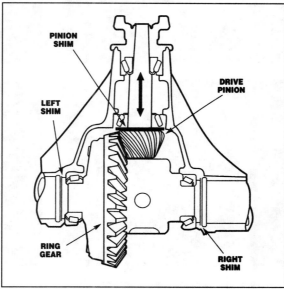

Backlash adjustments, Fig. 3

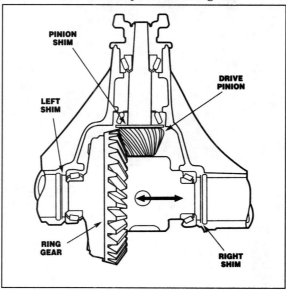

Adjustments Affecting Tooth Contact

Two adjustments can be made to affect the tooth contact pattern: backlash, and the position of the drive pinion in the carrier (Fig. 1). The effects of bearing preloads are not readily apparent on the hand-loaded tooth contact pattern tests; however, those adjustments should be brought into spec before proceeding with the backlash and drive pinion adjustments.

The position of the drive pinion is adjusted by increasing or decreasing the shim thickness between the pinion head and inner race of the rear bearing (Fig. 2). A shim can be used in the rear axle to compensate for manufacturing tolerances. Increasing shim thickness moves the pinion closer to the centerline of the ring gear while decreasing shim thickness moves the pinion farther away from the centerline of the ring gear.

Backlash is adjusted by means of the side bearing adjusting shims which moved the entire case and ring gear assembly closer to, or farther from, the drive pinion. Adjusting shims are also used to set side bearing preload. (See Fig.3.) If the thickness of the right shim is increased along with decreasing the left shim thickness, backlash will increase. Backlash decreases if the left shim thickness is increased along with a decrease in the thickness of the right shim.

Effects of Pinion Position on Tooth Pattern

When the drive pinion is too far away from the centerline of the ring gear, the pattern will be a high heel contact on the drive side and high toe contact on the coast side. Moving the pinion closer to centerline of the ring gear by increasing shim thickness will cause the high heel contact on drive side to lower and move toward the toe; the high toe contact on coast side will lower and move toward the heel. When the pinion is too close to the centerline of the ring gear, the pattern will be a low toe contact on the drive side, and a low contact on coast. Moving the pinion farther away from the ring gear by decreasing shim thickness will cause low toe contact on the drive side to raise and move toward the heel; the low heel contact on the coast side will raise and move toward toe. Pinion depth is correct when the contact on the drive side is directly opposite the contact on the coast side. As mentioned previously, readers who wish to study gear pattern in detail are advised to consult a repair manual.

Assembly of Eaton Positraction

The build-up of the optional Eaton Positraction differential GM 3863415 (Eaton ED12463-1) unit to replace the open differential unit in Suzy Q.'s differential carrier is shown in the following photos.

5. *When Ken New came to photograph the assembly operations, the pinion gear tolerances were set. It was an arduous task that required removing and reinstalling the pinion numerous times.*

6. *Eaton technician Ray Carver began the final assembly by lubricating the clutch plates and discs with a special positraction lubricant.*

7. *Five clutch plates and four clutch discs were stacked on the side gear, beginning with a clutch plate and alternating disc and plate, until all nine were on the gear. Two guide clips per pack held in place with a liberal amount of grease, were installed. A .020"-thick shim was selected and placed on the hub of the side gear disc pack subassembly. One side gear clutch pack assembly and shim was installed in the flange end of the differential case.*

8. *The pinion gears and thrust washers were positioned on the side gears while installing the pinion shaft through the case and gears.*

9. *A dial indicator was located on the case so the indicator tip rested against the pinion gear tooth face. With the clutch compressed, the pinion gear was rotated to obtain backlash. Tooth backlash should be .001" to .006". Had the set-up deemed a .020" shim improper, it would have been changed to obtain correct backlash. The side gear assembly was removed and the tooth backlash procedure repeated for the other gear pack on the opposite side of the case. The pinion shaft, gears and thrust washers were removed.*

10. *The first side gear clutch pack assembly and shim were reinstalled in the flange end of the case.*

11. *The pinion gears and thrust washers were installed.*

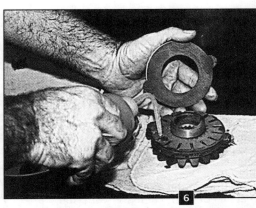

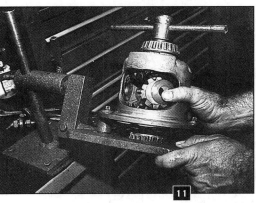

CORVETTE REAR AXLE SPECIFICATIONS

Gear backlash
(.005"-.008" preferred) .... .003"-.010"

Pinion bearing preload
New .... 20-25 in. lbs.
Used .... 5-15 in. lbs.

Lubricant capacity .... 3-3/4 pints

Bolt torques
Carrier Cover .... 50 lbs.-ft.
Ring Gear .... 50 lbs.-ft.
Differential Bearing Caps .... 55 lbs.-ft.
Filler plug .... 20 lbs.-ft.
Differential Pinion Lock .... 20 lbs.-ft.

POSITRACTION LUBRICANT

Positraction units invariably require the use of a special lubricant to maintain the correct slip characteristics between the surface of the clutch pack. Due to environmental concerns the original lubricant, containing whale oil is no longer available.

The lubricant level should be checked periodically and maintained at the level of the filler plug measured while the axle is warm. GM specifications list a lubricant capacity of 3 3/4 pints, using GM rear axle lube part 1052271 and four ounces of GM Limited Slip Additive part 1052358. If the wrong oil is used, the clutch plates in the differential will chatter.

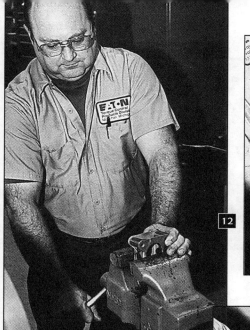

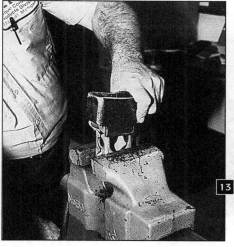

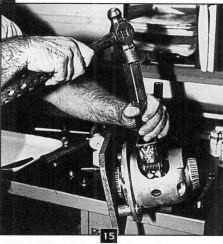

12-14. *The springs and load plates were assembled in a shop vise and the assembly compressed until the load plates touched. Ray Carver used a special tool of his own design to hold the clutch pack together to insert the pack into the proper position.*

15. *The spring pack was positioned between the side gears, then driven sufficiently into the side gears to retain the front springs. The tool was then removed.*

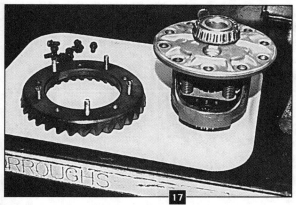

16. *The pinion shaft and lock screw were installed, then the lock screw tightened finger loose, because it had to be removed one last time when the splined yokes were installed.*

17. *Carver fabricated guide pins by cutting the heads from bolts, then slotting the ends. Then he screwed them into the ring gear. The ring gear mounting surface and mounting flange on the case were cleaned and the ring gear was positioned on the case pilot diameter.*

18. *Skipping every other bolt hole, the ring gear bolts (GM part 14003451) were run down, and tightened to raise the ring gear evenly until the gear was seated against the flange. The guide pins were then removed and the remaining ring gear bolts run down. All bolts were torqued to 50 lbs.-ft.*

19. *With this task completed, the assembly was ready for installation.*

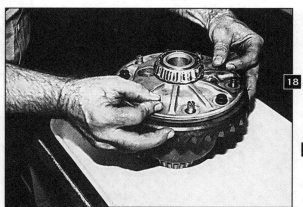

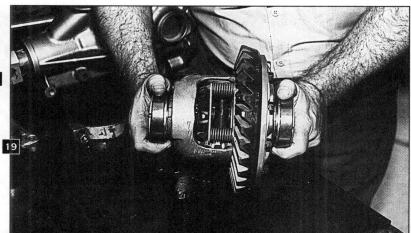

20

21

22

20. *The bearings were properly lubricated and the cups positioned on the bearings. Next the Eaton Positraction differential assembly was installed in the carrier. Production preloading of the differential bearings was accomplished by the use of cast iron preload shims. These shims should not be used when rebuilding the carrier as they may break when tapped into place.*

21. *The selected shims were installed between the carrier and bearing cap. A soft-face hammer was used to tap the shims into position.*

22. *The right and left bearing caps were installed and the bolts torqued to 55 lbs.-ft. Although not shown, a dial indicator was mounted on the carrier to check the backlash between the ring gear and the pinion. Backlash should be within the range of .004" to .010" with a reading of .005" to .008" preferred. Suzy Q.'s backlash was set at .006". The dial indicator was positioned so the indicator tip was perpendicular to the tooth face and in line with the gear rotation. If gear lash had not been within limits, decreasing the shim thickness on one side and increasing thickness of the other shim by the same amount would have corrected the problem. For example, decreasing the shim on the right side by .002" and increasing shim thickness on the left side by .002" would have decreased backlash by .001". The ring gear and pinion contact pattern was checked against acceptable patterns illustrated in GM manuals.*

23

24

23. *The new yoke bearings were tapped gently into the carrier.*

24. *Then, the new yoke seals, GM part 3820419, were pressed into the carrier outboard of the bearing.*

25. *The pinion cross shaft lock screw and cross shaft were removed from the differential. Both the right and left side gear yokes were installed making sure the snap rings secured the side gear yokes in the unit. The pinion cross shaft and lock pin were replaced and the lock pin torqued to 15.*

26. *The carrier cover gasket GM part 3818793 was installed on the carrier cover and the cover bolts torqued to 50 lbs.-ft.*

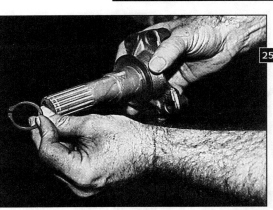

25

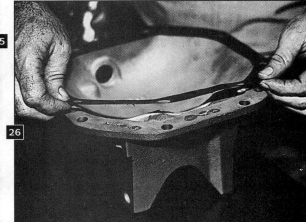

26

James B. DeWolfe

Helping people restore their old cars is "kind of a mission" for Jim DeWolfe, the 70-year-old retiree says. DeWolfe is a former quality control official with Eaton Corp., the company that supplied Chevrolet with the Positraction limited-slip differential unit originally installed in Suzy Q.'s drivetrain.

DeWolfe is a regular reader of *Cars & Parts*. When he read that we had chosen a 1963 Corvette as our restoration project, it brought back memories of his salad days and his involvement in the design and manufacture of the Vette's differential. Although very active in his area's Chamber of Commerce and the local historical society in Marshall, Mich., DeWolfe decided he could find time to examine and rebuild Suzy Q.'s differential unit as a special favor to *Cars & Parts* and a public service to the old car hobby. You may recall DeWolfe's name in association with similar restoration work he performed on our previous project cars, Vicky, the 1955 Ford Crown Victoria, and Peggy Sue, a 1957 Chevy Bel Air convertible.

DeWolfe graduated from Cass Technical High School in Detroit with a major in automotive engineering. During World War II, he served as a U.S. Navy carrier pilot in the Pacific. After the war, he married his high school sweetheart and in 1946 joined the staff at Eaton's Detroit facility as a lab technician in the company's experimental engineering department. There he became directly involved with the development of front and rear hydraulic pumps for automotive transmissions, in addition to designing, engineering and evaluating prototype power steering pumps for various vehicles. DeWolfe's face lit up as he recounted the first American production passenger car to offer power steering, the 1951 Chrysler. It used an Eaton unit on which DeWolfe had worked. Concerned with its performance in the field, it was over-engineered and used the most durable materials available. DeWolfe likened the over-built unit's application to "killing a fly with a sledgehammer."

At the Detroit facility, DeWolfe also taught service schools, wrote manuals and worked on the development and release of power steering for trucks and tractors. In 1956, he transferred to Eaton's production facility in Marshall, Mich., where he served as quality control supervisor and sales manager of hydrostatic pumps and motors. During that period of service, he was intimately involved with the development and manufacture of the limited-slip differential and viscous fan clutch designs that became part of Suzy Q.'s makeup. He knows the designs inside and out, and even remembers most of the part numbers of the parts and assemblies he worked on.

He still stays in touch with the current Eaton engineering staff. When reading the author's list of acknowledgements, you'll notice that he recruited several of his Eaton buddies in the execution of this restoration project.

DeWolfe and his wife of 49 years, Helen, have three grown children.

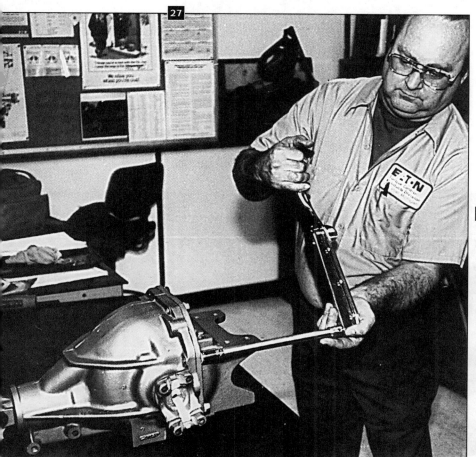

27. *Carver torqued the cover bolts to 50 lbs.-ft. Notice the case has been painted argent silver and the correct inspection marks were daubed in the proper places.*

28. *Carver demonstrates the proper method of filling a rear end with fluid. The carrier assembly will be filled with 3-3/4 pints of GM axle lube, part 1052271, and one four ounce bottle of GM limited slip additive, part 1052358 once the rear end assembly is bolted back onto Suzy Q.'s frame.*

Vette Resto

REAR SUSPENSION REASSEMBLY

By Eric Brockman

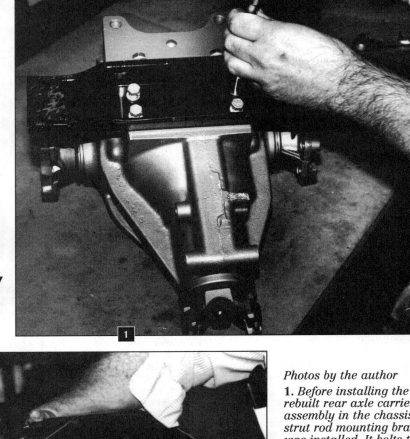

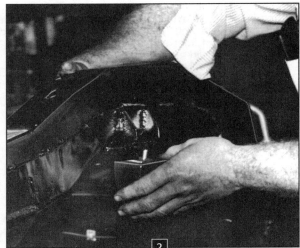

O ne of the highlights of the new Corvette Sting Ray that debuted for 1963 was the independent rear suspension. Critics had derided the previous Corvettes for their "crude" solid rear axle setup. With the introduction of the Sting Ray, Corvette enthusiasts could boast of a world class suspension.

Unfortunately, the independent rear suspension can also provide world class headaches for novice restorers not intimately familiar with its workings. We opted to let the Antique Auto Shop, Elsmere, Ky., which had handled the rest of the chassis restoration, reassemble the rear suspension of Suzy Q.

With the independent rear suspension, the axle carrier is mounted to a rear suspension crossmember at the rear and a support bracket at the front. The carrier lacks the cast-in axle tubes of a solid-axle setup. Axle "driveshafts" are attached to each side of the differential via U-joints. U-joints then connect each axle driveshaft to the spindle drive flanges, which, as the name implies, drive the spindles. The spindles drive the rear wheels. Each spindle and its accompanying support are contained in a control arm (sometimes also called a trailing arm). The front section of each control arm mounts to the frame on a pivot bolt. On each side, a strut rod mounts to the spindle support and the differential carrier. For springing, a single transverse leaf spring

Photos by the author

1. *Before installing the rebuilt rear axle carrier assembly in the chassis, the strut rod mounting bracket was installed. It bolts to the bottom of the differential case.*

2. *Bob Heeger began the reassembly by first installing the control arm bumpers on the frame.*

3. *Heeger and John Bastian then installed the rear suspension crossmember, to which the differential bolts.*

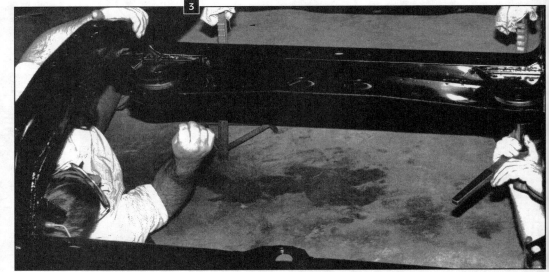

is utilized. It is attached to the differential via a clamp plate, and each end of the spring is suspended from a control arm.

This is referred to as a three-link rear suspension, with the axle driveshafts, strut rods, and control arms forming the three links at each rear wheel. According to Chevy, this setup reduced overall vehicle weight, reduced unsprung weight, and eliminated wheel tramp and torque steer.

To look at it, you wouldn't think this rear suspension setup would work very efficiently. But it got the job done, because Chevy used it with few changes for nearly 20 years.

With the installation of the rear suspension (and the brakes, which are covered elsewhere in this issue), it won't be much longer until the body is reunited with the chassis. 📷

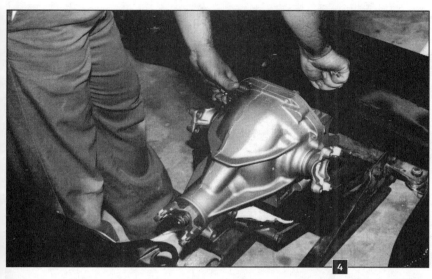

4. *The differential, supported on a floor jack, was moved into position and bolted to the crossmember.*

5. *The front differential support bracket was installed. It bolts to the underside of the differential and to a bracket on the frame.*

6. *The next step involved reassembling the control arms. First, new wheel bearing races were installed in the spindle supports.*

7. *Heeger bolted the spindle support and brake backing plate to the control arm.*

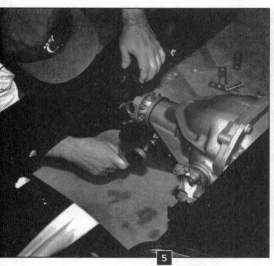

8. *Heeger and Tom Eggleston installed the wheel spindles using a press. Each spindle has a splined end, over which a drive flange fits and is bolted into place. The axle driveshafts bolt to these flanges, thus transmitting the power to the rear wheels.*

9. *The completed control arm (sometimes also referred to as a trailing arm) assembly was bolted into place on the frame.*

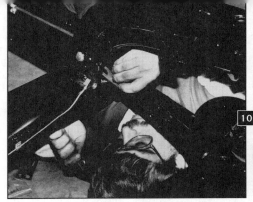

10. *The factory installed shims between the control arm and the frame to adjust rear wheel toe-out. Toe-out can be adjusted by adding or removing shims.*

11. *The strut rods were bolted into place on the strut rod bracket. The eccentric cam and bolt assemblies that hold them in place on the bracket are used to adjust the rear end camber. The bolt which holds the other end of the strut rod in place also serves as the mounting point for the shock absorbers.*

12. *Next, the transverse leaf spring was installed. With a floor jack supporting it, the spring was bolted to the differential.*

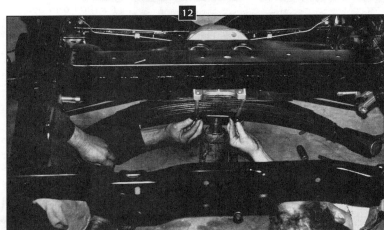

13. *Getting the spring link bolts into place on each end of the spring is tricky with the independent rear suspension. Antique Auto used a jack to lift the end of the spring while the bolt and spring cushions were mounted.*

14. *With the spring in place, the axle driveshafts were bolted into place. With the independent rear, U-joints are utilized at both ends of each shaft. At the control arm, the shaft mounts to the previously mentioned spindle drive flange.*

15. *Finally, the shock absorbers were mounted.*

16. *The fully reassembled rear end. The rear brakes could now be installed and the chassis prepared to receive the body.*

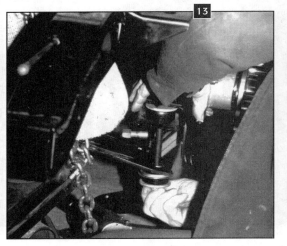

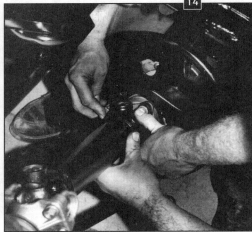

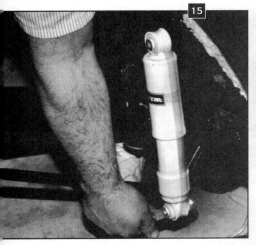

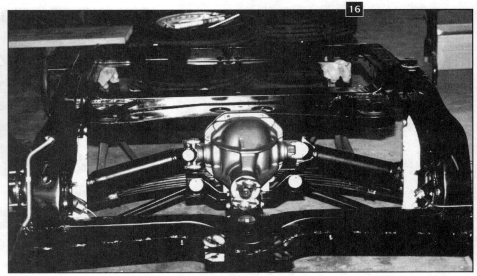

Suzy Q
Vette Resto

REBUILDING THE GAS TANK

By Bob Stevens

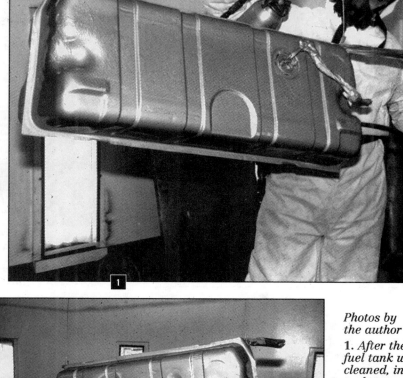

1

2

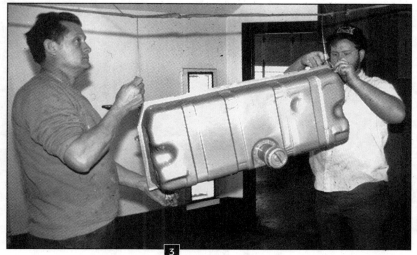

3

Refurbishing the fuel tank is a minor task, but an important one, in any restoration. A dirty tank contaminates gasoline, clogs fuel lines, ruins filters, and can even damage carburetors. Worse than that, an improperly rebuilt gas tank can leak fuel, creating a fire hazard, damaging paint, etc.

Suzy Q.'s tank, an all-steel affair, was in really decent shape. It hadn't been damaged or dented during its first 30 years of service. There was no need to search for a new or used tank, since this one was in need of no more than a cleaning and refinishing. This task was assigned to the Antique Auto Shop, Elsmere, Ky., where the chassis was being restored.

After thoroughly cleaning the tank, inside and out, the outside was sandblasted to remove all grime and rust scale. The tank cleaned up nicely. Then Jim Wietholter, the shop's paint expert, cleaned the tank again, applied a coating of self-etching primer, followed by a non-sanding primer-sealer. Then he sprayed the tank with an acrylic urethane paint, aluminum in color. Normally, the tank on a '63 Corvette was left in bare metal, but it was decided to prime and paint the tank to prevent any reoccurrence of the rust or scale.

After the tank was completely dried, Bob Heeger, of the Antique Auto Shop's mechanical department, removed the filler neck and the sending unit. A gas tank rebuilding kit from Quanta Restoration & Preservation Products, North East, Md., was then opened up. The kit consists of a new cork gasket and mounting screws for the filler neck, a rubber gasket and retaining cam for the tank gauge (sending unit), and a pair of anti-squeak mounting strips for the tank

itself. The reproduction parts fit precisely and mounted quickly and easily.

The tank is now ready to be remounted on the chassis, hooked up to a new fuel line, and filled with premium-grade petrol to feed that thirsty 300-horse Chevy small-block that is the beating heart of Suzy Q.

Photos by the author

1. After the steel fuel tank was cleaned, internally and externally, and the exterior was sandblasted, the Antique Auto Shop's ace painter, Jim Wietholter, squirted some acrylic urethane paint, aluminum in color, over a couple of freshly applied primer coats.

2. The painted tank hung in the spray booth until thoroughly dry and ready for handling.

3. Wietholter (left) is assisted by fellow Antique Auto Shop staffer Jack Morgan in removing the tank from the drying rack.

4. *Bob Heeger, a mechanic at the Antique Auto Shop, removes the filler neck from the gas tank.*

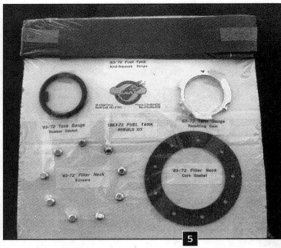

5. *A fuel tank restoration kit from Quanta Restoration and Preservation Products, North East, Md., was employed. It included a cork gasket and a set of mounting screws for the filler neck, a tank gauge rubber gasket and retaining cam, and a pair of fuel tank anti-squeak strips ... everything one needs to rebuild and reinstall a tank.*

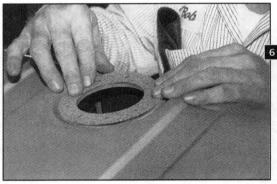

6. *The cork gasket slips right into the ready-made cavity. The new screws were then used to remount the filler neck.*

7. *Heeger reinserts the cleaned and inspected sending unit into the tank. A new filter was installed.*

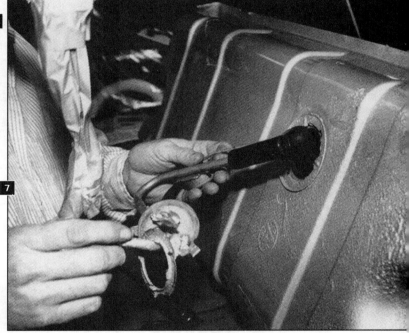

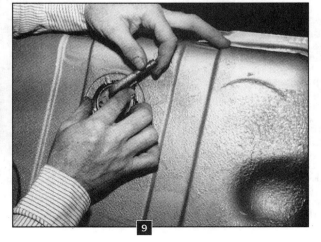

8. *The rubber gasket for the tank gauge was dropped in place; then the retaining cam was positioned over it.*

9. *Heeger completes the reinstallation of the gas tank sending unit. Everything went back together with no problem.*

Suzy Q 63
Vette Resto

PIPER'S A CORVETTE SPECIALIST

By Dean Shipley

"**J**.T.'s got it, but you'll pay for it."

J.T. Piper added a hoarse chuckle to that quote of some anonymous Corvette hobbyist who has dealt with him in the past. Piper, of Piper's Auto Specialties, Vermilion, Ill., attests to the statement. But what goes with the part, whether an NOS Corvette part or rebuilt drivetrain component, is the assurance the part is genuine Corvette and in the best condition in which it can possibly be.

Piper prides himself on being one of the best providers in the country of Corvette and other GM-make parts. He stands firmly behind any part that comes out of his warehouse on Water Street.

Piper has been in the Corvette parts business officially since 1978. His business grew out of his love of the Corvette that was enkindled as a boy. "My sister went with a guy who had one, and I always wanted one," he said.

His first one was a '58 model for which he paid $800. He initally had no intentions of selling it, but someone made him an offer he couldn't refuse: $3,000. "He paid me in one-hundred dollar bills. I didn't know that many one hundred dollar bills existed," he said.

He parlayed the gain on that first sale into a purchase of two more Corvettes. Yes, he sold them as well.

As he became more immersed in the Corvette culture, Piper, a long-time swap meet veteran, kept his eyes and ears open for parts. It paid off. He learned of a Corvette owner who had six cars and a cache of parts for which he was asking $27,000. Because he had a good day job

1. Piper's Auto Specialties is located on Water Street in the sleepy village of Vermilion, Ill., about nine miles southeast of Paris, Ill.
2. J.T. Piper, proprietor, points out the numbers to be cognizant of when buying a Borg-Warner T-10 transmission for a Corvette.
3. J.T. and the man responsible for his love of cars: his father, Perry Piper, who is well-known in the Edsel branch of the car hobby. Perry, 84, writes a weekly column, "Growing Up on Muddy Creek," carried by several area newspapers.
4. Shelves of transmissions, all tagged for easy reference, are included in Piper's inventory.
5. Not confined to trannies, Piper's has rear end third members, also dated for the discriminating Corvette restorer who wants all the correct build dates to coincide. Piper said that is an important factor in determining a car's value.

in those days, working for a natural gas pipeline company, he was able to borrow the money.

Then while visiting his grandmother in Bloomington, Ill., he heard about a Corvette meet held there. He took his parts to sell.

"We were selling parts left and right," he said. He found out later his prices were too low. "They took advantage of me. I was a virgin," he said.

But he still made money. Piper said when he took his receipts back to his grandmother's house and threw them on the bed where he was sleeping, "all she could say was 'my, my, my.'"

He paid off his loan in four months. At that point, he quit his good day job to go into the Corvette parts business full time.

Piper has learned the Corvette market well. No longer "a virgin," he knows the value of what he has (hence the quote at the beginning of this story).

But he knows the codes, has the correct parts with dates inventoried and doesn't ship what he calls "junk."

"The good stuff. That's what we're known for," he said with apparent pride.

Junk may be in the Piper lexicon, but *not* in his inventory.

He remains a Corvette enthusiast with 10 in his stable.

"I still care about the hobby," he said.

That's why he wants to provide the best Corvette parts and GM parts possible.

"It's gonna be done right!"

About the Shop
Piper's Auto Specialties is located at 3 Water St., Vermilion, IL 61955. The company specializes in restored Corvette and GM transmissions and rear ends and other parts. Tech Line 217-275-3743; 1-800-365-1102; FAX 217-275-3515.

Suzy Q

Vette Resto

TRANNIE TEARDOWN TRANS REBUILD PART 1

By Dean Shipley

Photos by the author

1. *Suzy Q.'s Muncie four-speed transmission, in its entirety, awaits the touch from the master's hand, Darrell Shepherd of 4-speeds by Darrell, Vermilion, Ill.*

For many people, part of the fun of driving a Corvette is running that baby through the gears. The author had the good fortune some years ago to have a friend, who had a '62 Corvette with a four-speed transmission. (That's the next best thing to having your own Vette). He felt me responsible enough to take the driver's seat from time to time and give me the pleasure of putting that Corvette through the paces. What a rush!

However, if that transmission is not going into gear and *staying* there, the pleasure of driving a four-speed-equipped Corvette is diminished.

One of our prerequisites for Suzy Q. was that she have a four-speed transmission. Since she was built late in the '63 model year, she was equipped with a Muncie four-speed gear box. Earlier-built '63 Corvette Sting Rays are equipped (or should be) with the Warner T-10 four-speed transmission.

When Darrell Shepherd, of 4 Speeds by Darrell, a division of J.T. Piper's Auto Spec, Inc., hefted Suzy Q.'s gearbox onto the bench, he was somewhat taken aback by the sizable globs of silicone sealer oozing from the trannie's joints.

"Someone's been in this one before (me)," he said.

It showed some of the earmarks of less than professional quality work thereon, but fortunately it did the transmission no apparent harm.

The long and short of it is, Shepherd pronounced the transmission in very good condition and would need just the basics in the rebuild process.

He said if he had found this transmis-

2. *The transmission number is stamped on the side of the case facing the shifting plate. The first digit, 3, indicates the model year, 1963. The second number 120317, matches or should match the numbers in the Corvette's serial number. It does. Shepherd and Piper check this number closely to confirm the transmission does indeed come out of a numbers-matching car. Muncie transmissions with letters in the number indicate they came from passenger cars.*

sion at a swap meet, pulled off the shift plate cover and given it a cursory examination, on a scale of 1 to 10, he would have given Suzy Q.'s Muncie a "9."

Well, as transmissions go, our four-speed will soon be dressed to the nines. But here following we'll give you a look at what was found when the transmission was opened up and inspected. We'll give you a few tips as well on some things to look for when you look at Muncie transmissions at swap meets.

3. *Another number on the transmission, in this case P05 17, indicates the build date. This Muncie transmission (P) was built May (05) seventeenth (17). Shepherd said in all the Muncie transmissions he has rebuilt, the earliest date he has seen is May 1 (05 01). In '67 the numbers on the Muncies changed.*

4. *A visual check of the splines tells you about the gear cluster inside. The notched spline on the right, indicates the transmission has a close ratio gear cluster, that is found attached to the higher horsepower engines. The smooth spline, left, Suzy Q.'s by the way, indicates a wide ratio cluster rotates therein. It was used for the base horsepower (250) and 300 horsepower engines.*

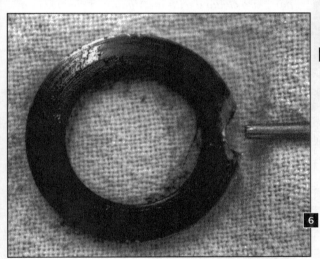

5. The screwdriver points to a large gouge battered out of the main drive nut on the front of the transmission. This confirmed the transmission had been gone through previously and that brute force, in the form of hammer and chisel, had been used to remove this nut. A gouge this severe will cause leakage of trans fluid and the ruination of the clutch.

6. A close up view of the damage to the main drive nut.

7. With the shifting plate off, the gears are visible. They are coated with a heavy black varnish-like substance. It indicates the car has been not used and has sat for "a long time," according to Shepherd.

8. Shepherd removes the main gear cluster after the tail piece had been removed. He found in disassembly the cluster shaft was loose in the case. This indicated wear, which is common flaw found in early-built transmissions. At this point proper diagnosis is not possible because of all the dirt.

9. *In disassembling the gear set, Shepherd removes a bearing retainer that is unique to the '63 model. It is of smaller diameter that retainers of succeeding years.*

10. *Filthy parts are loaded into baskets in preparation for cleaning.*

11. *Shepherd loads them into the washer. The parts are cleaned with an Aluminum cleaner in a jet-spray cabinet. The parts were so dirty, they had to be run through the machine several cycles. But Shepherd is an absolute stickler for these fine points. That's what makes him the best in the business.*

13. *A close up look at two second gears. The gear on the right shows damage to the shifting teeth indicated by the arrows. The second gear on the left, Suzy Q.'s shows there is no wear to the shifting teeth. Always inspect these,* not *the big gears when seeking a transmission. This is readily visible, when the transmission's shifting plate is removed. This is a must when negotiating to buy a transmission at a swap meet. If the seller says the trans is rebuilt, ask for proof by inspecting that set of shifting teeth.*

12. *The black marker arrow indicates where the main gear cluster had ridden up against the case, indicating it was loose in the case. This told Shepherd the case would have to be welded and a new set of cluster shaft holes drilled to spec. Again this is a common problem, but absolutely needs to be corrected properly to ensure long gear life.*

14. *Shepherd checks the main shaft for trueness. Suzy Q.'s was well within specifications. She needs new bearings and synchronizers, which will be shown in Part II of this series on the transmission rebuild.*

Suzy Q

Vette Resto

TRANS REBUILD

PART II

*Photos by
the author*

1. *Darrell Shepherd of 4-Speeds by Darrell, fits a synchronizer ring to the shaft. He often discards rings if the proper snug fit is not achieved. Since the ring acts as a brake on the gear, a proper fit is necessary for it to do its job well. If the gear doesn't slow down enough, the gears grind when shifted.*

2. *Initially, the '63 transmission had the ring pictured here on the left. But Shepherd uses the one on the right, found in a later version of the Muncie four-speed. Its shoulder is taller and makes the ring more sturdy.*

3. *The bearings, front, left, and rear "automatically" get replaced in a rebuild. Suzy Q.'s on top, showed wear. At bottom are the replacements.*

By Dean Shipley

Last time we relayed the good news Darrell Shepherd had for us. The Muncie four-speed transmission was basically in good shape and needed just the basics of a rebuild.

Now we'll continue with the reassembly with the new parts in the transmission.

Shepherd insists on excellent quality parts going into the rebuild of a transmission. Though he never said it, he lives by the saying: "If you haven't got the time to do the job right, when are you going to find the time to *do it over?*" Shepherd, of 4-Speed's by Darrell, a division of Piper Auto Specialties, Vermilion, Ill., makes *sure* it's done right the first time.

The transmission, in the skilled hands of Shepherd, went together without a problem. The shifter and linkage took more time to put in proper working order. That included bending the shifting rod for the reverse gear. It was very labor intensive. But as we said, Shepherd wanted to make sure it was shifting *perfectly* before this reporter hauled it back to Ohio. It was.

4. *Third and fourth gears go on the main shaft with Shepherd installing the bearing retainer that is unique to the '63 model Muncie trans.*

5. *First gear goes in place on the main shaft.*

6. *The washer that slips on behind first gear is installed.*

7. *Shepherd installs the rear bearing into the bearing plate, that is situated between the two cases.*

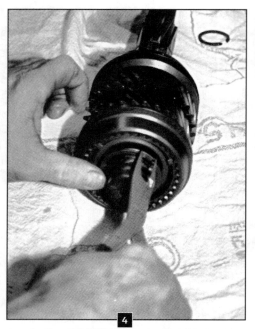

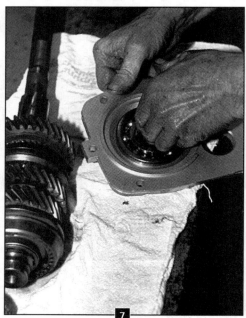

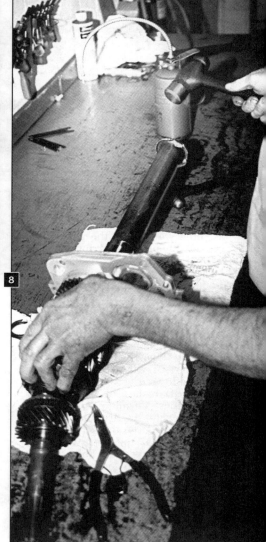

8. *The bearing is tapped in place and then it will be secured with new clips to hold it in place.*

9. *Reverse gear should slide in place easily, which it did. The small gear in the center of the shaft is for the speedometer. It is one of two gears that govern the speedometer.*

10. *The speedometer is governed by the groups of gears that are matched to the rear end gear ratio. On the bottom left is a gear with eight teeth. The plastic gears, green (left) has 22 teeth and is for the 3.70 gear, the yellow (right) has 24 teeth and is for a 4.11 gear. In the center, the large gear at the bottom also has eight teeth, but is thicker. Its three plastic mates are: left, brown, 18, 3.08; center, blue, 20, 3.36; right, red, 21, 3.55. At right, the gear has six teeth and is mated to a steel gear with 20 teeth for the 4.56 gear.*

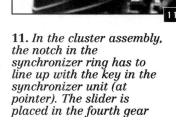

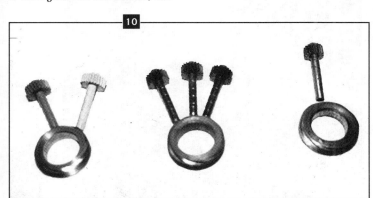

11. *In the cluster assembly, the notch in the synchronizer ring has to line up with the key in the synchronizer unit (at pointer). The slider is placed in the fourth gear position when it's loaded in the case. The cluster gear drives first through third gears. It determines whether a transmission is a wide ratio (2.56) or close ratio (2.20).*

12-13. *The cluster gear rides on 80 needle bearings, four rows of 20, with each group held in place by a washer. With the new bearings a new cluster gear shaft is also installed.*

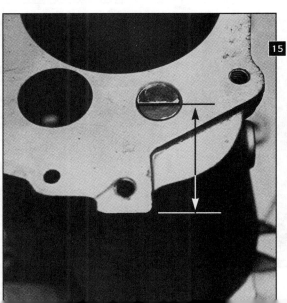

14. *The cluster gear is installed.*

15. *The notch in the cluster gear shaft must be aligned parallel to the bottom of the case. The tanged front reverse thrust washer must have the tang engage that notch for a proper fit.*

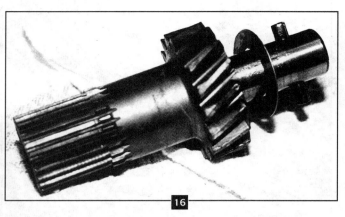

16. *The rear reverse idler is shown with a thin flat washer installed. Shepherd said it's important to be sure the washer is installed.*

17. *Kenny Quinn, of Piper's Auto Specialties, cleans up the tail piece to prepare it for reassembly.*

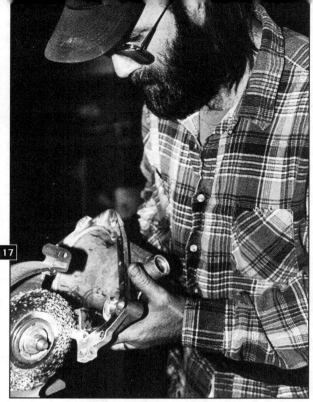

18. *The rear bushing, on which the driveshaft yoke rides, is installed.*
19. *The rear seal is tapped into place.*

20. *With the main shaft slipped into place, Shepherd installs the rear reverse idler gear.*

21. *With the gasket in place, the tail piece is positioned on the back of the main case.*

22. *A beautiful sight! Fresh synchronizers, immaculately cleaned parts, assembled by a pro in a clean case that nearly sparkles. It almost seems a shame to bolt it underneath Suzy Q.*

23. *The side plate with the shifting forks is lowered into place. The transmission must be in second gear to slip it properly into place.*

24. *Shepherd works with the shifter and linkage. This was the most hellacious part of the rebuild as the reverse rod had to be bent and rebent numerous times to allow the shifter to spring back to neutral without a hangup. He also raided his spare parts bins to make the linkage fit properly. Shepherd remarked as tough as this part is for a professional with all the skills, tools, etc., imagine what it would be for the home-garage restorer to attempt?*

25. *Proudly, Shepherd shows off his latest rebuild and for good reason. It's a beautiful job inside and out.*

Suzy Q.
Vette Resto

THE VETTE STOPS HERE

By Eric Brockman

The brakes are probably the most important feature of an automobile. There's not much point in being able to go fast if you can't stop the car. But because they are hidden away behind the wheels, the brakes tend to be neglected more often than not.

Brake components, especially in drum brake systems such as Suzy Q.'s, live in a harsh environment laden with dirt, moisture and extreme heat. Brake lines and hoses are also exposed to the worst conditions the roads have to offer. When restoring a car, it makes sense to replace *all* the brake hardware. Why cut any corners here, and risk destroying your pride and joy, not to mention risking injury because of brake failure?

So the stoppers got new shoes, mounting hardware, wheel cylinders, lines and master cylinder. Kanter Auto Products (76 Monroe St., Boonton, N.J. 07005; order line 800-KANTERS; fax 201-334-5423) supplied all the hardware, including the rubber hoses, while Fine Lines (650 W. Smith St., Unit #2, Medina, Ohio 44256; phone 216-722-7641) provided the new metal brake lines. The brake drums, in decent shape, were turned, cleaned and painted. Antique Auto Shop, Elsmere, Ky., installed everything, except the master cylinder, which will be installed after the body is remounted on the chassis.

Now Suzy Q.'s "whoa" will match her "go!"

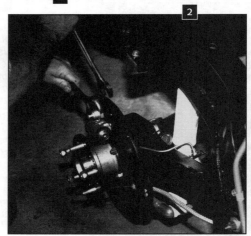

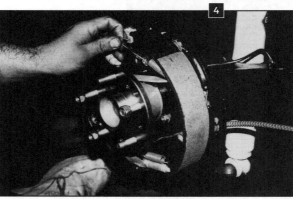

Photos by the author

1. *John Bastian, of the Antique Auto Shop, Elsmere, Ky., fits the new metal brake lines to Suzy Q.'s chassis. Fine Lines, of Medina, Ohio, provided the brake lines, as well as the new fuel lines.*

2. *With the suspension reassembled, the brakes could then be fitted to the chassis. The first item to be attached to the backing plate was the wheel cylinder. Kanter Auto Products, of Boonton, N.J., supplied the brake hardware.*

3. *Here, Bastian fits the new brake shoes into place.*

4. *With the shoes in place, the related mounting hardware was attached.*

5. *An assembled brake assembly, ready to accept the refinished brake drum.*

Suzy Q Vette Resto
INSTALLING THE ENGINE & TRANSMISSION

By Dean Shipley

With the 327-cubic-inch, 300-horsepower engine finally mated to the Muncie four-speed transmission, the time had come to install the drivetrain components in the freshly refurbished and rolling chassis. The latter was trailered to Comer & Culp Engines, where the installation would take place.

It did not appear to be a difficult operation. But, with any job on a car, you have to be sure to have all the parts needed to complete the work.

That way the work can proceed without the interruption of running out to the local parts supply store for the part you "forgot."

With the body off the car, the installation was a proverbial "piece of cake." The engine, which was hung by cables on the rolling and telescoping hoist, was rolled into position near the chassis. Glenn Culp, operating the hoist, positioned the engine to drop into place. The necessary mounts were bolted in place and the mounts were secured to the chassis.

Though Culp was able to perform the operation mostly alone, one or two helpers to assist would certainly be welcome to the primary installer. Anytime you're dealing with a pair of heavy, bulky components, such as an engine and transmission, which together weigh around 600 pounds, extra hands are always welcome.

These photos illustrate the installation procedure.

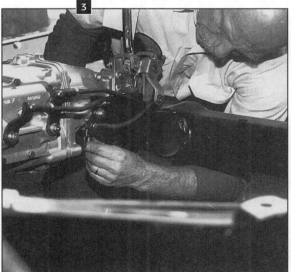

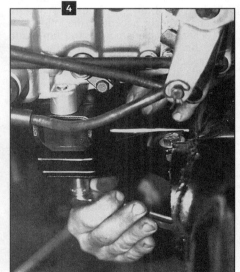

Photos by Eric Brockman and Dean Shipley

1. *With a cable bolted into the top of the engine through the intake manifold, Glenn Culp positioned the hoisted engine for its descent onto the completed chassis.*

2. *The engine mounts were put in place on the engine itself, then the mounts were bolted to the brackets on the chassis. They were not snugged up at this point, because some movement on the transmission end of the assembly was necessary.*

3. *At this point, the drivetrain assembly was being supported by the bolts in the top of the bell housing. This allowed for the installation of the transmission mount on the bottom of the transmission.*

4. *With the transmission bracket now in place, the holes in it and the transmission were lined up. Culp bolted down the transmission to the mounting bracket. Then the engine mounts were snugged up.*

VISCOUS FAN CLUTCH BUILD-UP

By James B. DeWolfe

When it was announced that *Cars & Parts* had chosen the 1963 Corvette Sting Ray as its restoration car, I realized that Eaton Corp.'s Marshall, Mich. plant had furnished two major products for the production of the vehicle. Before retirement, your correspondent was a quality control official at Eaton and a *Cars & Parts* reader.

Having had first-hand experience with the production of both components, this writer contacted *Cars & Parts'* editor, Bob Stevens, and offered to rebuild or replace the viscous fan clutch and the limited slip differential for the restoration project. He felt appropriate text and photos would provide readers an understanding of the Eaton viscous fan clutch and its mission on air-conditioned passenger cars as well as those like Suzy Q., which were built without the option. Stevens eagerly accepted the offer and the original viscous clutch and fan blade and the Positraction rear end were shipped to the Eaton Corp. Proving Grounds in Marshall.

In this article, we concentrate on the build-up of a new fan clutch. Next month, the restoration of the Positraction rear end will be featured in detail.

Prior to getting into the details of the construction of the viscous clutch, it is appropriate to tell about the development of the product. In the late 1950's air conditioning began to be offered as an option on a wide range of American passenger cars. While adding considerably to passenger comfort, it strained engine cooling requirements greatly. Automakers began to look for an answer to solve the problem. A quick fix appeared to be the addition of a larger capacity fan blade, how-

ever, additional fan noise and the loss of horsepower at elevated engine speeds resulted. The problem of high speed fan noise and horsepower loss had to be solved.

At Eaton Corp., the viscous fan clutch, as found on Suzy Q., was developed to control the speed of the engine fan blade.

Photos by Ken New

1. The original viscous fan clutch from the 1963 restoration car was date coded F25D (June 25, 1963) indicating use by a late-built vehicle. The original viscous clutch was dynamometer tested and found to still meet original cooling requirements after 30 years, however, it was determined that the restoration vehicle should have a new fan clutch.

2. To begin the build-up of a new replacement unit, a small "o" ring was assembled to the valve arm shaft prior to inserting the shaft into the cover plate. Then the bimetal coil was placed onto the end of the valve arm shaft and the tab of the coil located in the clip attached to the cover plate. The end of the valve arm shaft was lightly staked to retain its position.

3. The pump plate was then assembled to the cover plate after being adjusted so the valve arm will open over the fill port in the pump plate at the specified temperature. The pump plate contains two detents, that act as scoop pumps to remove fluid from the clutching area back into the reservoir area, that is formed between the cover plate and the pump plate.

4-5. *A special sealed ball bearing was then pressed into the viscous clutch body and a retaining bead rolled over.*

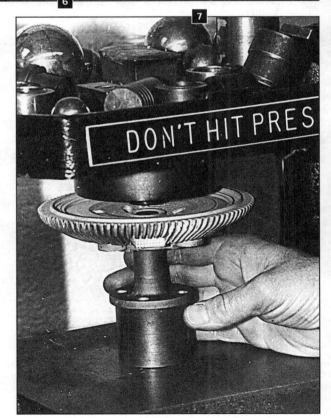

6-7. *The drive shaft was then pressed into the ball bearing and the clutch disc pressed onto the shaft.*

8-9. *A special gasket ring was assembled into the body and the unit was ready to be filled with the correct amount of the specified viscous fluid.*

DON'T HIT PRES

10-12. *Eaton lab technician Mike Hazel placed the cover and pump plate subassemblies into position on the body and sealed the unit by rolling over a bead of metal. The final viscous fan clutch assembly was now ready to be tested, date stamped, and shipped to the customer.*

While original designs did not utilize the temperature sensing capability, within a short time, the addition of a bi-metal coil attached to an internal valve gave engineers the ability to control the working of the viscous clutch. It could be designed to monitor the air temperature passing through the radiator core so as to engage the clutch only when cooling was necessary and establish limits on the high speed fan blade. The maximum speed of a given fan blade based upon torque characteristics could be tailored by adjusting the viscosity of the silicone fluid that served as the driving force in the viscous clutch.

Since the viscous clutch is a sealed unit and there is no appropriate rebuild procedure, plans were set in motion by this writer to build a new 1963 unit. The accompanying photos and captions record the building of a new "1963" unit.

13. *Reattached to the restored fan, the new viscous fan clutch is stored face-down to prevent the possibility, however slight, of the silicone fluid leaching into the ball bearing and contaminating the grease. The strip of white tape at right, was applied to the fan by DeWolfe as part of the testing procedure of the old unit.*

Suzy Q
Vette Resto
FAN CLUTCH ALTERNATIVE

By Eric Brockman

As outlined in the March issue, we replaced Suzy Q.'s original, correct viscous fan clutch with an all-new replacement unit.

Normally, an item like this wouldn't be restored, but if absolute correctness for showing an automobile is desired, it can be done. Having seen the article on the construction of the new fan clutch, Fred Oliva, president of Vintage Automotive Research (2602 NW 94th Ave., Coral Springs, Fla. 33065; phone 305-755-1161) offered to restore the original fan clutch to NCRS and Bloomington Gold specifications. The major difference between the original and the replacement unit is the front of the housing.

The accompanying pictures illustrate the end product.

Photos by Ken New

1-2. *This is Suzy Q.'s original fan clutch, as restored by Vintage Automotive Research. In most instances, a fan clutch would be replaced with a new unit. If exact originality is required, though, the old unit can be redone. The cover plate of the replacement unit and the cover plate of the original have* *a slightly different pattern to the raised area. The unit shown here is also correctly painted. "F25D" is the date code for the piece: June 25, 1963. For a comparison of the two units, see the March '95 issue.*

3. *Vintage Automotive Research also supplied an exact reproduction flasher capacitor for Suzy Q.*

Vette Resto

SUZY Q. GOES TO BROADWAY ...VIRGINIA

By Eric Brockman

"Do you know where WW Motor Cars is?" asked Walt, as we rolled into Broadway, Va.

"No, not really," I replied "Hey, look at all those old cars over there — wait, I bet that's it."

That's how Cars & Parts' publisher Walt Reed and I found WW Motor Cars & Parts, Inc., of Broadway, Va. Once you make it to Broadway, you *will* be able to locate Jack Wenger's restoration shop. Trust us on this one. If all the vintage automotive signs on the main building don't catch your eye, the row of old cars out front will. The day we arrived with Suzy Q.'s body in tow, that row included a '56 Continental Mark II, '57 & '59 Fords and a '50 Chrysler, just to name a few.

Jack's shop will be performing the bodywork and paint, restoring Suzy Q.'s exterior to its former beauty and glory. The split-window Sting Ray body is definitely in good hands. Jack and his 15 employees are old-car people through and through. This small town, located in northwest Virginia, is a hot-bed of collector car activity, due largely to the presence of WW Motor Cars. The surrounding mountains are literally crawling with old cars, and Jack knows the location of every single one of them.

Jack has been involved in the old-car hobby since he was 16. He began his restoration business 17 years ago, working out of a small shop next to his home. The shop has been at its present location on Main Street in Broadway for nine years. WW Motor Cars occupies two large buildings, one of which originally served as a grain elevator. The other, appropriately enough, used to be a

Chevrolet dealership. Several warehouses around the area hold cars that are for sale and vehicles awaiting restoration.

Currently, about 18 cars are under restoration in the shop, with many more "waiting in the wings." While WW Motor Cars has restored quite a few early '30s Packards and other makes from that decade, the shop also takes in projects considerably older and newer.

In addition to restoration work, Jack is constantly buying, selling and swapping cars, parts and auto-related memorabilia. In fact, his restoration shop is a virtual treasure trove of original automotive service signs and dealership neon signs. As a result of these activities, you can usually find him set up at major events such as Auburn, Hershey, Carlisle, etc. If all that isn't enough to keep the man

busy, Jack has a new son, Kyle Wenger, born July 7.

Judging by the quality of work done on the cars we viewed at the shop, Suzy Q. will undoubtedly look far better than she did when new!

About the shop

WW Motor Cars & Parts, Inc. is located at 132 Main Street, Broadway, VA 22815, and the phone number is 703-896-8243. Broadway is located north of Harrisonburg, Va., just off Interstate 81. Jack P. Wenger is the owner and president, and the shop offers full restoration services, including specializing in the recasting of steering wheels for collector cars. The hours are Monday through Thursday, 7 a.m. to 5:30 p.m.

Photos by the author

1. Upon making our way to Broadway, Va., finding WW Motor Cars & Parts, Inc. was no problem. Could it be the row of vintage cars out front that gave it away?

2. Directly across the street, WW Motor Cars & Parts also occupies what was once the town's Chevrolet dealership. The picture window at the far right of the building still bears the words Fawley Chevrolet.

3. Walt Reed, left, Cars & Parts *publisher, and Jack Wenger, owner of WW Motor Cars & Parts, discuss the work to be done on Suzy Q. Old automotive signs, posters, and neon lights such as the Chevy piece at the left, adorn nearly every corner of the shop.*

4. The main building is a converted feed mill, and although a bit cramped, provides ample room for working on several cars. Workshops and parts storage occupy the upper floors of the structure.

5. The shop's specialty is the recasting of steering wheels for a wide array of collector cars. In fact, they handled the steering wheel restoration for Cars & Parts' *last project car, Peggy Sue.*

6. Restoration work ranges from classics and antiques to more-recent muscle and special interest cars. Here, employees Paul Sherman (left) and Paul Salyards work on a Mustang convertible.

Vette Resto
Suzy Q. Un-Masked

By Eric Brockman

It was time to see just what was underneath the aging, flaking paint on Suzy Q. Our Corvette was about to bare it all.

After Suzy Q. had been safely delivered to WW Motor Cars & Parts, Inc., of Broadway, Va., the first step in restoring the curvaceous fiberglass body was getting all that old paint off. Then we'd know what we were going to be up against, in terms of body work, to prepare the car for new paint.

For stripping chores, WW Motor Cars farms its work out to Maple Hill Body Shop, also of Broadway, Va. Owner Jeremy Turner specializes in glass and plastic media stripping, and has been operating his business for three-and-a-half years. WW Motor Cars has sandblasting equipment, but after seeing the results of plastic media blasting, WW Motor Cars owner Jack Wenger doesn't plan on doing any sandblasting any time soon.

Plastic media blasting was detailed by Matt Joseph in his Nov. '93 "On Restoration" column, but for those unfamiliar with the process, here's a brief description. The media used looks like fine sand, but is in fact plastic. The advantage in this being that plastic will remove paint with less damage to the underlying material than sand. And of course it's less environmentally hazardous than chemical stripping. Another advantage of plastic media over sand is that the media can be "reclaimed" and reused several times before it is "burnt up."

Air pressure is provided by a large industrial compressor, and the plastic media is fed from a hopper into the line. The actual stripping process is similar to sandblasting. Once the hopper is depleted, the plastic media can be swept up and shoveled into another hopper that feeds it into a reclaimer. The reclaimer

Photos by the author

1. *Prior to blasting, shop owner Jeremy Turner applied degreaser to the underside of the body to remove as much dirt and grease as possible.*

2. *Having successfully made the trek to WW Motor Cars & Parts of Broadway, Va., Suzy Q.'s dismantled body was delivered to nearby Maple Hill Body Shop to have the old paint removed, via plastic media blasting.*

3. *After being allowed to soak in, the degreaser and much of the underside grunge were washed away with water.*

4. *A garage bay at one end of the body shop serves as the blast booth. Air is fed from an industrial compressor outside, and the plastic media comes from the large hopper at the right of the picture. In the center is the inlet for the reclaimer, located behind the shop, which cleans the plastic media and feeds it back into the hopper.*

5. *The entire body was rolled into the garage bay on its dolly for stripping.*

6. *A portable stand is used for blasting smaller pieces. Here, Turner begins stripping the Corvette's passenger-side door.*

7. *The plastic media easily removes the paint without damaging the fiberglass, making it an ideal way to strip Corvettes. Under the paint, we discovered the front portion of the door will require some major body work.*

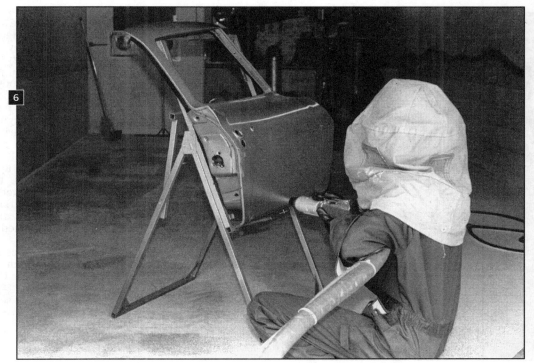

8. *The left fender provided the biggest surprise when it was stripped bare. Two separate patch pieces made up the lower part of the fender, and a significant amount of plastic filler occupied the upper part of the fender.*

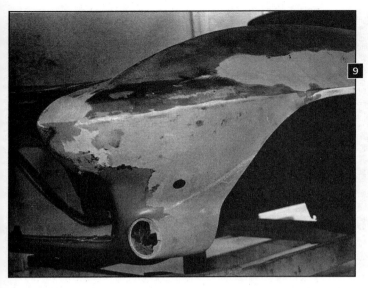

9. *We knew Suzy Q. had been knocked around some, but we were a little surprised by the amount of body work that had previously been done to the front clip. Patch panels had been grafted in at both front corners. In addition, much plastic filler had been used to fill cracks and wavy panels.*

10. *One of the advantages of plastic media is that it's reusable. When the supply of media in the hopper was depleted, the used media was swept up and shoveled back into the hopper. To save time during stripping, the media is run through a sieve — to remove large pieces of debris — straight into the hopper. Once a stripping job is completed, the plastic media will be thoroughly cleaned in the reclaimer.*

thoroughly cleans the dirt and debris from the media, allowing it to be used again.

Plastic media can be used to strip a variety of surfaces, including metal, fiberglass and wood. Different grades of media are used, depending on the material being stripped. For example, a courser media would be used on sheetmetal than on fiberglass.

Turner said he uses about 250 pounds of media when stripping a car, and that with the Corvette, about 10 pounds was "burnt up" in the process. A larger amount of media would be lost stripping a metal car. It took 14 hours to strip Suzy Q., at a cost of around $700. Metal cars can be stripped in less time, at an average cost of $400-$500, depending on the condition of the paint and the amount of filler in the body.

If that sounds like a lot of money for stripping, you should see the results. The plastic media is very gentle on the body of the car, so there are no worries of damage. The results are worth the money spent.

Suzy Q. presented a few surprises once all the paint was gone. The back end of the body was in fairly decent shape, but the nose was a real mess. We knew the right front corner had sustained some damage, but it looked good compared to the driver's side fender. Two separate patch panels made up the lower part of the left fender, and a good bit of filler had been applied to the upper part of the panel. Our girl appears to have been involved in a more serious accident than we first suspected. The areas around both headlight cut-outs had been patched, as had the lower right front corner.

Once the body was devoid of paint and old undercoating, it was back to WW Motor Cars, where Suzy Q. will undergo some "plastic surgery." Next month, you'll see the "operation."

About the shop
Maple Hill Body Shop is located in Broadway, Va., and is owned and operated by Jeremy C. Turner. The address is Route 1, Box 74, Broadway, VA 22815, and the phone number is 703-896-9024. The shop is open Monday through Friday, 9 a.m. to 6 p.m., and specializes in plastic and glass media stripping, as well as complete or cosmetic restoration services.

11. *Once the body was stripped, two specially constructed stands were attached to the body, allowing it to be tilted to strip the undercoating.*

12. *Now totally "naked," Suzy Q. was then loaded back on a truck and returned to WW Motor Cars for body work.*

Vette Resto

PLASTIC SURGERY

By Eric Brockman

In our "last episode," Suzy Q.'s body had been stripped bare, revealing a need for a sizable amount of body work to be performed before a fresh coat of silver blue paint could be applied.

WW Motor Cars bodyman, Paul Salyards, began what would be several weeks of "surgery" on Suzy Q. In his skilled hands, the Vette's battered fiberglass was smoothed out and prepared for priming and painting.

At first, working with fiberglass would seem like an intimidating proposition, mainly because it's a medium that is a bit foreign to most people. In reality though, the basics of fiberglass repair aren't difficult. But getting a finished product that looks good does require skill. The items used and principles involved in fiberglass repair are relatively simple and straightforward. The area to be repaired is sanded; sheets of glass fiber are cut to size and a resin is applied to them. This creates the actual "fiberglass" that is then applied to the damaged area.

Like any body work, it's a slow, painstaking process. The condition of the body will determine how painstaking and slow the process is. Fiberglass repair is a matter of slowly building up new layers of fiberglass over a damaged area. Each successive layer is sanded smooth and inspected for imperfections that would require an additional layer. Then body filler must be applied over the fiberglass to smooth out any remaining minor imperfections that sanding couldn't eliminate.

Sanding is one of the primary tasks required for good results when tackling fiberglass repair. It takes a good hand with a sander to get panels smooth and to maintain proper body contours. The latter is especially important on the front clip of a Corvette. It's definitely a plus to

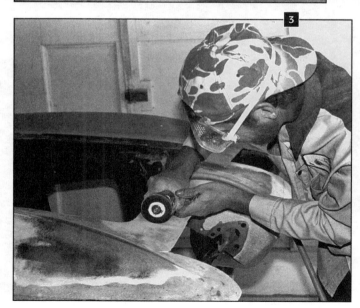

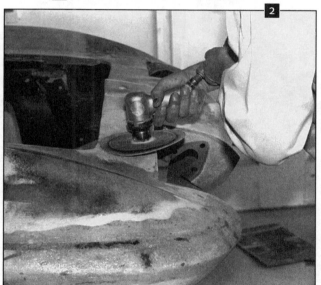

Photos by the author

1. *This old patchwork was one of several spots on the nose of Suzy Q. that would need attention before new paint could be applied. This and other such spots would be sanded and filled in with new fiberglass.*

2. *The first step in the process was sanding down the areas to be repaired, in order to remove as much of the old fiberglass as possible. This also provided a smooth surface on which to begin repairs.*

3. *A cutting wheel was then used to "V out" the cracks to see how bad they were and how deep they went. Cleaning out as much old material as possible also would allow the new fiberglass to more completely fill the cracks.*

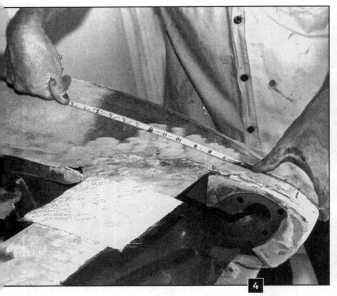

4-5. *Once the areas to be repaired were prepped, measurements of those areas were taken, and sheets of glass fiber were cut to the proper size for each area. Two sheets were initially applied to each area to create a stronger repair.*

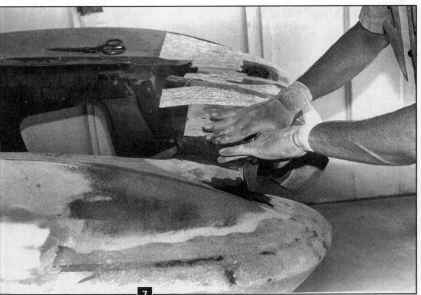

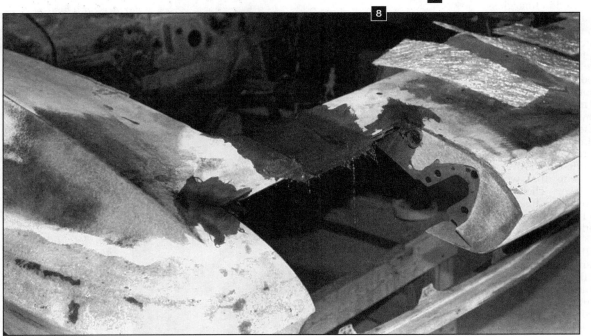

6. *A polyester resin was mixed with a liquid hardener, and then applied to the previously cut sheets of glass fiber.*

7. *The pliable fiberglass was then laid over the damaged area and smoothed into place.*

8. *Once in place, the new fiberglass took about one-and-a-half to two hours to dry. Drying time depends on the temperature and how well the resin and hardener are mixed.*

9. *As can be seen from this photograph, quite a bit of new fiberglass was applied to the front of Suzy Q. The central nose section and the cutouts around the headlights needed a good deal of repair work.*

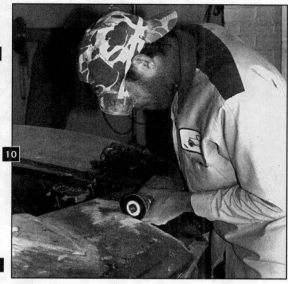

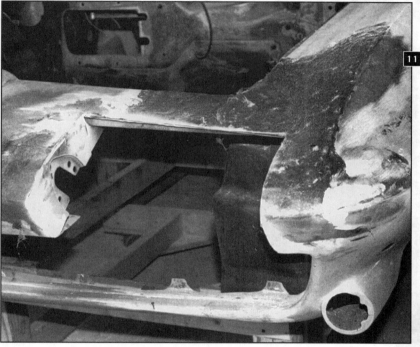

10-11. *Once the new fiberglass dried, the cutoff wheel trimmed the excess fiberglass away around the headlight door openings.*

12. *The rough fiberglass was then sanded smooth.*

13. *With the new fiberglass trimmed and sanded, the headlight doors were test fitted. One of the trickiest parts of repair work in this area is getting the fiberglass thickness right to allow proper operation of the headlight doors.*

15-17. *Once the fiberglass repairs were completed, a layer of special fiberglass reinforced body filler was applied over those areas to help smooth out any slight imperfections in the new fiberglass.*

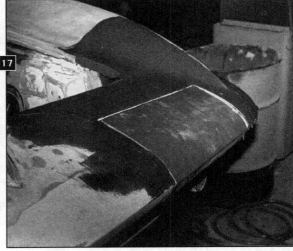

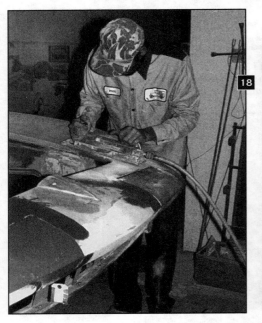

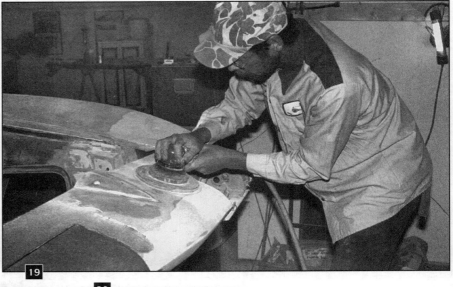

18-19. *Once the filler dried, it too was sanded smooth. If any low spots appeared after sanding, additional filler was applied to those areas.*

20. *The final step in the process was the application of a coat of glazing putty over the body filler. Once sanded, Suzy Q.'s front end would feel as straight and smooth as the day the car left the factory. The next step from here: primer and more sanding.*

use air-powered sanders when doing this sort of work, too.

While a good deal of body work was done to Suzy Q., both top side and bottom side, for this article we concentrated on repairs to the nose of the car. As we discovered in the stripping process, this was the area that would require some of the most extensive repairs. Not only were there several patches and cracks in the nose and front fenders, but also the inner fender-wells were quite battered.

Follow along as Suzy Q.'s bruised and battered exterior is "massaged" and smoothed back into shape.

Suzy Q Vette Resto

PAINTING THE BODY

By Eric Brockman

With the "plastic surgery" finally completed on Suzy Q.'s body, it was time to apply the paint. WW Motor Cars & Parts, of Broadway, Va., topped off the excellent body work with an equally fine coat of the correct silver blue paint. Paul Salyards, who handled the body work, stuck with Suzy Q. to the end, also applying the many coats of primer, paint and clear coat.

The first step once the body work was completed, was a good rubdown with wax and grease remover. This was followed by successive coats of epoxy primer and then primer surfacer. PPG paint products were used throughout the entire priming and painting process, by the way.

The body was then sanded to search for any low spots or other problems in the body work, and additional coats of primer surfacer were applied as necessary. The cars was then shot with a second type of primer surfacer, which was also sanded. Finally, Salyards meticulously wet-sanded the car until the primer nearly looked glossier than some finished paint jobs we've seen over the years.

After masking off the interior, inner fenders, and any other areas that weren't to be painted silver blue, the body was wheeled into the paint booth. After another application of wax and grease remover, the entire body was then sprayed with an acrylic urethane sealer.

For the final paint, we chose to use a basecoat/clearcoat system in the interest of appearance and durability. Purists might frown upon the use of a clearcoat, because it's not "original." True, but the results looked absolutely fabulous. Silver blue isn't exactly what you would call a real "grabber" color on its own — the word glossy doesn't exactly come to mind when describing it. But the addition of

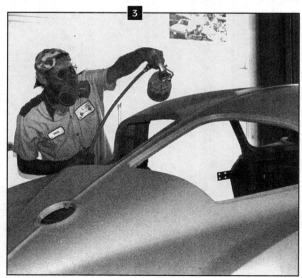

Photos by the author

1. *Once the body was ready for paint, body man Paul Salyards wiped it down with wax and grease remover to clean the surface and looked for any additional spots that might need sanding or filled with a catalyzed glazing putty.*

2. *Once the body was deemed ready, two coats of PPG DP40 epoxy primer were applied to the fiberglass. All of the painting materials were supplied by PPG.*

3. *Next, three coats of K200 primer surfacer were applied.*

4. *Suzy Q. was looking considerably better than she had been for a while. All one color — even if it was only primer — the body was just about ready for another round of sanding to eliminate any minor defects that escaped detection prior to priming.*

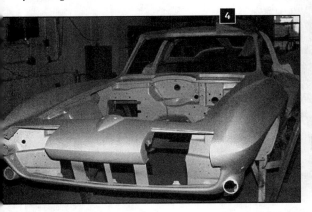

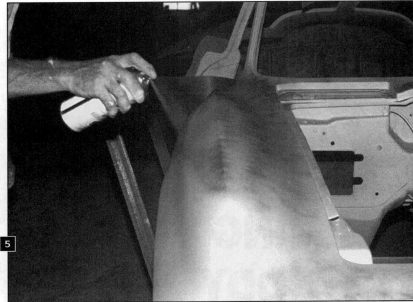

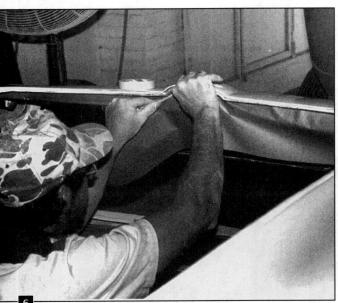

5. *Before Salyards began sanding he "misted" a light layer of black spray paint over the primer. This would help him locate any low spots in the body work after the primer was sanded. After sanding came another application of K200, followed by more sanding. A second primer surfacer, K36, was then applied and sanded in a similar manner.*

6. *After a final wet sanding of the K36 primer surfacer, the body was ready for the color coat. Salyards masked off the areas of the body that would not be painted silver blue.*

7. *The body was then wheeled on its dolly into the controlled environment of the paint booth.*

8. *Before painting, the final masking of the door areas was completed.*

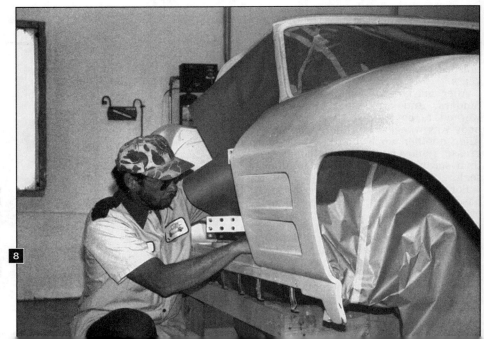

9. The body was wiped down with wax and grease remover before final painting began. An acrylic urethane sealer, NCS 230, was then sprayed on the body just prior to the first basecoat application.

10-11. At last the silver blue paint was laid onto Suzy Q. Three coats of color were applied, with about 15-20 minutes of drying time in between coats. Deltron DBU 2772 paint was used to return Suzy Q.'s appearance to its former glory.

12. Between color coats, a tack rag was lightly run over the fresh paint to remove any minute particles of foreign material that might have settled onto the surface. The final coat of color was allowed to dry for about half of an hour. Then three coats of Concept 2001 clearcoat were applied. While not 100 percent authentic, the clearcoat really "wakes up" a "sleepy" color like silver blue.

13. The finished product, ready to be wet sanded and buffed. The remainder of the body components (hood, doors, etc.) were painted separately.

> Paints used (all manufactured by PPG):
> • DP40 epoxy primer
> • K200 primer surfacer
> • K36 primer surfacer
> • Deltron DBU 2772 basecoat
> • Concept 2001 clearcoat

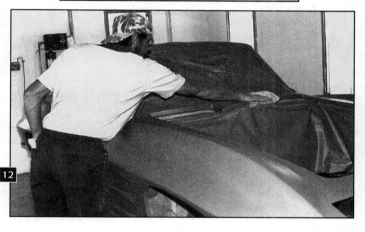

the clearcoat really made the metallic color shine.

Three coats of paint were applied, with a short drying time allowed in between coats. Before each successive coat, a tack rag was run over the car to pick up any foreign matter that might have found its way into the paint booth and onto the body.

Finally, three coats of clearcoat were applied over the paint. After the paint was allowed to "cure," the body was then wet sanded and buffed to remove any minor imperfections in the surface.

Even straight out of the paint booth, the results were stunning. With the paint but a few days old and not yet sanded and buffed, the nearly finished body made its debut at the Corvettes at Carlisle show in Carlisle, Pa. It drew curious onlookers more quickly than wet paint draws dust. Suzy Q. is definitely beginning to "shine."

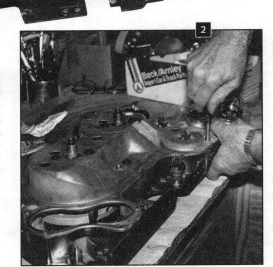

Suzy Q
Vette Resto

GAUGE RESTORATION

PART 1

By Eric Brockman

While most of Suzy Q.'s interior looked presentable, the gauge cluster was in sorry shape. Time had taken its toll; not only did it look shabby, but the functional aspects of the cluster also left something to be desired.

Faded and worn paint abounded on the gauge cluster. We wanted the cluster to complement the restored interior, not detract from Suzy Q.'s fresh appearance, so cosmetic freshening topped the agenda.

More importantly, however, we wanted to be able to accurately monitor Suzy Q.'s vital signs once the motor is returned to "life." When we purchased the car, the speedo didn't work at all and the accuracy of the tachometer's readings seemed a bit suspect (not to mention the fact that both were incorrect '64 gauges). As for the rest of the gauges, well, the fuel gauge serves as a good example. It gave a reading when the car was turned off, but immediately fell to empty when the ignition was turned on. The other gauges didn't work much better, if at all.

Enter Vintage Vette, of Woodbridge, Va. This one-man operation specializes in the restoration of gauge clusters for solid axle (1953-62) and mid-year (1963-67) years? other resto work? Corvettes. Neil Russell works out of a shop in the basement of his home, located in eastern Virginia, south of Washington D.C. We paid a visit to watch him resurrect Suzy Q.'s gauge cluster. Russell began redoing Corvette gauges in 1985 and he has no problem keeping busy via a word-of-mouth reputation.

After a visual inspection to size up the situation, Russell began the disassembly

Photos by the author

1. *Suzy Q.'s gauge cluster, in all its shabbiness. The ignition switch, oil pressure gauge and temperature gauge had already been removed at this point.*

2. *The two sets of smaller gauges on each side of the cluster came out as pairs. The bolts holding the backing plate were removed and the entire assembly lifted out of the main housing.*

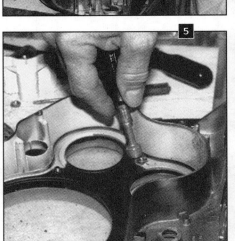

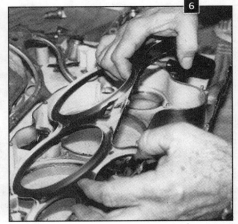

3. *The main housing was then unbolted and lifted away from the back of the cluster. The speedometer and tachometer are attached to this section.*

4. *The mounting bezel (above the cluster housing, already removed) was unbolted from the cluster and set aside for cleaning in a later phase of the restoration.*

5-6. *Underneath is the bezel holding the instrument lenses in place. A series of small hex-head screws hold it in place. Once the screws were removed, it too was removed from the cluster. It will be bead blasted and then repainted.*

7. *With that piece removed, the lenses were next removed from the cluster housing. TrimParts, Inc., of Milford, Ohio supplied new lenses, which will be installed when the cluster is reassembled.*

8. *Devoid of its "innards," the cluster housing was ready to have its tattered old paint stripped off.*

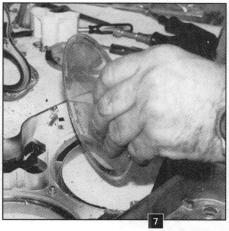

9. *The speedometer/ tachometer housing was removed from the gauges.*

10-11. *After testing the speedometer and tachometer to make certain they worked correctly, Russell removed the "guts" of both. The mechanicals will be attached to correct '63 gauge faces, replacing the incorrect '64 units in our cluster.*

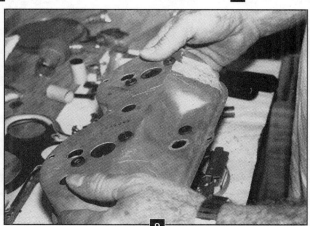

of the unit. The procedure is pretty straightforward, starting on the backside of the cluster. Screws hold successive "layers" together, until you're down to the gauge lenses.

Russell tested all the gauges to determine which ones functioned properly and which ones needed repairs or replacement. After that, he disassembled the gauges for any necessary mechanical repairs, and to clean or redo the gauge faces and needles.

The cluster housing received a coat of paint stripper to remove the old paint on the front side. The rubber seals that go around the back side of the gauge openings also received a coating of stripper to help get them out.

Fasteners, bezels, and backing plates for the gauges were either bead blasted or chemically cleaned.

Fortunately, our cluster was in relatively decent shape, with most of the parts only needing a good cleaning. The cleaning process requires slow careful work, because the needles and paint on the gauge faces are delicate.

With the cluster disassembled and cleaning underway, next month we'll follow along as the cluster is repainted and assembled. 📷

About the shop
Vintage Vette is owned and operated by Neil Russell, 14831 Honor Court, Woodbridge, Va. 22193. The phone number is 703-670-7489. Russell specializes in the restoration of gauges for solid axle and mid-year Corvettes.

12. *Russell tests the operation of the fuel gauge. It worked fine, so its problems must have stemmed from a loose ground somewhere. The temperature gauge also checked out okay, but the battery gauge was kaput. The oil pressure gauge seemed to function alright, but the line into the back of it was seized, so it will require some additional work.*

13. *Russell applied paint stripper to the front of the cluster housing with a small brush. He left the stripper on for 20 minutes, rinsed it off, and then applied a second coat.*

14. *While the stripper was doing its job, the rest of the gauges were disassembled for cleaning and repairs.*

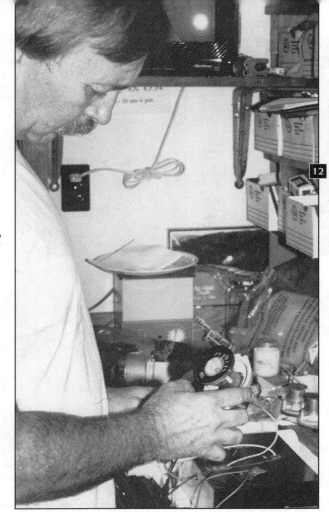

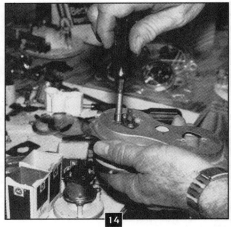

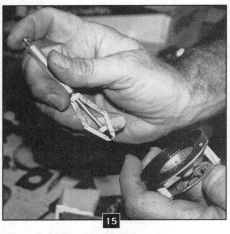

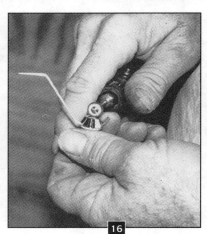

15. *A special puller is used to remove the needles from the gauges. Care has to be taken here, because the needles are fragile and expensive to replace.*

16. *The chrome centers of the needle assemblies are polished, one by one. The needles themselves are repainted or touched up as needed.*

17. *After the stripper had sufficiently soaked in, Russell rinsed the cluster housing with water.*

18. *The rubber seals that go between the gauge lenses and the housing become hard with age and are difficult to remove. Russell gives them a coating of stripper as well, which loosens them up, making them easier to remove.*

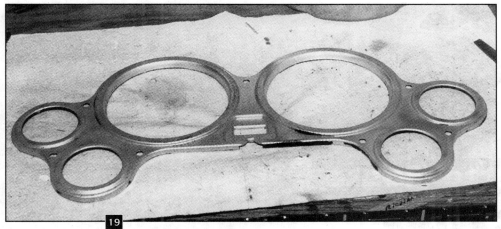

19-20. *The lens bezel, which was painted, and the various fasteners received a trip through the bead-blasting cabinet, and are now ready for detailing.*

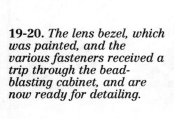

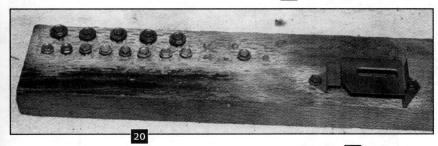

21. *The housings for the four smaller gauges were chemically cleaned. The clean unit, on the right, is shown next to the other housing, which had not yet been cleaned.*

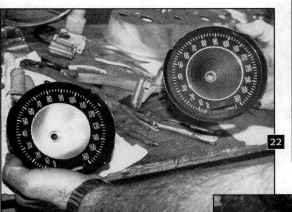

22. *The new speedometer is displayed on the left, next to the '64 unit that came out of our cluster. Note the difference in the centers of the gauges.*

23. *The centers of the gauges are cleaned with care, so not to damage the delicate cones.*

24. *All stripped down, the cluster housing is nearly ready to receive new paint. Next month, we'll follow the painting and assembly of our renovated gauge cluster.*

SUZY Q.
Vette Resto

GAUGE RESTORATION

PART II

By Eric Brockman

In our prior installment, Suzy Q.'s aged gauge cluster rested in the capable hands of Vintage Vette, Woodbridge, Va., a one-man operation that specializes in the restoration of gauges for solid-axle and mid-year Corvettes.

Owner Neil Russell is a long-time auto enthusiast, as evidenced by the solid-axle Corvette and first-generation Camaro in his garage. A couple more early Camaro project cars rest under tarps outside. Russell's also fond of the two wheelers, and has a pair of vintage motorcycles, a Triumph and a BMW.

Russell remarked that our worn cluster was in better shape than many units that he receives for restoration work. While at his shop, he pointed out one particular mid-year cluster in for refurbishment that looked like it had been exposed to the elements for quite a while.

Going into the disassembly of the cluster, we knew the speedometer and tachometer needed replacement, and that the operation of most of the gauges seemed a little suspect. Disassembly and inspection revealed what the problem areas were, as detailed in the first part of the gauge restoration.

The gauge housing was stripped of paint and cleaned. All the assorted bezels, housings and associated hardware were also cleaned, either chemically or via bead blasting. Any necessary repairs were made, and the incorrect speedo and tach were substituted for the correct items. TrimParts, Inc., of Milford, Ohio, supplied new lenses for all the gauges.

Once all the parts were thoroughly cleaned, the gauge housing received a

Photos by Neil Russell, unless otherwise noted

1-2. *When we last saw the gauge cluster, this was its condition. Having had its paint stripped, the housing was ready for additional cleaning prior to the repaint.*

3. *With new paint applied and brightwork cleaned and polished, the housing looks immensely better than it did before work began.*

new coat of black paint. Any necessary gauge face touch-ups or repaints were performed. The faces of the four smaller gauges were all in good shape, and only needed some cleaning. The tach and speedo, of course, were replaced with fresh new units.

Reassembly is pretty straightforward — putting everything back into the housing in the proper order. Once completed, Russell shipped the restored gauge cluster back to us. It looks great, and will look even better installed in Suzy Q. Now we can rest assured that her vital signs will be properly monitored.

4-5. *Our incorrect '64 speedo and tach (photo 4), versus the correct units (photo 5). The center cones are now the correct style, and the worn and faded redline is bright, and in the proper location for the 300-hp engine. The oil, fuel, temperature and battery gauges are reassembled and ready to join the speedo and tach in the freshly restored housing. Only the temperature gauge required any mechanical refurbishment, while the oil pressure gauge needed a new fitting.*

6. *TrimParts, Inc., of Milford, Ohio, supplied new lenses for the gauges and the trip odometer. The restored gauge cluster in shown here in all its glory. By the time Spring arrives, it will have returned to its former space in the dash of Suzy Q. (photo by Eric Brockman)*

About the shop
Vintage Vette is owned and operated by Neil Russell, 14831 Honor Ct., Woodbridge, VA. 22193. The phone number is 703-670-7489. Russell specializes in the restoration of gauges and clocks for 1953-67 Corvettes.

Suzy Q

Vette Resto

RESTORING THE RADIO

1

2

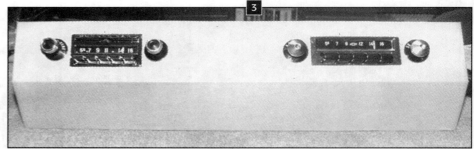

3

By Bob Stevens

Although it worked, the AM-FM radio, mounted vertically in Suzy Q.'s aging dash, was lacking in performance. Its volume was weak, its tone diluted, its controls a bit sloppy, its faceplate marred, its knobs cracked or missing, and its aftermarket speakers scratchy and vibrating. It obviously needed professional attention.

With 25 years in the automobile radio repair business on a full-time basis, John Sheldon needed no introduction to the uniquely shaped dual-band radio found in a 1963 Corvette. The AM-FM unit, a late model year introduction in 1963, was ordered by 9,178 Corvette buyers that year, while 11,368 opted for the standard signal-seeking AM radio. That left 967 Corvettes with no radio at all in 1963. Sheldon, who owns Radio & Wheel Cover World, Sterling Heights, Mich., in conjunction with his junior partner, son Jim, feels as though he's treated all of those Corvette radios as patients at one time or another over the past quarter century. The Sheldons do a lot of work on Corvette radios; it's one of their prime specialties.

A visit to this shop, which is quartered in the basement of the senior Sheldon's residence (one reason walk-in traffic is discouraged as opposed to mail-order), is a real eye-opener. The place is filled with modern tools and equipment, everything needed to repair old or new radios, tape players, etc., as well as upgrade vintage radios to modern specs in terms of performance, reliability, and capability (cassette, CD, etc.). And there's a staff of six full-time radio technicians, including the two Sheldons, all of whom are kept extremely busy keeping up with the huge and steadily growing volume of work.

Currently, the staff's time is split about 40 percent in regular service and repair work and 60 percent in upgrading old

Photos by the author

1. *John Sheldon (right), co-owner of Radio & Wheel Cover World, Sterling Heights, Mich., waits on a customer in his shop. Very little of the firm's business is attributed to walk-in; more than 95 percent is derived from mail-order. Sheldon started the*

operation some 25 years ago.

2. *Jim Sheldon (right), a partner in Radio and Wheel Cover World, and the son of the founder, John Sheldon, checks out a radio with one of the shop's six full-time employees.*

3. *A unique counter display shows a '58 Chevy Wonder Bar deluxe signal-seeking AM radio (left) and a regular pushbutton AM radio out of a '56 Chevy (right). Both have been upgraded to AM-FM with no changes in the outward appearance of the units.*

4

5

4. *Tagged units are either ready to return to the customer or awaiting service.*

5. *A huge supply of radio tubes feeds the repair operation.*

6. *The business also stocks a full range of vintage radios for the hobbyist who has nothing more than a hole in his dash, or a blank faceplate covering the hole. Most customers, though, have a radio to be rebuilt or upgraded.*

7. *There's a sizable inventory of knobs, bezels, faceplates, mounting hardware, etc.*

8. *When new or reproduction parts are not available, there's a room full of radios that can be raided for spare parts, some of which are seen here.*

radios or customizing auto sound systems. At one time, John Sheldon recalls, about 80 percent or more of his work was in simply rebuilding or repairing radios. The appeal of modern cassette and CD systems, however, has worn down the puritan attitude of staying totally stock, especially since most radios can be converted to handle cassette and CD players without losing their stock outward appearance.

All the customizing work is confined to the innards of the system, or to the back of the unit, which is concealed under the dash. The controls for the accessory equipment are generally located behind the stock radio buttons. Watching a system or two operate is proof enough that the modifications not only work extremely well, but in no way compromise the factory appearance.

The average turnaround, whether a unit is being repaired, restored, upgraded, or whatever, is about 30 days. Even older units don't present much of a problem, as the shop has a huge supply of tubes, knobs, chassis, and parts radios for units from the '30s all the way up through the '70s. All types of units are serviced, including 6 and 12 volt, positive and negative ground, AM, AM-FM, eight-track tape, cassette, CD, etc.

In the past 10 years, the hobby has changed, and so has the radio repair business, John says. The 1955-57 Chevys are still pretty hot, and all years of Corvette are strong, but other than that, the radio business has pretty much shifted away from the '30s, '40s and '50s to the '60s and '70s. The '30s and '40s in particular have dropped off sharply in the past few years, he adds, but "the '50s have gotten pretty quiet, except for the tri-year Chevys." Mopar is quite healthy right now, he says, especially the '60s. "Mopars are being restored with a passion that was formerly reserved for Corvettes; in fact the Mopar people are

6

7

8

9. *An employee repairs an old radio. The shop's six-man staff handles some 2,000 radios a year, with about 40 percent of them rebuilds and the remainder upgrades to cassette, AM-FM, CD player, etc.*

10. *Two radio repair technicians work on different projects, both major upgrades for vintage radios where the owners wanted to retain the pure stock appearance.*

11. *Another service offered by Radio World is speaker reconing. Here again, the speaker can be reconed to stock specs, or an OEM-quality replacement speaker can be supplied. Also, modern units are available for anyone wanting to upgrade the sound system's speaker capabilities.*

even bigger spenders when it comes to custom sound systems for their vintage cars," John observes.

In terms of repairs, upgrades and supplying a complete radio for a car that didn't come with one, the Sheldons typically satisfy a customer's search 85 percent of the time, or better. When they aren't able to help, it's usually because the radio is such a rare or oddball piece.

Again, nearly all of their business is by phone or mail, with very little walk-in.

Jim Sheldon, who handles all the company's computer work, prides himself in the fact that all the repair work is done on the premises. No outside contractors, subcontractors or parts vendors. The only exception is cadmium plating for cases, but in all their years in business, they've only had one request for a plated chassis, which is usually just cleaned up and painted silver, or left in its natural state if it's a particularly clean unit. Cad plating is attractive, but "that's not the way it came from the factory," Jim asserts. Besides, he says, it doesn't affect the radio's performance and nobody sees the case anyway since it's hidden behind the dash. Even so, cad plating is available, at about $125 to $150 per unit.

When a unit is repaired or upgraded, it is returned to the customer ready to install, plug in and enjoy. Each piece is carefully inspected, tested and packaged so there are no surprises at the customer's end.

John's wife, Ruth, helps with correspondence, shipping, billing, accounting, etc., as well as handling phone inquiries. The Sheldons prefer telephone inquiries, as they are quicker and more direct. Particularly helpful are complete descriptions of the radio (type, voltage, and condition) and its application (year, make, model, body style, etc.)

Or, you might get lucky and catch them at a show. The Sheldons haven't been attending car shows and swap meets since the early '80s, since the events generated very little real business for them. But just recently they've started hitting a few select shows, primarily Chevy, Corvette and Mopar events, to introduce some new products they've created in the conversion area.

It appears that Suzy Q.'s AM-FM link with the outside world is in capable hands. Next month, we'll watch those hands do some magic on the radio's internals, and its cosmetics.

Next Month:
Restoring a Vette radio

About the shop
Radio & Wheel Cover World is located at 2718 Koper Dr., Sterling Heights, Mich. 48310, phone 810-977-7979 or 810-268-2918, fax 810-977-0895. Shop hours are 9 a.m. to 5 p.m., Monday thru Friday, and the contacts are partners John and Jim Sheldon. Mail inquiries should include an SASE and both daytime and evening phone numbers.

12. *John and Jim Sheldon's shop updated this '49 Olds AM radio to AM-FM without sacrificing its totally stock appearance. FM is accessed by using the pushbuttons.*

13. *The only external signs of modification are at the rear of the radio, which is hidden from sight, even from the prying eyes of car show judges.*

14. *An AM-FM radio and eight-track tape player for a 1970 Chrysler 300 appears totally stock, but has been converted to handle cassettes and CDs. The cassette player has been ingenuously installed in the built-in housing for the eight-track tape player, and the compact disc player is hooked into the basic sound system, with everything operated via the buttons and knobs on the radio, which have been re-keyed to a light touch control system.*

15. *All visible evidence of customizing is limited to the back of the radio, which is hidden from view, unless one is on his back on the floor with his head on the pedals looking up into the maize of wires behind the dash, an uncomfortable position and one avoided by all but the most fanatic of judges. The workmanship on such conversions is top notch.*

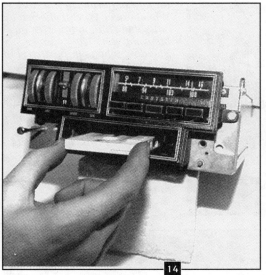

16. *In addition to radio work, the Sheldons also stock wheel covers ... thousands of them. About 4,000 of the 20,000 wheel covers in inventory are new-old-stock, and the shop has the cap the customer is inquiring about roughly half the time — pretty good odds.*

17. *This is the object of our attention at the Sheldon shop, the stock Delco AM-FM pushbutton radio extracted from Suzy Q.'s dash with surgical precision. Now it's up to the professionals to recondition the 30-year-old sound system.*

Suzy Q Vette Resto

RESTORING THE RADIO

PART 2

By Bob Stevens

Restoring the Delco AM-FM radio that Chevrolet installed in Suzy Q. more than 30 years ago, proved to be a relatively simple chore. The technicians at Classic Car Radio Co. Sterling Heights, Mich., tested the unit every way it could, and it passed every exam with high grades. There simply wasn't anything major wrong with it.

Before readers think that we changed radio shops in the middle of the project, we should explain that Classic Car Radio Co., is the former Radio and Wheel Cover World, the very same shop presented in the previous part of this radio restoration series. And it's still under the ownership and direction of John Sheldon and his son, Jim.

One is unable to get his vintage car radio repaired just anywhere. Most regular radio and electronic shops don't want to fool with the old stuff, Sheldon says, simply because it takes much longer to diagnose the problem and fix it. A shop can't just replace a chip and fix the unit, or call the distributor and have new parts delivered the next day. Classic Car Radio Co. often has to make its own parts from scratch, or raid a parts radio. In addition, it can take an experienced technician a whole day to troubleshoot an old radio.

The antique radio industry has overcome most of the old problems surrounding the equipment, "but we haven't quite resolved all of the deficiencies of the six-volt positive ground system." Jim Sheldon admitted, "But technology is moving at such a rapid pace, anything is possible tomorrow.

As for the future of the renamed Classic Car Radio, the Sheldons hope to attend more shows in the future, and offer their radio conversion packages through more independent vendors. Jim would also like

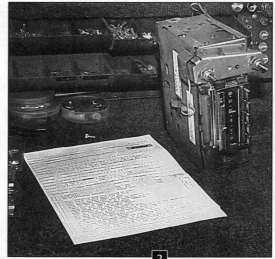

Photos by the author

1. *Jim Sheldon, Classic Car Radio Co. (formerly Radio & Wheel Cover World) checks out some catalog updates on his computer. The younger Sheldon, who is in partnership with his dad, John, handles the firm's marketing, sales, and customer relations.*

2. *A work order is drafted for each incoming radio, detailing the year, make and model of car, and the type of radio, its condition, any known problems, and specifically what the customer wants done to the unit.*

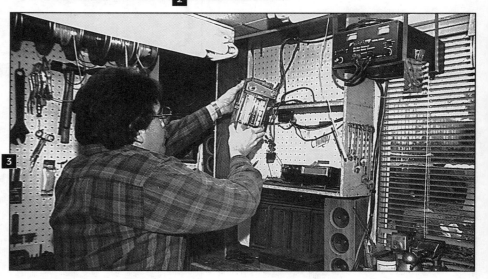

3. *Chris Springstead, Ferndale, Mich., was the technician assigned to Suzy Q.'s radio. Springstead, who has been with Classic Car Radio for more than eight years, is shown here plugging in the AM-FM radio for a test run. It worked fine in both* modes, AM and FM, *although the tuner was a bit slow and jumpy and the face was worn and scratched. Performance, though, was more than satisfactory. All the buttons worked correctly, but the knobs and bezels were cosmetically marred. The unit was hooked up* to a signal wave generator to set all the tolerances. The radio was then operated for 14 hours, being turned on and off several times and having all controls used during the marathon test session.

4. Included in the restoration of Suzy Q.'s radio will be cosmetic surgery; she'll get a whole new face. Included in the kit from Corvette Central, a major Corvette parts vendor based in Sawyer, Mich., are a new dial, knobs, face plate, front bezel, etc. Most of these items were made by TrimParts, Milford, Ohio.

5. The first step in any radio work, of course, is the removal of the exterior covers, which is accomplished quickly and easily. Since a radio is mounted under the dash and not exposed to the outside elements, nuts and screws remain relatively rust-free. A power nut driver made short work of removing the two outer case panels.

6. Since nothing was amiss with this radio, there was no need to troubleshoot the unit. Many troubleshooting sessions with antique car radios can require a full day, or longer. Lots of potential here for problems given the old style circuit board and all its attendant wires and hookups. Modern radios and stereos are much easier to troubleshoot; sometimes a simple chip replacement can cure up to 25 different ailments. Plus, this particular radio has separate AM and FM tuners, making it that much more difficult to troubleshoot.

7. A corner of the radio's case had been damaged and the plastic plug had been bent. The unit had likely been dropped at some point. Springstead was able to straighten out the case and plug with miniature pliers, but a little more damage would have required replacement of the plug receptacle.

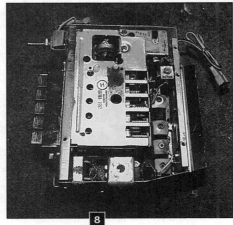

8. The flip side of the unit, with cover removed, looked fine. No physical damage was present.

to equip an old sedan delivery with a variety of sound systems as a rolling demo of the company's capabilities.

During an hour-long conversation with Jim Sheldon, he received about a dozen phone calls concerning vintage radio installations, including inquiries from owners of a 1948 Ford, '35 Studebaker, '68 Dodge, '57 Chevy, '79 Pontiac Firebird Trans Am, '50 Buick, '84 Corvette, '70 Mercedes, etc. Obviously, he has to have a lot of knowledge and computer aids to intelligently converse with enthusiasts who won such a wide variety of vehicles, all with their own peculiar radio and sound system installations.

In respect to Suzy Q.'s radio, the AM-FM unit worked perfectly, and needed just a cleaning, some paint touch-up and a new face kit. The latter, supplied by Corvette Central, Sawyer, Mich., came complete with knobs, bezels, face plate, face bar, etc., and everything fit according to original specs. Most of the pieces in the kit were manufactured by TrimParts, Milford, Ohio. The radio, featuring 18 transistors and 9 diodes, was checked out in every possible manner without a single complaint or flaw. The manual tuning now works a lot better, and the buttons set precisely. The new cosmetics, of course, dress up the unit tremendously.

Suzy Q. came to us with a set of after-market speakers jammed into the rear compartment. So Classic Car Radio supplied an original, reconed 10-ohm, 6 x 9-inch speaker that is as good as new in appearance, and better than new in function. This type of speaker has its own built-in transformer, and the technicians at Classic Car Radio advised against using a non-original spec radio.

Follow along as we go through the entire procedure of inspecting and restoring a Delco AM-FM radio at a professional radio shop to ensure listening pleasure for the next owner of Suzy Q. 📷

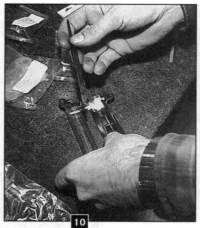

9. Springstead used a portable power drill to remove the face plate.

10. *The new face plate requires assembly. The kit includes a new bezel, pushbuttons, selector bar, radio lens, pair of radio knobs and volume/tone and tuning bezels. Because the parts are plastic, caution must be exercised in assembling* the face plate. *Springstead uses this special tool to secure the bar to the face plate without breaking it. The tabs on the bar must be gently spread apart, per instructions.*

11. *One thing not recommended in the instructions is the use of* glue to hold the bar in place, but the technicians at Classic Car Radio liked this added touch because it ensures that the bar will stay in place during the radio's reassembly, shipment, installation and use.

12. *A long hex wrench is used to loosen the retaining screw on each knob to remove the knob and replace it.*

13. *Pliers hold each lever steady while the knob is popped free, after loosening the hex-head attaching screw. A small threading bar is used to clear out the screw holes on the new knobs to ensure proper seating. Each knob is then pushed to check for function, clearance, etc. Then the hex key is used once again to check for tightness.*

14. *One of the shop's favorite weapons, a Dremel Moto-Tool, is used to grind down the tabs so the slide can travel its full vertical length. Two spring retainers are then used, one at each end, to secure the entire faceplate assembly together.*

15. *The new faceplate is bolted to the radio.*

16. *A small square of black electrical tape is placed over a hole in the bottom of the case, which is the way the radio was shipped from the factory, probably to block out light.*

17. *The veteran radio technician hooks up Suzy Q.'s AM-FM radio for a final test and antenna trimming (which must be done again once installed in the car). The unit dialed in nicely. Each button was set on a certain station and all were tested several times for function and accuracy.*

18. *The antenna sticker, which was originally white with red lettering but is now reproduced in orange with black lettering, points out where the adjustment screw is, and provides the advice: "Make antenna adjustments for maximum volume on weak AM stations between 1500 and 1600."*

MAKE ANTENNA
ADJUSTMENTS →
For Maximum Volume on Weak AM
Stations Between 1500 & 1600 KC

19. *The knobs are then pushed on the shafts with the bezels already in place. These will have to be removed later for installation in the car, but installing them will help keep them from getting lost.*

FRONT SPEAKER
FRONT

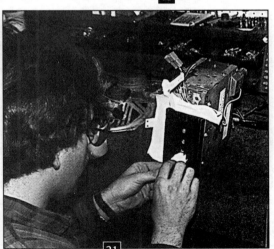

20. *Each wire is inspected for condition and then tagged to make sure that the in-car installation is done properly.*

21. *Springstead takes off the radio in preparation for painting the heat sink, a ridged panel at the rear of the radio.*

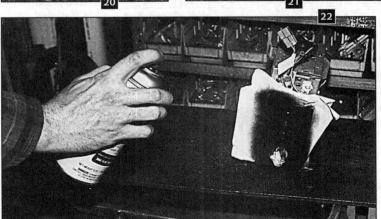

22. *Black paint is sprayed on the heat sink, restoring its factory finish.*

23. Springstead gives the unit one final inspection, making sure that all screws, bolts, clips, etc., are securely fastened and that nothing was left off.

24. The volume/tone and tuning bezels will be attached when the radio is installed, in order to avoid damaging them.

About the shop

Radio and Wheel Cover World has changed its name to Classic Car Radio Co. The firm is located at 2718 Koper Dr., Sterling Heights, Mich. 48310, phone 810-977-7979, or 810-268-2918. The proprietors are John and Jim Sheldon.

25. The finished product is released from the shop, ready for installation back into Suzy Q.'s dash.

26. There wasn't an original speaker core in Suzy Q. when we got her, so the Classic Car Radio Co. kindly provided this reconed unit, a correct style speaker. It is very important to match up the proper speaker with the radio. Quite often, improper matching leads the customer to think he has a problem with the radio, when it's actually trouble with the speaker. Suzy Q.'s speaker was to be an 8 to 10 ohm unit with a built-in transformer rated at 1.4 to 1.8 ohms.

27. The speaker looks too nice to hide behind the dash. In addition to the correct OE style of speaker, the technicians at Classic Car Radio in Sterling Heights, Mich., say that a quality antenna, properly installed and trimmed, is a requisite to superior radio performance.

28. This '41 Cadillac AM pushbutton radio has been converted to FM, and cassette and CD player can also be added without altering the stock outward appearance. The digital display on the dial is also an option. The neat trick with these units is that virtually all of the functions can be activated and controlled through the basic AM radio's standard pushbuttons. Hearing a demonstration is quite a treat ... witnessing the blending of modern audio technology with the antique appearance of a 25, 40 or even 50-year-old radio. (Photo courtesy Classic Car Radio Co.)

RESTORING THE CLOCK

Photos courtesy Instrument Services, Inc.

1. *This was Suzy Q.'s clock prior to any restoration work. Its inner workings were no longer operable.*

2. *The back was was removed, exposing the old works, an electromechanical movement.*

3. *The hands were then removed from the center hub.*

4. *Next, the face was separated from the dial plate, to which the movement is attached.*

The clock in Suzy Q. had completely stopped operation, and a restoration was clearly in order. The movement, or inner works, needed to be replaced. Investigation showed that a previous owner had tried to repair and clean the original movement, but this had failed the test of time. The options were either a new electric movement, or an upgrade to a quartz mechanism. The restorers selected the quartz option for several reasons, including greater accuracy, better reliability, and the fact that no maintenance would be required.

From a cosmetic and physical integrity point of view, the clock was in fairly good shape and simply needed some tender-loving care and attention to detail.

Physically, the outer body, or case, was in good shape, except for a missing mounting stud on the back of the case. It was added during the restoration. The case itself was stripped and repainted to its original machine gray color.

Cosmetically, the clock was in reasonably good shape, but in need of a face lift. On the bezel assembly, the flush face area of bright chrome was in excellent condition, and needed just hand polishing. The sides of the bezel, painted dull aluminum, showed minor surface discoloration and scratches. This surface was stripped and repainted to original colors.

The set knob was in excellent shape, but the set stem had surface rusting and abrasions. This was probably caused when an earlier owner aggressively used pliers on it. Polishing and buffing could restore the original shine, but in this case it was replaced with a duplicate of the original.

The lens, made of clear acrylic and slightly concave in shape, was in good condition, with no scratches or cracks. However, it had a cloudiness that could be removed with hand polishing and a soft buffing wheel. In this case, the restorers chose to replace it.

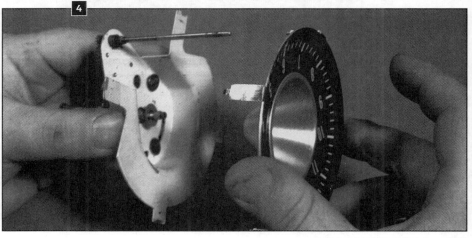

5. *The technician removed the old movement from the back of the dial plate.*

6. *The new quartz movement was mounted on the dial plate*

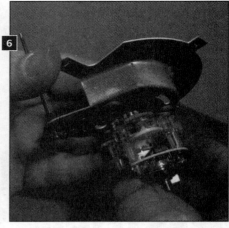

7. *The reassembled face and hands were reattached to the dial plate. The clock face was cleaned, polished and buffed. The hands were stripped and repainted to the original colors, and a new set stem was installed.*

8. *After reattaching the bezel/lens assembly to the face, the case was reinstalled.*

9. *The completed clock is ready for testing. Each customer's clock receives a brand new mechanism, never a rebuilt or repaired movement. Either quartz or NOS electro-mechanical movements are used, with the original appearance and cosmetics preserved.*

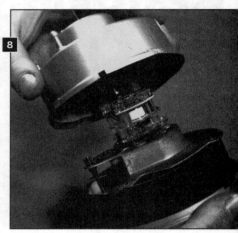

10. *All restored clocks are run on the test stand for a minimum of 12-16 hours to ensure all components are in working order, and the clock is keeping accurate time. This clock now has a maintenance-free movement, is accurate within plus or minus one to two seconds per day, draws about 1/4,000 of the amps of the electro-mechanical movement clock, and will provide years of trouble-free, accurate performance.*

The lens retaining ring just inside the lens had slight scratches on its painted surface of semi-flat black. It was stripped and repainted to original colors.

The pointers (hands) were faded and tarnished. The bright red-orange minute and hour hands were severely faded, and were stripped, painted to original colors and baked to firmly set the paint on the surface of the hands.

The metallic second hand was faded and dull, but hand polishing restored it to its original shine.

The face and numbers were in excellent condition and only required cleaning with a soft cloth.

The center of the face, a recessed area made of brushed aluminum, was stained, but responded to gentle hand polishing with a non-abrasive cleaner/polish.

Time had taken its toll over the years, but the clock's time had not yet come. Its suffering was minute. With some gentle handling however, Suzy Q.'s time piece has been given a second chance and should prove to be a punctual timekeeper for some time to come. 🔧

Vette Resto

MID AMERICA DESIGNS

Photos by the author

1. *Mid America Designs is a Corvette parts specialist, as the sign out front indicates. What the sign doesn't tell you, however, is that Mid America Designs is one of the nation's largest and oldest Corvette parts suppliers.*

By Bob Stevens

Driving through the countryside of southwestern Illinois just north of Effingham, the miles and miles of cornfields are suddenly interrupted by a two-story building and landscaped grounds that look like they belong in the fashionable business district of a large metropolitan area. The impressive facility is home to Mid America Designs, Inc., one of the Corvette hobby's largest and oldest suppliers.

Currently, Mid America employs 70 full-time people, ships some 350,000 packages a year, has a customer list numbering more than 600,000, offers 7,000 items through a 300-page catalog, and sells $20-25 million a year in Corvette parts and accessories. But founder and President Mike Yager remembers when he sold items out of the trunk of his car at local swap meets and had his entire inventory listed on a 3 x 5 card.

When Yager started Mid America Enterprises in 1974, as it was then known, he was a tool and die maker. In just two years, though, the part-time Corvette parts business became a full-time occupation.

The new business kept growing, and 22 years later it's still expanding. Mid America recently added 15,000 square feet of office space and an impressive 16,000-square-foot automated distribution center. The company plans to add another 27,000 square feet of space to its manufacturing operation. Mike Yager has come a long way since the days of hawking Corvette caps and T-shirts from the trunk of his car. But one senses that he's not done yet ... far from it!

2. *A modern two-story structure near Effingham, Ill., houses Mid America Designs. The finish line from the imaginary "Corvette Speedway" is replicated on the lawn to the front of the building.*

3. *With an illuminated dealership sign from Ray Trinkle Chevrolet overhead, the customer service center, where orders are placed and received, looks similar to the parts department of a large, successful Chevrolet dealership.*

4. *The fully automated warehouse features carousels and conveyor systems. Up to 1,000 packages are shipped and mailed each day from the company's Effingham operation.*

About the firm

Mid America Designs, Inc., is located at One Mid America Place, P.O. Box 1368, Effingham, Ill. 62401, 217-347-5591, and normal business hours are observed for showroom visitors. The toll-free, 24-hour order line is 1-800-500-VETT (8388). Mike Yager is the owner.

Vette Resto

CHROME PLATING

By Eric Brockman

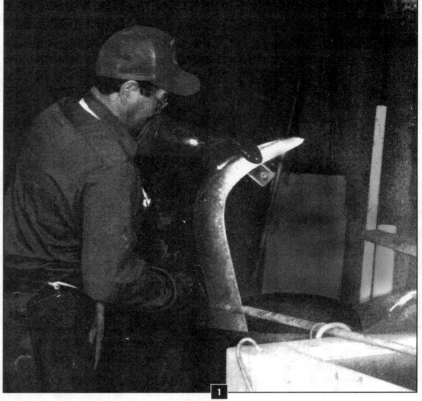

Anybody who has restored an old car in recent years will tell you that good chrome platers are getting hard to find.

For one thing, new cars have worn less and less chrome over the past few years, making for a shrinking base of people who need the services of chrome platers. But environmental regulations have taken the greatest toll on chrome plating operations. The chrome plating process involves using large of amounts of toxic, corrosive chemicals, and increasingly stringent regulations regarding the use and disposal of those substances have lead to spiraling operation costs.

Fortunately for Suzy Q., one of the top restoration platers around offered its services to return the shine to her chrome. Paul's Chrome Plating, Inc., of Mars, Pa., deals exclusively in chrome plating for the restoration hobby. Located near Pittsburgh, Paul's Chrome Plating has been in business since the mid-70s, and has been owned by Fred Hespenheide since 1982. Paul's deals mainly in triple plate show chrome, but less-expensive triple plate custom finish plating is also available.

The plating process itself involves numerous steps. Space limitations dictated that we couldn't show every single step in the process, but we've included illustrations of the main ones and detailed the steps not shown. The whole process of rechroming Suzy Q.'s bumpers, exterior door handles, and interior handles and window cranks involved several days. The staff is meticulous in its work. If a part shows the smallest imperfection in it after the plating process is complete, it goes back to be redone.

When parts arrive at Paul's Chrome, they are unpacked, labeled, and photos are taken of each item. The first step in the plating process involves stripping the

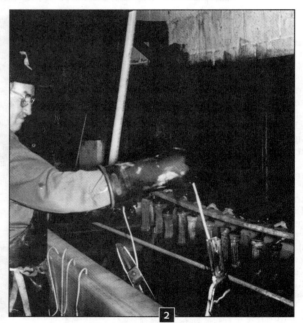

Photos by the author

1. *The first step in the chroming process is to chemically strip the old chrome. Here, Wayne Davidson immerses one of Suzy Q.'s bumpers in a muriatic acid solution to remove rust.*

2. *After rinsing them, the pieces go into a sulfuric acid solution to strip the Chrome. Like the plating tanks, this solution is electrically charged, but with the opposite polarity. This arrangement works the opposite of the plating operation, actually removing the old plating. The Corvette bumpers required about 45 minutes in the sulfuric acid solution.*

3. *After the acid bath and another rinsing, the pieces take a trip through the blasting cabinet to remove any remaining material, and clean the back of the part.*

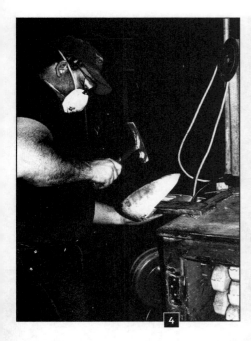

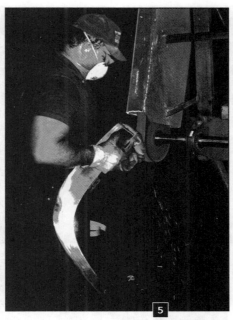

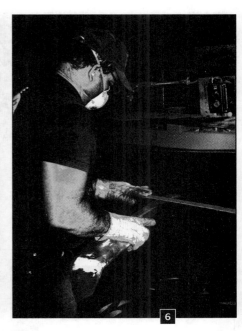

old plating. The parts go through a solution of muriatic acid to remove rust, then a sulfuric acid solution to remove the old plating. This stage takes around 45 minutes to an hour. The parts then go to a blasting cabinet to remove any remaining plating, rust, etc.

Once the parts are stripped, they must be sanded and buffed, so that any dents, cracks or other imperfections can be worked out of the metal. This also removes any remaining nickel plating on the pieces. Having a perfectly prepped piece is critical for satisfactory results to be achieved in the plating process.

The stripped parts must first be thoroughly washed to remove any dirt or grease, so that the plating metals will properly adhere to the steel. After washing, any remaining soap residue is removed by immersing the parts in a sulfuric acid solution.

Plating is accomplished by immersing a piece to be plated in an electrolytic solution. The part to be plated acts as the cathode in the electrical circuit, and a bar composed of the metal to be applied to the piece serves as the anode. The actual plating metal is suspended in baskets in the solution. The electrical current flowing through the completed circuit "dissolves" the plating metal and deposits it on the piece to be plated. For the plating operations, the parts are attached to copper hooks, which complete the electrical circuit in the tanks.

The term "triple plating" refers to the number of different types of metals that are applied in the plating process — copper, nickel and chromium. Plated parts actually receive several varying layers of some of the metals.

The plating steps vary somewhat, depending on the part being plated. Suzy Q.'s bumpers, which are the main focus of this story, followed the order described in the next few paragraphs.

The first metal applied in the plating process is called cyanide copper. After

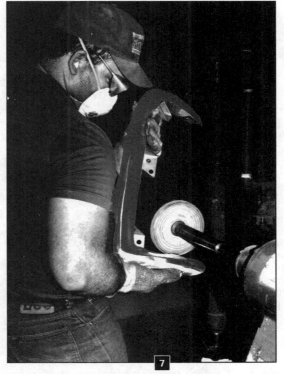

4. *Once the pieces are stripped, they have to be polished and any imperfections have to be corrected. Before polishing a bumper, John Williams levels out some waviness in the metal with a hammer.*

5. *Using a belt sander, Williams first works the bumper on the end piece of the sander, in order to remove any pits and remaining nickel plate.*

6. *Then the bumper is "side-belted" on the belt sander to smooth it out. Initially, the bumper is sanded with a 60-grit belt, then 180 grit and finally 240 grit. Removing all imperfections before plating begins is an absolute must to achieve satisfactory results.*

7-8. *Various types of buffing wheels are also utilized to help get the surface to be plated as perfect as possible.*

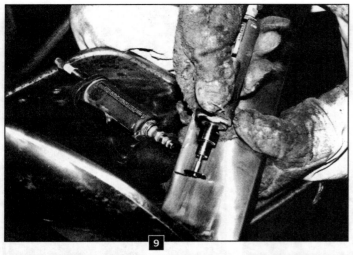

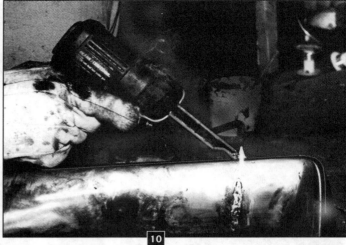

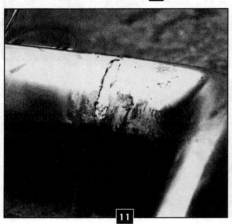

that, a layer of nickel is applied, then another layer of cyanide copper. A second type of copper, called acid copper, is then applied. The cyanide copper leaves a dull finish on the metal, but the acid copper leaves a shiny, chrome-like coating, but copper colored, on the metal.

After coming out of the acid copper tank, parts are then buffed and checked for signs of any imperfections in the surface of the metal. If any problems are found, they are corrected and the part is returned to the acid copper tank for replating.

Once deemed satisfactory, the parts are then returned to the plating room, where they are washed and then dipped in the sulfuric acid solution again. They then receive another coat of cyanide copper, followed by another coat of nickel. The actual "chrome" of chrome plating is a thin layer of chromium that is applied last.

Unlike the other plating tanks, the anode rod in the chrome tank is made of carbon, and the chromium is in powdered form and mixed into the solution.

Finished parts are then cleaned and inspected. Once they pass inspection, they are carefully wrapped, packaged and shipped back to the customer.

Suzy Q. may not wear much chrome, but what she has now shines beautifully, thanks to the talented, consciencious staff at Paul's Chrome Plating.

9. *On one bumper, a deteriorated factory weld needed some attention. A cutting tool is used to remove the old metal in preparation for repairs.*

10-11. *The old weld is filled with silver solder. The repair (photo 11) will then be sanded and buffed smooth.*

12. *Once all the polishing and repairs are completed, the pieces are ready to go to the plating room.*

13. *In the plating room, Rick Feil first thoroughly cleans and rinses all the parts before the plating process begins. The part is rinsed and then goes through a mild sulfuric acid rinse to remove any remaining soap residue.*

14

15

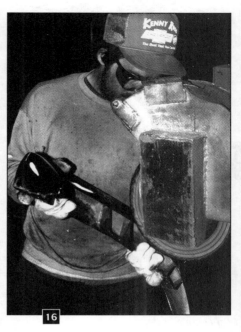

16

14. *Triple plating involves many steps, and space limitations preclude illustrating every single step of the process. The next several photos will show the main steps. The first of those steps is a coating of cyanide copper, which acts like a sort of "primer" for the metal. After the piece is removed from the cyanide copper it goes through two rinse tanks.*

15. *Next, the bumper goes into the nickel plating tank. After coming out of the nickel tank, the bumper is rinsed and then receives another coating of cyanide copper. Then it is rinsed and dipped in the sulfuric acid solution again. After that the bumper is placed in the acid copper tank.*

16. *Once the bumper is removed from the acid copper tank and rinsed, it must be buffed prior to the final steps in the plating process. Jeff Boyle buffs one of Suzy Q.'s bumpers. Any additional repairs that might be needed are also made at this point.*

17. *Once buffing is completed, the piece is washed, then dipped in the sulfuric acid solution. The piece then*

17

receives another coating of cyanide copper, a rinse, and another coating of nickel. After removing one of the bumpers from the nickel tank and rinsing it, Scott Whitfield is shown here placing it in the chrome plating tank.

18. *After coming out of the chrome tank and being rinsed again, the shiny*

About the shop
Paul's Chrome Plating, Inc., is located at 341 Mars-Valencia Rd., Mars, Pa. 16046. The phone number is 412-625-3135 or 1-800-245-8679, fax 412-625-3060. Fred Hespenheide is the owner. Triple plating services include custom finish chrome plating and show chrome plating.

18

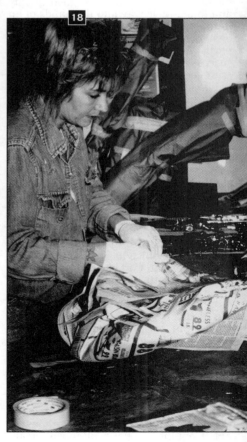

like-new pieces go upstairs for inspection, cleaning and polishing by Larue Rinehart. If any defects are found in the plating, the piece is sent back to be redone. If the pieces pass inspection, they are wrapped and packaged for shipment to the customer.

Suzy Q
Vette Resto
CORVETTE CENTRAL

By Dean Shipley

This year, Corvette Central of Sawyer, Mich. is celebrating its 20th anniversary. Over the course of those 20 years, the Corvette parts supplier has, indeed, come a long way. But its genesis is not so different from that of any other business that has stood such a test of time.

Jerry Kohn, the owner, started small. His first few products were essentially for his own use. They were of good quality and found their way into the hands of an initially small cadre of Corvette owners/customers, who needed the same parts. Word got around. Kohn built the success of Corvette Central on meeting the needs of Corvette owners across the nation and around the globe.

Those needs, it turns out, are many these 20 years hence. The company lists over 10,000 parts in a catalog that looks like the yellow pages of a small city. Telephone calls for Corvette parts have the proverbial switchboard lit up like Times Square. The helixes of the sales staff are curiously shaped like phone receivers (just kidding, but they *do* spend much of the day on the phone).

In fact, Corvette Central, is expanding its sales staff to better handle the thriving volume of calls. To better accommodate the staff, the office has been remodeled.

Stepping into Corvette Central's showroom throws the visitor back to the '60s. One Corvette in Jerry Kohn's collection, a dazzling '62 model, sits on a checkered tile floor. It's the centerpiece for the showroom, which displays Corvette accessories to embellish the Corvette driver's home, garage or wardrobe.

It's the icing on the cake.

That "cake," of course, is the Corvette itself. And nearly all the ingredients needed to create a detailed show car or a snappy driver are available through Corvette Central. And what isn't available from the company, often isn't avail-

Photos by the author

1. *Corvette Central is located in Sawyer, Mich. in spacious facilities convenient to I-94.*

2. *The showroom uses Jerry Kohn's '62 Corvette as a centerpiece. Corvette Central carries numerous accessories and apparel items for the Corvette enthusiast.*

3. *Service with a smile; that's Jim Simmons with customers, Rufus Winfield and his daughter, Precious, of Benton Harbor, Mich.*

4. *Sara Kohn, Jerry's daughter, is a member of the sales staff.*

5. *Here's where it all started. Jerry Kohn holds some die cast Corvette grille teeth, fresh from the machine. It was his first product and the one that got Corvette Central started.*

6. *Lois Allwood prepares an order for shipping. The inventory, order and billing systems are all computerized.*

7. *Kohn's piece de resistance: a reproduction '57 Corvette body that is a perfect replica of the original. Ten years of work culminated in its debut earlier this year.*

8. *Patty Naragon prepares a Corvette muffler for shipment. Corvette Central manufactures complete exhaust systems for Corvettes '53-82. The company is planning to expand to '84 and up models.*

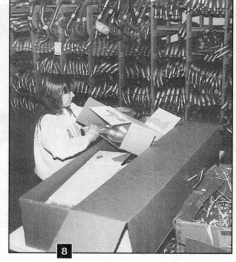

able *anywhere.*

They carry parts from numerous high quality suppliers. But there's more to it than that. Corvette Central itself manufactures parts under the banner of CC Industries. Making so many of its own parts naturally follows since the owner, Jerry Kohn, is both a Corvette lover/driver and has a strong background in manufacturing. CC Industries melds the two. Five vendors run parts under its banner.

In 1974, Kohn had a '58 Corvette in need of some "bridge work." But replacement grille teeth were impossible to locate. Finding no one who made replacements, Kohn, a tool-and-die man by profession, set out to make his own. He "reverse engineered" one (used an existing tooth and built the mold from it) and set it up to be made on a small die cast machine. Kohn's then partner bet him a steak dinner it couldn't be done on that machine. After a successful initial run of grille teeth, Kohn said, "make mine medium rare."

The grille teeth were taken to Corvette swap meets and shows and sold like hotcakes. Emblems for Kohn's '64 Sting Ray were next on the list to be manufactured. From that point on, Kohn continued to increase the number of items he manufactured. At the present some 1,000 items are manufactured in the Sawyer, Mich. facility. The remaining items manufactured, numbering approximately 1,000, are produced by shops that have contracts with Corvette Central.

Kohn said CC Industries has recently reached its apex and now offers what he calls "the ultimate reproduction Corvette part:" a complete body for a 1957 Corvette. The body culminates 10 years of research, development and manufacturing expertise. It is a dimensionally-exact duplicate of the original '57 body. But it is much stronger, has a much nicer finish and will endure much longer than the original. It also has an advantage of being made with superior materials than those available nearly 40 years ago. It is

designed to use all original and reproduction parts, from the headlight bezels to the taillamp lenses. Hoods, trunk lids and doors are interchangeable from body to body. So if one of those is damaged, replacing it is no problem. The original '57 Corvette bodies had those parts essentially hand built to fit properly. Getting a replacement to fit correctly can be a problem.

Corvette Central will continue to try and take the problems out of Corvette restoration. Kohn said the manufacturing company will continue to develop more reproduction parts the Corvette owner has difficulty in finding.

They are not just focusing on the older Corvettes either. "Half the Corvettes out there have been made since '84," Kohn said. Corvette Central has recently added a section to its catalog that caters to this newer segment of the Corvette movement.

Riding right along with Corvette Central's movement through the generations of Corvette, is Kohn's son, Scott. He has been working with dad since the outset. While dad's die casting company was producing grille teeth and emblems on die cast machines, Scott, at age 12, was wrapping them for shipment and filling orders.

Scott has literally grown up in the Corvette parts business. Having done so, Kohn endearingly refers to his son as "the proverbial granddaddy of Corvette

parts." Scott remains the point man for the increasing number of parts that appear in the catalog.

Corvette Central's catalog sales operations, as well as inventory control, billing, etc., have been computerized to make processes flow more smoothly. Kohn's wife, Beverly, took up the challenge to complete that computerization conversion some years ago. Kohn said the entire system works extremely well.

Fulfilling the role of general manager at Corvette Central is Mike Samson, who keeps the operation moving throughout the day.

Another member of the Kohn family can be counted in the ranks of the more than 40 employed there. His daughter, Sara, serves on the sales staff. They, along with the rest of the crew, have one goal: to keep your Corvette lookin' good. They pride themselves on being called "America's Leader in Corvette Parts."

About Corvette Central

Corvette Central is located at 5865 Sawyer Rd., Sawyer, MI 49125. Phone: 616-426-3342; toll free: 800-345-4122; fax: 616-426-4108; toll free fax: 800-635-4108. Showroom hours: Mon.-Fri., 9 a.m. to 5:30 p.m. ET, Sat., 9 a.m.- 1 p.m. Phone orders: Mon.- Fri., 8:30 a.m. to 6 p.m., Sat., 9 a.m.- 1 p.m. Most orders shipped within 24 hours. Various payment methods are offered.

Suzy Q.
Vette Resto

INTRODUCING D&D RESTORATION

By Bob Stevens

For the final phase of her renewal, Suzy Q. will be surrounded by the very best of company ... Rolls-Royces, Bentleys, Marmons, Cadillac V-16s and other full-blooded classics. No, she hasn't forgotten her roots as an American sports machine of "neo-classic" status. But then she doesn't mind being seen with the royalty of automotive history either.

Taking up a relatively small chunk of floor space at D&D Classic Auto Restoration in Covington, Ohio, Suzy Q. is now amongst future concours winners in the classic and antique ranks. The shop's walls are decorated with color photos showing former projects that received honors at Pebble Beach, Meadow Brook, Rolls and Bentley national meets,

Photos by the author
1. At the helm of D&D Classic Auto Restoration in Covington, Ohio, are three knowledgeable, skilled and energetic partners: (from left) Dale Sotzing, Dave Myers, and Roger James. Dave and Dale, who have worked together for 26 years, are the two Ds in D&D, having started the business in 1985. Roger signed on as a third partner about four years ago.
2. D&D Classic Auto

Restoration, Inc., is quartered in a pair of large buildings in an industrial park in Covington, Ohio. This is the main structure, which contains the offices and the body shop where the primary metal work is done. The business moved into its new custom-built facilities in 1988.
3. The second building in the D&D complex is where vehicle reassembly work is concentrated; it also contains an in-

house but independent upholstery shop. Altogether, the two buildings afford some 10,000 square feet of space.

4. The shop specializes in Rolls-Royce and Bentley from the prewar years, as well as other British marques from Aston Martin and Jaguar to MG and Triumph. But it will restore any car, partially or fully, body-on or body-off, etc. This '37 Rolls

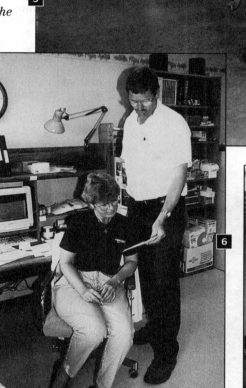

Phantom III is a rare V-12 model (the only series of V-12s ever built by the British maker of luxury cars). Rescued from another shop, this rare specimen is receiving a complete restoration.

5. Being treated to a cosmetic restoration is a '37 Rolls 25-30. All Rolls-Royces in those days were custom-bodied creations, with only the best in coachwork mated to the exceptional Rolls chassis. All Rolls-Royce models handcrafted during the 1925-48 classic period are genuine classics.

6. Dave Myers checks over some paperwork with office manager Brenda Grigsby. "She just about runs the place," Dave quips, only half joking.

7. Roger James (right) is assisted by Jeff Mitchell in slipping a windshield into a '37 Rolls. All three partners in D&D are hands-on owners and perform skilled restoration work themselves. This example of the exclusive English make sports a Belgium-built body refinished in two-tone dark and royal blue.

and other equally impressive and exclusive affairs. The resto shop, formed in 1985 by Dave Myers and Dale Sotzing, is one of the world's leading Rolls-Royce and Bentley specialists, having produced numerous national winners. The business has developed a solid reputation for quality paint work, handcrafted body panels, custom built parts and a parts locating service focusing on Rolls and Bentley pieces.

Dave and Dale, who had worked together on cars in various capacities dating back to 1969, formed their partnership in 1985 using their first initials for the company's title. A third partner, Roger James, came on board in 1991, but the three owners haven't figured out how to smoothly blend in an R; D&D&R sounds like a Madison Avenue ad agency and DD&R sounds too much like a railroad.

Dave Myers started working on cars at any early age. He painted his first car at 14; that was some 40 years ago and since then he has worked on hundreds of cars, first as a sideline, then as the owner of a conventional body business and now as the operator of a restoration shop. He had already developed a pretty healthy interest in cars by the time he went to work for John "Red" Elson, a well-known southwestern Ohio Ford dealer and vintage car collector. "He really sparked my interest in old cars, especially the classics," Myers remembers. He still sees Red Elson every now and then at car meets, and just recently custom fabricat-

ed a handcrank for Red's 1906 Cadillac. Myers' brother, Chris, is still running Elson's body shop in Versailles, Ohio, even though the Ford dealership there, of which the body shop was a part, was closed a year or so ago.

Dale Sotzing had worked with Myers since 1969. So when the two opened their restoration business on June 5, 1985, they were well acquainted with each other's work habits, ethics and capabilities. They complemented each other in several ways. Sotzing, who is 49, enjoys the fabrication end of car restoration and can often be found at the business end of a grinder, cutter, welder,

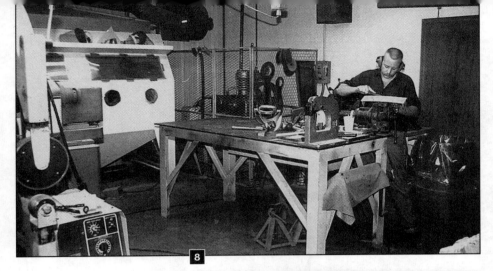

8.

8. *The shop is very well equipped with everything from a huge sandblaster, a paint booth and modern welding equipment to an English wheel.*

9. *Not all of the classics at D&D are of English origin, as witnessed by this 1931 Marmon V-16 now undergoing restoration.*

10. *A classic beauty, this '29 Rolls-Royce PI dual cowl phaeton is painted a distinctive maroon and red.*

11. *The D&D crew provides some motivation for Suzy Q.,* the Cars & Parts *1963 Corvette project car. The shop is handling the final assembly of the split window coupe.*

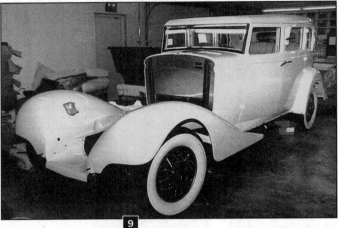

9.

10.

11.

sander, etc. He just enjoys working with sheet metal, especially when it's attached to a prewar Rolls, Bentley or other illustrious British motor car.

Sotzing likes the business at its current size and pace. There are 10 full-time employees, including the three partners, and he thinks that's sufficient. There are also 18 customers' cars in the shop right now, including 12 undergoing a total restoration, and that's also sufficient, he says. Myers, however, wouldn't mind seeing the business expand just a bit more with a marginally larger staff and a lot more space.

Even though they're inspired and captivated by antique and classic cars, neither Myers nor Sotzing owns a collector vehicle. But the third point of the partnership triangle, Roger James, is a typical car hobbyist. The pride of his collection is a 1941 Graham Hollywood. He also owns a nice '41 Ford sedan delivery and is currently restoring a '56 Ford pickup.

It was James' interest in the old car hobby that got him into the business. By day, he was a plant manager for a plastics manufacturer in Fairborn, Ohio. But he spent his evenings and weekends out in the garage restoring his cars, something that didn't go unnoticed by one of his neighbors, Dale Sotzing. In fact, he was often helping James work on his old vehicles. It wasn't long before the casual hobby talk became serious and Roger found himself restoring cars on a full-time permanent basis as a partner in D&D Classic Auto Restoration.

It's a good match. Myers manages the day-to-day operation and does much of the custom parts fabrication and parts locating work, while Sotzing runs the body shop, especially the fabrication work, and the 50-year-old James takes care of the final assembly and detailing tasks. All three get involved in painting, either directly or in a supervisory role.

All three owners travel extensively. Myers has been a regular at Hershey since his first appearance there in 1973, and has been attending the big Auburn extravaganza almost as long. Myers, Sotzing and James all attend the major events, like Hershey and Auburn, and also such exclusive affairs as Pebble Beach, Meadow Brook and the national Rolls club meet.

The trio of restoration experts represents a wealth of knowledge and experience. The management triangle at D&D is now complete! 📷

**Next Month:
Making their own parts**

About the shop

D&D Classic Auto Restoration, Inc., 2300 Mote Dr., Covington, Ohio 45318, is owned and operated by three partners, Dave Myers, Dale Sotzing and Roger James. The shop's phone number is 513-473-2229, and the fax number is 513-473-5433. Normal business hours are observed, and customers and prospects are welcome to tour the shop with advance notice.

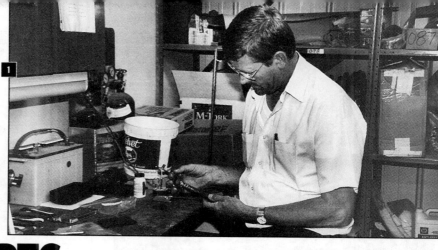

CUSTOM PARTS FABRICATING AT D&D RESTO

By Bob Stevens

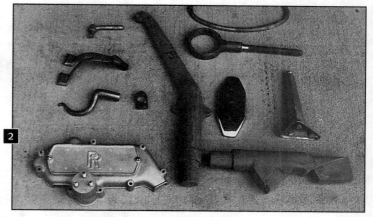

One tour through D&D Classic Auto Restoration convinced us that the well organized, fully equipped and adequately staffed operation could handle the reassembly of Suzy Q. in stride. Our first impression was right.

As our 1963 Corvette coupe project entered the final assembly stages, Suzy Q. found herself surrounded by classics, from Marmon and Cadillac V-16s to Rolls-Royces and Bentleys of prewar vintage. She has enjoyed the ritzy company.

As revealed last month, D&D specializes in the restoration of Rolls-Royce and Bentley automobiles from the prewar era, but also works on other classics, as well as postwar cars, both domestic and foreign. If it rolls, D&D will restore it to its original eminence. The highly skilled 10-person staff is backed up by a corps of suppliers covering virtually every facet of parts design and manufacture, explains Dave Myers, speaking for the three-man partnership that also includes Dale Sotzing and Roger James.

One of the shop's most admirable and valuable qualities is its ability to reproduce, or have reproduced, about any part imaginable. Of course, it can also be quite expensive, but when there's no new or rebuildable used parts available, there are few options for the restorer to take. Along this vein, the shop has become known for its parts cache of reproduction Rolls and Bentley items, such as the radiator shutters that were so vulnerable to damage and are impossible to find in new or usable shape.

Quite often the only choice is to make a part by hand, from scratch, utilizing key suppliers. The right contacts are very important, Myers says, and he's

Photos by the author

1. *Dave Myers, one of the three partners in D&D Classic Auto Restoration, Covington, Ohio, examines a hood hold-down for a 1931 Marmon V-16 the shop is restoring. Myers will reproduce this part, which is impossible to find in new or usable condition.*

2. *This group of vintage Rolls-Royce and Bentley parts is representative of the wide variety of reproduction undertaken by D&D Classic Auto. The resto shop uses a cadre of highly skilled suppliers for reproducing everything from wood body frames and engine castings to taillight housings and lenses. (The piece at the upper left is a Chrysler nameplate that the shop had replicated for a project; the taillight stand at the center, right, was made for a Marmon.)*

3. *Dale Sotzing, one of the shop's three owners, does a little grinding on the rear of a body for a 1934 3.5-liter Bentley three-position drophead coupe. Employee Chris Smallenbarger works on a wheel well. This Bentley, a 1934 factory show car, was won in a poker game some 25 years ago.*

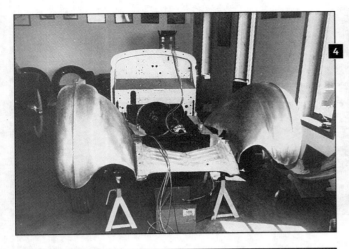

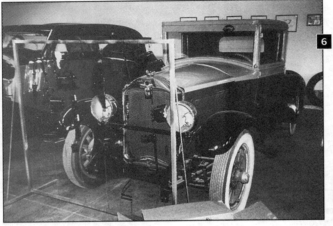

4. This is the rest of the '34 Bentley, the chassis, cowl and fenders. This car has some history to it, being the actual factory display car for the 1934 London Auto Show. It was originally sold to one A.B. Briscoe in England. The exquisite coachwork was by H.J. Mulliner.

5. D&D can have about anything reproduced, especially if there's a pattern to follow. This Buick radiator shell (left) was made to replace an original (right). The new shell was stamped in several pieces and then shipped to D&D for assembly.

6. Not all of the cars restored at D&D are classics, as witnessed by this 1928 Buick coupe.

7. The shop was about ready to put the finishing touches on this chassis for a 1909 Buick being restored for a doctor.

8. The body for the '09 Buick awaits some new upholstery.

9. Joe Smith, who operates Upholstery Unlimited, the in-house upholstery shop at D&D, shows how he trimmed the material for the '09 Buick to a pattern he developed himself from the original button-tufted design. The padding had to be hand stuffed. Smith is an independent contractor, although most of his work is done for D&D.

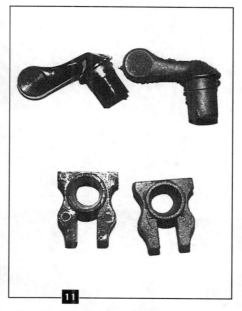

extremely proud of his primary suppliers. Among them are Crystal Engineering, Piqua, Ohio, where D&D gets a lot of its specialized castings; Dayton Carbide, Troy, Ohio, which supplies one-off machined pieces; Custom Chrome, Elyria, Ohio, where the resto shops sends all of its plating business; Tom Willis, Miamisburg, Ohio, a pinstriper; and Upholstery Unlimited, which performs all of the trim work.

Upholstery Unlimited, which is a one-man operation located within D&D, shares the same quarters and address, but works for anyone. Owner Joe Smith relocated to D&D from the Cleveland area because a major chunk of his business was coming from the Covington restoration shop some 250 miles away. But the shop is independent of D&D and accepts upholstery and trim work from any customer, again specializing in prewar antiques and classics. Currently, some 75 percent of the shop's trim work is performed on cars from D&D.

Prior to saddling up with Joe Smith, D&D used Brown's Auto Trim, Troy, Ohio, which was owned and operated by R.J. Brown, who retired some four years ago. "Brownie," as he was known by almost everyone, handled virtually all of D&D's business.

Having a corps of quality suppliers is paramount to success in the restoration business, Myers admits, but the most important asset is still the customer. "We've developed a large and very loyal clientele. I've met some of the nicest people in this business," Myers says. He credits one regular customer in particular with getting his shop interested in prewar Rolls-Royce and Bentley restoration work. It was Dick Scott, a construction equipment executive in Sidney, Ohio, who first brought some high-quality Rolls and Bentley business into D&D. As Scott's cars began to win at Pebble Beach, Hershey and elsewhere, the word spread quickly about D&D.

D&D has expanded well beyond the borders of Ohio, where most of its work originated at the beginning. Today, about 80 percent of its restoration work comes in from out-of-state. From producing local show winners, the shop has developed into a creator of blue ribbon beauties at the hobby's highest levels. The shop was scheduled to take nine cars to the classy Meadow Brook Concours in Detroit in August of 1995.

Suzy Q. lacks the blood lines for a Pebble Beach Concours appearance, but she's certainly enjoying the high class company during her stay at D&D Classic Auto Restoration. Maybe some of that concours quality restoration normally reserved for genuine classics will rub off on the proud little American sports car.

10. *Michael Fullerton does a little grinding work on the body of a 1953 MG TD roadster.*

11. *An original Pierce-Arrow ignition lever (left) had worn out, but it was good enough to serve as a model for a new one (right). The shop will frequently have an extra part made to serve as a pattern for future projects. A part can be made in any quantity, from one up to 100 or more, depending on the part's salability.*

12. *Undergoing a full restoration is a 1936 Cadillac V-16 sedan.*

13. *Roger James, the third partner, checks out the quality on some parts that had just been rebuilt, replated or refinished for a 1934 Marmon V-16.*

About the shop
D&D Classic Auto Restoration, Inc., can be reached at 2300 Mote Dr., Covington, Ohio 45318, 513-473-2229, fax 513-473-5433.

Suzy Q
Vette Resto

SPARE WHEEL REFINISHING

By Bob Stevens

Since Suzy Q. isn't equipped with run-flat tires, she'll need to carry a spare wheel and tire assembly everywhere she goes.

The spare tire carrier mounted under the tail end was empty when we acquired Suzy Q., so we first had to hunt for a replacement. Actually, it didn't take long, just a phone call and a plea for help to Dan Mershon, owner of Mershon's World of Cars, a Corvette dealership in Springfield, Ohio.

Mershon had a member of his crew remove a used tire from a spare 15-inch Corvette wheel. Then we transported the

Photos by the author
1. *The spare wheel, donated by Mershon's World of Cars, Springfield, Ohio, is an original five-bolt Chevy wheel in the correct 15-inch size. It was in fine shape, having just recently been taken off a Corvette, but it needed to be refinished.*

2. *John Bastian, Cincinnati, Ohio, readies the sandblasting booth at the Antique Auto Shop, Elsmere, Ky., for stripping the wheel.*

3. *The wheel prepares for a blast of sand.*

4. *After blasting and painting by the resto shop, the wheel was ready for mating with a new reproduction Firestone 6.70 x 15 polyester blackwall tire from Lucas Automotive, Long Beach, Calif.*

wheel to the Antique Auto Shop, Elsmere, Ky., where it received a thorough cleaning, a quick trip through the sandblast cabinet, and a fresh coat of black paint.

The wheel was then married with a 6.70 x 15 Firestone blackwall polyester four-ply tire provided by Lucas Automotive, Long Beach, Calif. The tire matches the four already on the car, although those tires are mated to reproduction knock-off wheels.

In the unlikely event that Suzy Q. should ever suffer a flat tire, the spare wheel and tire will be ready to get her back up on all fours in a jiffy.

5. *A high-performance anti-sway bar and handling kit was supplied by Performance Suspension Technology (PST), Montville, N.J., but not mounted on the chassis during restoration. Although it provides a major boost in handling, the kit also represents a departure from stock and requires some drilling into the frame, so we elected to let the new owner of Suzy Q. mount the kit at his convenience and in the way he wanted. The attaching hardware is not shown.*

Suzy Q Vette Resto

FITTING THE BRAKES

By Eric Brockman

The brakes are probably the most important feature of an automobile. There's not much point in being able to go fast if you can't stop the car. But because they are hidden away behind the wheels, the brakes tend to be neglected more often than not.

Brake components, especially in drum brake systems such as Suzy Q.'s, live in a harsh environment laden with dirt, moisture and extreme heat. Brake lines and hoses are also exposed to the worst conditions the roads have to offer. When restoring a car, it makes sense to replace *all* the brake hardware. Why cut any corners here, and risk destroying your pride and joy, not to mention risking injury because of brake failure?

So the stoppers got new shoes, mounting hardware, wheel cylinders, lines and master cylinder. Kanter Auto Products (76 Monroe St., Boonton, N.J. 07005; order line 800-KANTERS; fax 201-334-5423) supplied all the hardware, including the rubber hoses, while Fine Lines (650 W. Smith St., Unit #2, Medina, Ohio 44256; phone 216-722-7641) provided the new metal brake lines. The brake drums, in decent shape, were turned, cleaned and painted. Antique Auto Shop, Elsmere, Ky., installed everything, except the master cylinder, which will be installed after the body is remounted on the chassis.

Now Suzy Q.'s "whoa" will match her "go!"

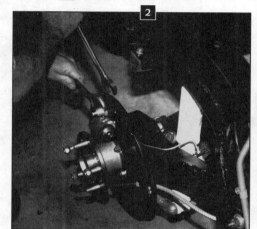

Photos by the author

1. *John Bastian, of the Antique Auto Shop, Elsmere, Ky., fits the new metal brake lines to Suzy Q.'s chassis. Fine Lines, of Medina, Ohio, provided the brake lines, as well as the new fuel lines.*

2. *With the suspension reassembled, the brakes could then be fitted to the chassis. The first item to be attached to the backing plate was the wheel cylinder. Kanter Auto Products, of Boonton, N.J., supplied the brake hardware.*

3. *Here, Bastian fits the new brake shoes into place.*

4. *With the shoes in place, the related mounting hardware was attached.*

5. *An assembled brake assembly, ready to accept the refinished brake drum.*

Suzy Q

Vette Resto

Final Chassis Assembly

By Eric Brockman

After many months of looking at piles of random parts in the office and at various restoration shops, things are starting to come together now. The parts piles are growing smaller, and Suzy Q. is slowly but surely beginning to look like an automobile again.

With the engine and transmission back in the chassis, it was time to finish up the last few niggling things that needed to be done to the chassis prior to mounting the body back on it.

We transported the chassis, along with many boxes of parts, to D&D Classic Auto Restoration in Covington, Ohio, where final assembly would be taking place.

Shop co-owner Roger James, assisted through much of the work by Jeff Mitchell, set about putting the final touches on the chassis. Among the items needing installation were the exhaust system, driveshaft, fuel tank, parts of the steering and emergency brake assemblies, along with as many engine compartment accessories as could be installed before mounting the body.

Once the rolling chassis was complete, the body could then be placed back on the frame.

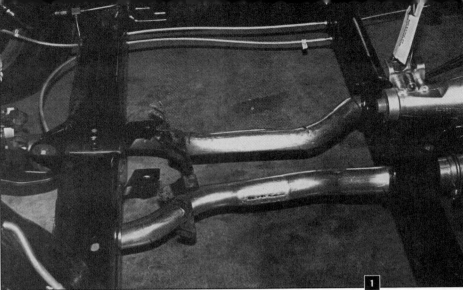

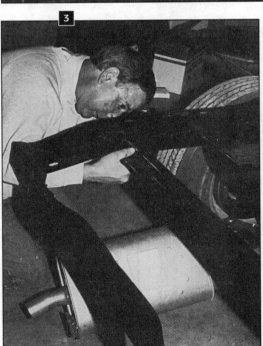

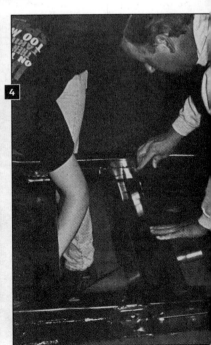

Photos by the author

1. *Upon its arrival at D&D Classic Auto Restoration, the first item installed on the chassis was the new exhaust system, supplied by Kepich Exhaust.*

2. *The heat riser valve was cleaned up and reinstalled on the passenger-side exhaust manifold.*

3. *Roger James then began the reinstallation of the gas tank. Because of its location, it's much easier to install prior to mounting the body. James first re-installed the chassis crossmember which supports the tank.*

4. *Anti-rub strips for the gas tank were then installed on the chassis.*

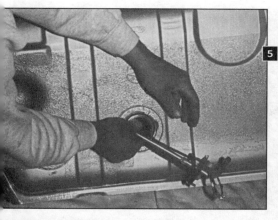

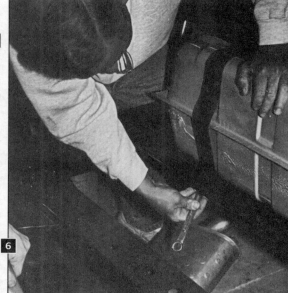

5. *Prior to installing the tank, James re-installed the fuel gauge sending unit.*

6. *With the tank in place on the chassis, the hold-down straps were bolted into place.*

7. *Moving to the front of the chassis, James assembled the linkage for the clutch. The linkage could have been installed after the body was back on the chassis, but its much easier to do prior to mounting the body. In addition, there is less chance of accidentally damaging the paint on the body.*

8. *The pivot bracket for the parking brake was also reassembled at this time.*

9. *C Central supplied new components for the steering. Shown here is final assembly of the components for the steering relay rod, which attaches to the pitman arm. Also supplied, but not shown, was a new steering damper.*

10. *Jeff Mitchell installed the new coil and distributor cap. The spark plugs and wires were also installed at this time.*

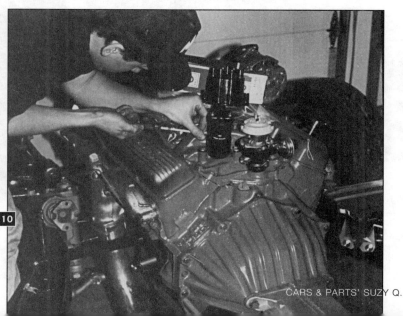

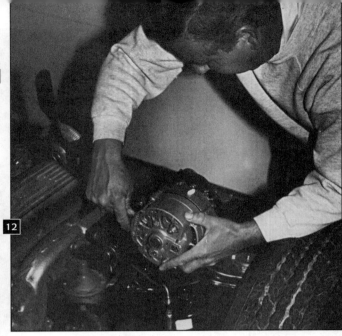

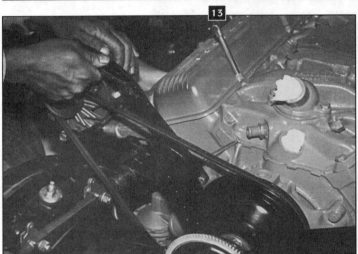

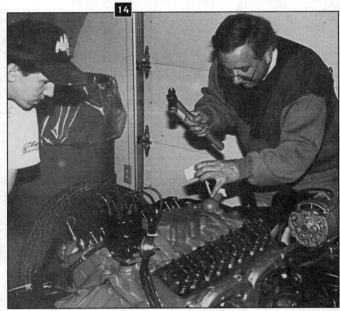

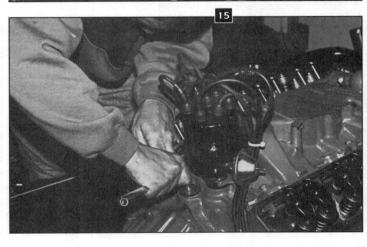

15. The road draft tube and grommet were installed in the block behind the distributor.

16. C Central supplied the correct-style valve covers, which were painted Chevy orange and then installed by Mitchell.

11-13. The repainted fan and the new fan clutch were installed, along with the alternator, supplied by Chicago Corvette Supply, and the fan belt, supplied by Quanta Restoration and Preservation Products.

14. A few careful taps from a hammer, and the oil filler tube, also supplied by C Central, was in place. James placed a small piece of 2x4 wood on the top of the tube so the hammer blows would not damage it.

SUZY Q

Vette Resto

REMOUNTING THE BODY

By Eric Brockman

Finally, the time had come. After months of separation, the body and chassis would be, at last, reunited. Suzy Q. would actually resemble a whole, complete car — for the most part at any rate.

Putting the body back on the chassis isn't exceedingly difficult. But it requires a great deal of care and patience. If the body isn't slid perfectly into place, that beautiful new paint and body work could be seriously damaged. The last thing anyone wanted to hear was the sickening sound of cracking fiberglass.

D&D Classic Auto Restorations used an overhead hoist to support the body and lower it into place. Several of the shop's technicians stood at strategic points around the body and helped guide it into place, making certain the body adequately cleared all the chassis components.

As you may recall from the disassembly of the car, each body mount point contained a number of shims to level out the body on the chassis. Once the body was set in place, the proper number of shims were slid in between the body and chassis at the mount locations. Comparison measurements were taken on each side of the car, to make certain the body sat level on each side after the shims were installed. The mounting bolts were then installed and torqued down.

Now that Suzy Q. is starting to look like her old self again — only much better now — final assembly of the trim, interior, glass, etc. can begin. There's still a long way to go, but the end of the restoration road is finally in sight. 🔧

Photos by the author

1-2. With the body securely attached to an overhead hoist and spotters positioned at strategic points to make certain everything went alright, it was lifted off the dolly. The dolly was then slid out of the way. The body is heavy, so it's important to make certain your method of lifting the body is capable of handling the weight. Also make certain your lift points are strong enough to stand the strain.

3. The chassis was then carefully slid into position under the suspended body. Care was taken to be sure all components on the chassis cleared the underside of the body.

4

4-6. *The body was then lowered onto the chassis. This step must be taken slowly, so that the body is properly lined up on the chassis and clears all items on the chassis. Don't forget to check that the shifter lines up with the hole in the transmission tunnel.*

7. *With the body in place on the chassis, the body alignment shims were inserted between the body and chassis.*

5

6

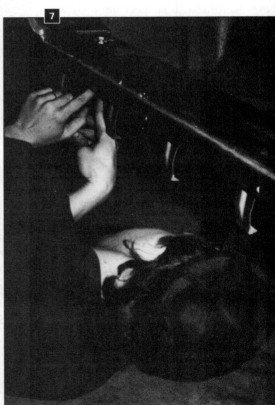

7

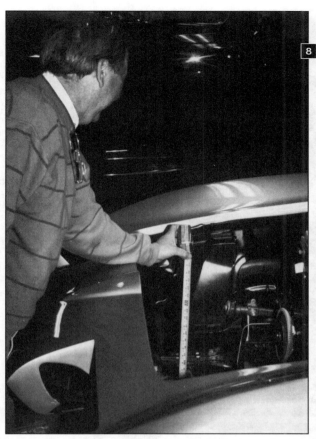

8

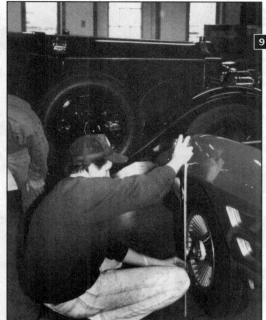

9

8-11. *Once the shims were in place, comparative measurements were taken at various points around the car, to make certain the body sat level on the chassis.*

12-13. *When everything was deemed kosher from side to side, the body bolts were inserted and tightened down.*

10

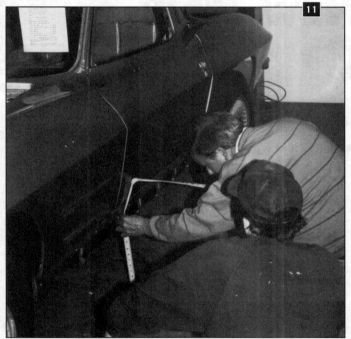

11

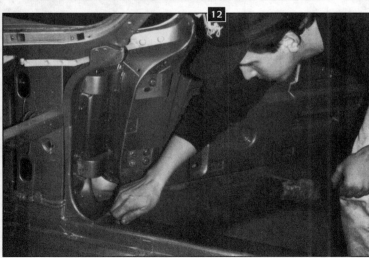

12

13

Vette Resto

BABY NEEDS A NEW PAIR OF SHOES

By Eric Brockman

Photos by the author

1. *C Central of Sawyer, Mich. supplied the reproduction knock-off aluminum wheels for Suzy Q. The company also supplied the necessary hardware — adapters, cones, spinners, center caps, and knock-off pins.*

After a flashy paint job, wheels are the next biggest contributors to a car's appearance. Wheels can change the whole demeanor of a car, transforming it from a sedate-looking piece of mere transportation to something wild and exciting to behold.

With Suzy Q.'s original wheels and wheel covers long gone when we got her, we knew correct wheels would have to be tracked down. Right away we determined the plain jane wheels and wheelcovers used on '63s just wouldn't do for our lady. Those sharp knock-off aluminum wheels available during mid-year Vette production were the only "shoes" for Suzy Q.

To that end, C Central of Sawyer, Mich. supplied the reproduction knock-off wheels and associated hardware. For the rolling stock, Lucas Automotive of Long Beach, Calif., donated a set of five reproduction blackwall 6.70-15 Firestone Deluxe Champion tires. Sidney Tire Service, Sidney, Ohio, handled the chore of mounting the tires on our shiny new knock-off wheels.

The wheels garnered many admiring comments just sitting on the tire changer at Sidney Tire Service. Wait until they're on the finished Suzy Q.

2. *Lucas Automotive of Long Beach, Calif. donated the correct reproduction tires for Suzy Q. They're 6.70-15 Firestone Deluxe Champions.*

3. *At Sidney Tire Service, Jamie Simpson installed the tires on the aluminum rims. Here, a valve stem was being installed in one of the rims.*

4. *Next, the tire was carefully coaxed over the wheel.*

5. *Once the tire seated against the rim, Simpson inflated it to the proper pressure.*

6. *Each wheel and tire received a "spin" on the balancing machine.*

7-8. *The balancing machine registered the amount of weight needed to properly balance each wheel, and Simpson then installed the necessary weights on the inside of each rim.*

9. *C&P writer Dean Shipley shows off Suzy Q.'s new footwear in front of Sidney Tire Service. Now all we have to do is reassemble the car, so we can see how they look on Suzy Q.!*

SUZY Q

Vette Resto

MOUNTING KNOCK-OFF WHEELS

By Eric Brockman

Corvette knock-off wheels look dynamite, but require a little more time and attention in the installation process than ordinary wheels.

Because each wheel is held in place by a single knock-off spinner (hence the name), instead of five lug nuts, extra care must be taken to properly secure the spinners. Failure to adequately tighten the spinners — and recheck them at regular intervals — could have dire consequences: a wheel (or wheels) could come off, severely damaging the car and injuring you.

The wheels come with detailed instructions and recommendations, to help insure they perform satisfactorily. D&D Classic Auto Restoration, Covington, Ohio, mounted the knock-off wheels once the car's body had been reunited with the chassis.

Photos by the author

1. *A special adaptor for mounting the knock-off wheels bolts to the brake drum. The adaptors are side specific, and marked as such. Jeff Mitchell, D&D Classic Auto Restoration, tightens the lug nuts with an air impact wrench.*

2. *The directions recommend a bead of silicone adhesive to help hold the center cone in place on the wheel. Since the spinner doesn't tighten down far enough to secure the cone, we found this to be necessary.*

3. *The wheel and tire are then slid over the knock-off hub, and the center cone is positioned in place.*

4. *With the center cone in place, the spinner is threaded onto the hub by hand, and then snugged down with a mallet. A small center cap snaps in place over the end of the hub. The directions recommend checking and retightening the spinners after the first 10 miles of operation.*

Suzy Q

Vette Resto

Building the Wiring Harness

By Dean Shipley

Lectric Limited is "wired." But its customers of some 20 years have come to expect it from the automotive specialty company, that calls Justice, Ill. home (somewhere west of Chicago).

Lectric Limited makes wiring harnesses. It's the company's specialty. "We build harnesses for GM and Chrysler cars," said co-owner Ken Hanna.

Not only does the firm build them, but Lectric Limited builds them to duplicate exactly the application for which the harness is to be built. That original harness, connectors and all, has become a product for which demand has been steadily increasing. Allen Fierke, co-owner with Hanna, said as car show judges increasingly scrutinize their judgments, the correct harness can help the car owner score valuable points. But even for the non-concours car guy, it makes sense, when restoring a car, to have a harness that duplicates the original.

Lectric Limited has *original blueprints* for the harnesses it builds. That's a great

1

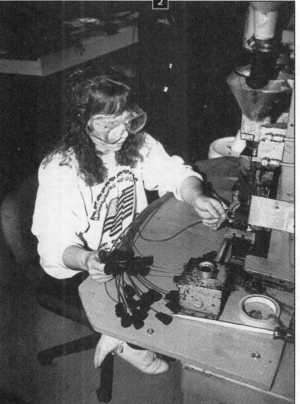

2

3

Photos by the author

1. *Lectric Limited partners, Allen Fierke, left, and Ken Hanna are "wired" into the car hobby with their many wiring harness applications. To say they get a charge out of conducting this business would certainly not blow a circuit.*

2. *Lectric Limited's Debbie Clemens assembles part of the wiring harness that will be installed on a '73 Corvette with automatic transmission. Connectors and wires are made to duplicate the look of the originals.*

3. *Lectric Limited produces exact replica T-3 headlamps for GM applications. They are look-alikes to the originals, but have been technologically upgraded to meet current standards for candle power and photometry.*

place to start, but a duplicate harness is more than just blueprints on paper. The wire and the connectors all have to duplicate the originals as well. Hanna said they buy enormous quantities of Packard components and stock pile them to ensure the company can continuously produce quality wiring harnesses. "We've become very good scroungers," said Hanna with a chuckle.

Hanna said Lectric Limited builds thousands of harnesses per year. The company can produce so many because many of the operations are mechanized. They have numerous presses that crimp terminals on the ends of wires. "We carry this to a major extreme to minimize changeover time, which diminishes efficiency," Hanna said.

But Hanna said time is taken to make sure each harness conforms to the blueprint and every wire has been plugged into a circuit tester to make sure it works. "Every harness is plugged into all the circuits found on the car to make sure all connections work before it is shipped," Hanna said.

Lectric Limited's products include the harnesses, plus spark plug wires, battery cables and the now-famous T-3 headlamps, which were original equipment in many GM vehicles.

Hanna said Lectric Limited had to perform months of behind-the-scenes work to secure permission to build and market the lamps. They look like the original lights, but meet contemporary standards for candle power and photometry.

Lectric Limited's products are distributed through a network of 200 dealers. "We also sell factory direct to hobbyists and restorers," Hanna said.

Lectric Limited has the utmost confidence in its products. "I like to think we're leading the way," Hanna said. 📷

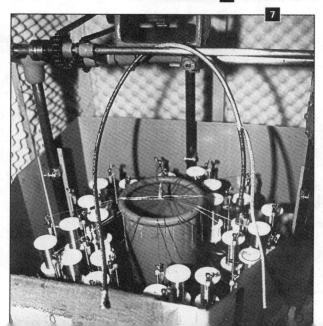

4. *The wiring harnesses are built to exacting standards as set forth by the original blueprints. Here, Pete Partridge, shop foreman, checks out a harness against its blueprint. Lectric Limited holds many, many original blueprints from which it builds harnesses.*

5. *The building of the wiring harnesses and components is mechanized as much as possible. Mechanization speeds the process so less time is needed without sacrificing quality. As they say, "time is money."*

6. *"Testing one, two ...." To the left of Ken Hanna, lays a wiring harness about to be tested, on the circuit testing board. He holds upright another wiring harness circuit testing board, to show "the business side." Every harness is completely plugged in and tested before it is shipped to the customer.*

7. *If the original wires wore braiding, the duplicates built by Lectric Limited are braided as well. This braiding machine is a mechanical marvel that weaves the threads into braids. Note the spark plug wire in the foreground that wears a braided wrap.*

About Lectric Limited
Lectric Limited is located at 7322 South Archer Rd., Justice, Ill. 60458; phone 708-563-0400.

Suzy Q
Vette Resto

INSTALLING THE WIRING HARNESS

By Dean Shipley

When the wiring harness for Suzy Q. came out of the package, the multi-colored wire strands appeared to be more numerous than the asps in the "well of souls" in the movie *Raiders of the Lost Ark*.

But the restorers at D & D Classic Auto Restoration, Covington, Ohio, didn't act the least bit snake bit or even intimidated by the wiring harness built especially for Suzy Q. by Lectric Limited of Justice, Ill.

Roger James, restorer, said putting in a new wiring harness is easier when the preparation is thorough. That includes completely labeling the *old* wiring harness before it is removed. Yes, this is a time consuming process, but doing it will save time when installing the new one.

It should also be noted if the old wiring harness passed through the body, as it did in Suzy Q.'s case, or underneath it. In the case of the latter, according to James, make sure all the wiring is in place before the body is set on the chassis.

Label, label, label each and every wire as it is unplugged. "You can't have too much information," James said. So it follows also to have a legible copy of the wiring diagram from either a shop manual or a restorer's guide.

Make sure you also have all the necessary straps and fixtures needed to attach it properly. In fact, when ordering the wiring harness, make sure either the straps and hangers come with it, or arrangements can be made to purchase a kit. Assume nothing when ordering. It's better to ask right up front and know for sure if the harness comes with all attaching "hardware," than to assume it does and *not* have it. It will certainly slow down your progress.

Photos by the author

1. D&D restorer, Tim Henderson, studies a wiring diagram in the midst of his installation of the wiring harness in Suzy Q. Gather all sources of written material possible before this stage of the restoration begins. You can't have too much information.

2. Where does installing a new wiring harness start? With the removal of the old wiring harness—provided it is properly labeled. Any information that can be gathered prior to the harness installation is valuable.

3. The new harness is threaded into place. It goes through the body on this car. Be sure you have gathered all the necessary hangers and fixtures for installation. "Correct" fasteners are available from various vendors and are not always included in the purchase of the harness.

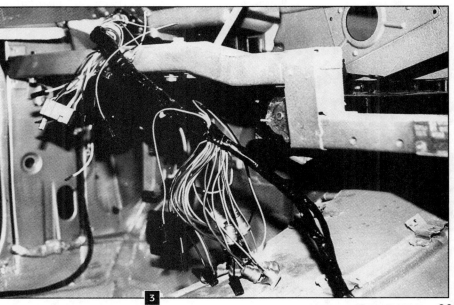

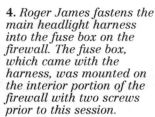

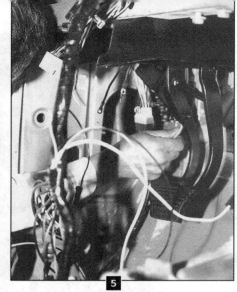

4. *Roger James fastens the main headlight harness into the fuse box on the firewall. The fuse box, which came with the harness, was mounted on the interior portion of the firewall with two screws prior to this session.*

5. *Roger James presses a grommet in place after the wiring harness has been brought through the hole in the firewall on the driver's side of the car. James advises taking the harness one connection at a time, so as not to be intimidated by the enormity of the job.*

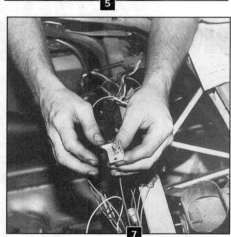

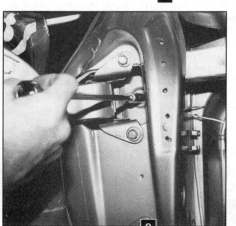

6-7. *Henderson inserts the various bulbs that will light the instruments and accessories on the dashboard.*

8-9. *Henderson threads wire through the body, photo 8, to the junction point with the courtesy light switch. In photo 9, he snugs the nut that holds the switch in place.*

10. *During the process of installing the wiring harness, a meter was used to check various circuits and switches — in this case, the switch to operate the headlight motors. The meter is a very handy tool to have for wiring harness installation, especially if any of the old underdash switches are reused. It*

can track down problems and effect solutions before it's so late in the project that solutions become major hassles.

11. *The bulbs are in and various sections of wire have been routed in anticipation of the installation of the dash.*

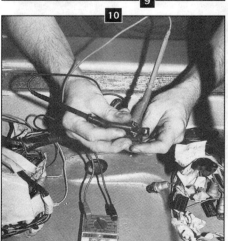

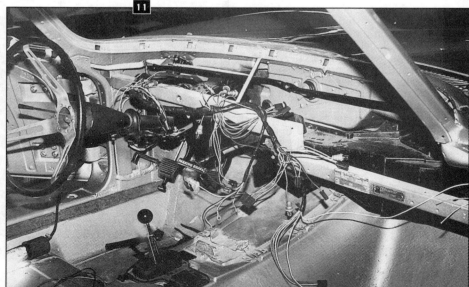

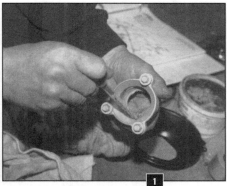

Suzy Q
Vette Resto

INSTALLING HEADLIGHT MOTORS

By Eric Brockman

With a couple of major exceptions, mid-year Corvettes are not exceedingly complex automobiles. One of those exceptions, the independent rear suspension, was covered in a previous issue.

This month, our attention turns to the other exception: the hidden headlight mechanism. Ever wonder why so many mid-year Vettes had custom headlights installed in the grille? Here's a clue: the hidden jobbies can be a real pain to repair.

Being mounted in the nose of the car, the wiring, mechanisms and motors are relatively exposed to the elements. After many years of service, this can lead to problems. Upon first trying out the headlights after purchasing Suzy Q., we discovered they definitely needed attention. One side opened, and the other did not. After a little fiddling with the switch, the latter opened. But then they both refused to close.

Chicago Corvette Supply provided us rebuilt headlight motors on an exchange

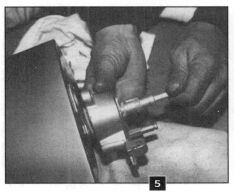

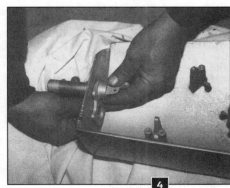

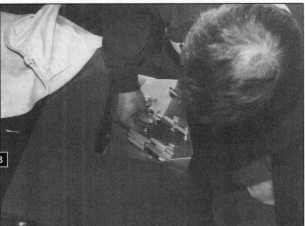

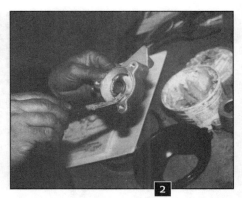

Photos by the author

1. *Roger James, D&D Classic Auto Restoration, performed most of the installation work for the headlight assemblies. First, the inside of the* headlight pivot support *was given a coating of grease before the pivot ball was inserted.*

2. *Once the pivot ball was installed, it too received a coating of grease. The* pivot seals were then *installed over the ball.*

3-4. *The inner (photo 3) and outer (photo 4) pivot shafts were installed on the headlight buckets. The headlight motor mounts onto the inner shaft.*

5-6. *The pivot assemblies were mounted onto their respective shafts. The inner and outer pivot assemblies differ, and can't be interchanged.*

7-8. *With the headlight bucket in place, it's attached to the nose. On each side of the bucket, three screws attach the pivot assembly housing to the nose. The hole in the side of the headlight bucket allows access to the screws.*

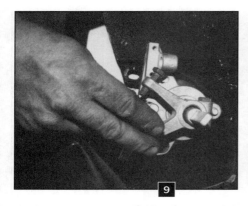

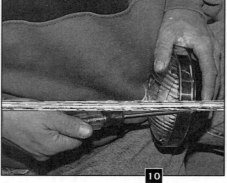

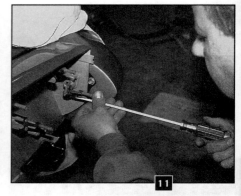

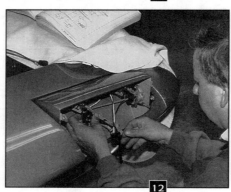

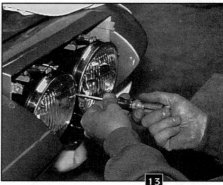

basis, and Corvette Central provided new limit switches, which "tell" the motors when to shut off. The rest of the parts of the mechanism were in reasonably good shape and only required some cleaning.

The system itself really isn't all that complicated, once you've studied the diagrams in a good shop manual. Copious photos and notes while disassembling the system are a must, because it is a bit tricky getting all the pieces apart and back together again.

The only real problem is the location — crawling up into the nose of the car is awkward and difficult. We waited until the body was off the chassis to disassemble the system. Reassembly commenced following mounting the body back on the chassis at D&D Classic Auto Restoration. As you can see from some of the photos, getting the pieces back in was a tight squeeze at times.

Once everything was installed came the moment of truth. The new headlight motors worked beautifully, raising and lowering the headlights without a glitch.

9. *The headlight motor stop mechanism was then slid onto the inner shaft. The stop bolts allow adjustment of the position of the headlight bucket in relation to the nose of the car.*

10. *With the headlight buckets in place, the headlights could be installed. The reproduction T-3 headlights, supplied by Lectric Limited, were installed in the mounting ring, and the retaining ring was attached with screws.*

11. *The headlight bracket hardware was installed in the headlight buckets.*

12. *The headlight wiring harness was threaded through the access hole and attached to the main harness.*

13. *The headlight assemblies were then plugged into the harness and attached to the brackets.*

14. *Jim Dotson drew the short straw (just kidding), and got to crawl up in the nose of the car to install the new headlight limit switches and the headlight motors.*

15. *Headlights up! The refurbished system worked without a glitch, successfully raising and lowering the headlights.*

Suzy Q

Vette Resto

FITTING A REPRO HOOD

By Eric Brockman

The Corvette reproduction parts industry has progressed to the point that it is possible to replace nearly any worn out part on a vintage Corvette (there are a few exceptions).

When it comes to body parts, it's gotten to the point where suppliers such as Corvette Central can even sell you a complete reproduction body for a '57 Corvette. With mid-year Vettes such as Suzy Q., most any badly damaged or deteriorated body component can be replaced with new, high-quality reproduction components.

While the body man at WW Motor Cars in Broadway, Va. managed to smooth out Suzy Q.'s battered front clip, the prognosis wasn't so good for the car's hood. It had taken too much of a beating over the years, and bringing it back to top-notch shape was just not feasible. Fortunately, the previously mentioned Corvette Central was able to supply a reproduction hood.

But it's not quite as simple as bolting on a new hood and shooting a coat of paint. Because of manufacturing variances when the Vettes were originally assembled, the repop hood has to be produced to a dimension guaranteed to fit each and every Vette produced. Hence, for most applications, the hood must be custom sized and trimmed to fit an individual car.

This is *not* a job for an amateur — it takes a skilled hand to get everything just right. To discourage the foolhardy, a large warning is attached to the hood, proclaiming that once you cut it, it's yours! Paul Salyards of WW Motor Cars skillfully trimmed and shaped the hood, then prepped it for painting.

1

Photos by the author

1. *Paul Salyards started by installing the new hood hinges. The new hood needed to be test fitted to determine what work would need to be done to it. Because of specification variances in the manufacture of Corvettes, the reproduction hoods have to be made large enough to guarantee they will fit all Corvettes of a given year.*

2. *The hood was bolted into place for a "trial run" to see how much trimming would be necessary. All the necessary holes — for hinges, prop and latches — were in place when the hood arrived.*

2

3. There was a remote chance the hood might fit without trimming it, but that was not the case. After taking measurements, Salyards used masking tape to mark how much had to come off each side of the hood. That might not seem too difficult, but when material was removed from the sides, the contours of the rounded front corners had to be reshaped to match the nose of the car. That was where a bit more bodywork skill than the average hobbyist would possess was needed to do the job properly.

4. Using a cutting wheel, Salyards carefully removed the excess material from the hood. Once cutting has started, the hood can't be returned. As they say, "You break it, you bought it."

5. The hood hinge holes also had to be elongated a bit to provide some extra room for adjustment.

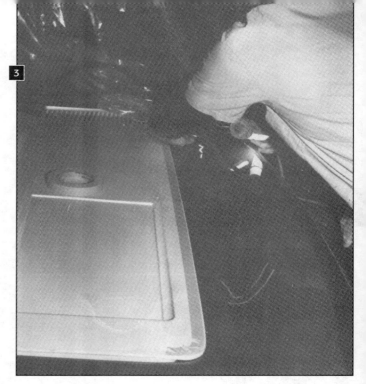

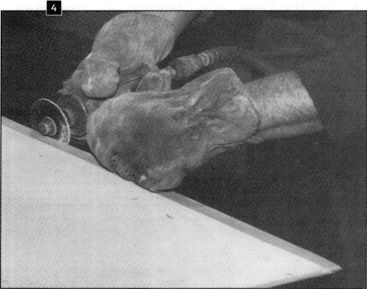

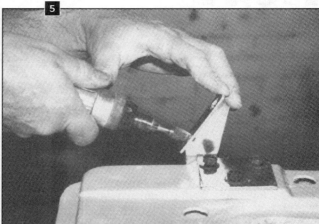

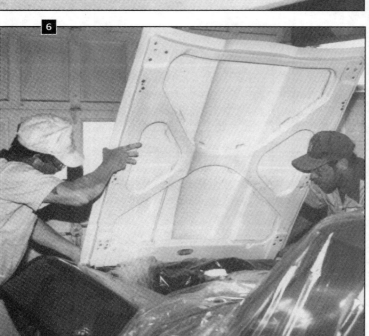

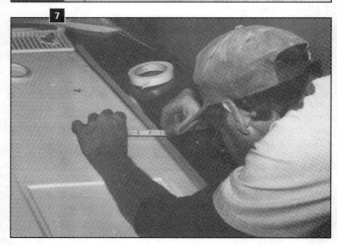

6. Salyards test fitted the hood several times along the way to check his progress.

7. Measurements were taken to check that the gaps on each side matched once the hood was installed.

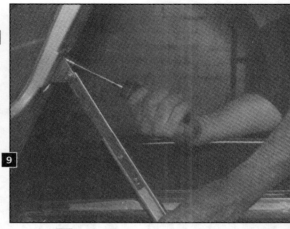

8. *Once trimmed, the hood was ready for a test fit with all the mounting hardware in place.*

9-10. *The hood prop and the hood catch were installed, along with new latch assemblies. Once it was determined everything worked properly, the hood was removed in preparation for painting.*

11. *The hood was sanded prior to priming to remove any surface imperfections.*

12-13. *The hood was primed and a guide coat sprayed in the manner described in the article on painting the rest of the body.*

14-15. *Sanding then began, with checks to make certain the surface was level and free of imperfections.*

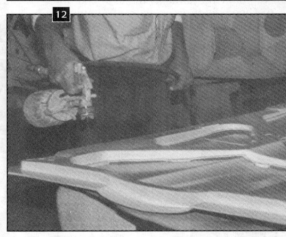

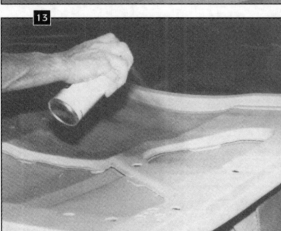

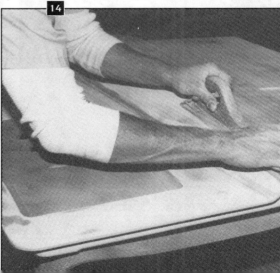

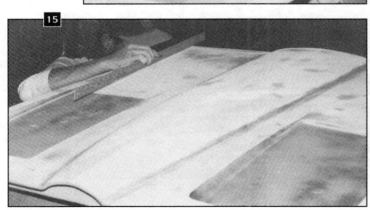

Suzy Q

Vette Resto

HOOD TRIM INSTALLATION

By Eric Brockman

While '63-67 Corvettes are very similar in appearance, there are significant differences from year to year. The '63s present certain obstacles not found on other mid-year Vettes, because of a number of items unique to that model.

One such area is the hood. While essentially the same as the '64 hood, the '63 hood features a pair of simulated "grille" inserts that are purely decorative. Many thought they looked a bit tacky — especially since they served no actual function — and Chevy eliminated them after one year. Tacky or not, they are unique to the '63 and therefore have to be installed.

Photos by the author

1. *Using a piece of thin cardboard, Henderson cut it to the shape of the trim panel and pushed it over the mounting studs on the trim panel.*

2. *He then placed the template in the proper location on the hood, and used the holes in it as guides to mark the locations for the mounting holes to be drilled in the hood.*

3. *Before drilling, he double checked the marks on the hood against the mounting studs on the trim panels. Everything lined up alright.*

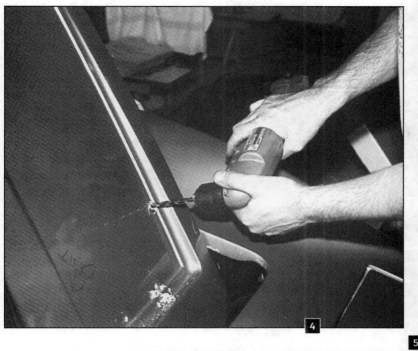

4

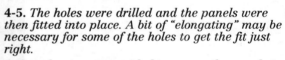

5

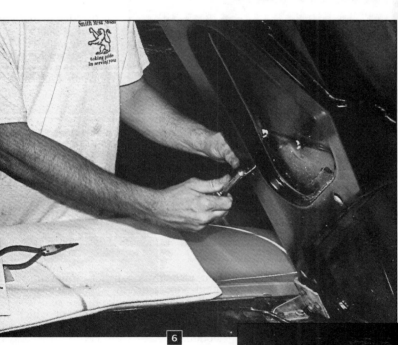

6

4-5. *The holes were drilled and the panels were then fitted into place. A bit of "elongating" may be necessary for some of the holes to get the fit just right.*

6. *Speed nuts are provided to secure the panels to the hood. But with the reproduction hood, the panel studs were just a bit short for the speed nuts to hold things in place. Henderson ended up tapping the studs and securing the panels with regular nuts.*

7. *To get the nuts on the leading edge of the trim panel tightened, Henderson had to close the hood and reach up from underneath with the wrench.*

7

The hood inserts on Suzy Q. were fairly battered after 30-plus years exposed to the elements, since they consist of fairly thin anodized aluminum. Reproduction inserts were ordered from Corvette Central, but the installation was not as easy as it would seem. Since the reproduction hood fitted to Suzy Q. doubles for both '63 and '64, the holes for the trim pieces are not predrilled.

Locating and drilling the new holes was not a particularly difficult procedure, and Tim Henderson at D&D Classic Auto Restoration capably handled the job. He made a template to mark the location of the mounting holes and then drilled them in the hood. The hood panels are held in place by nuts on the panels' mounting studs.

Suzy Q
Vette Resto

C.A.R.S. WEST SETTLES IN L.A.

By Bob Stevens

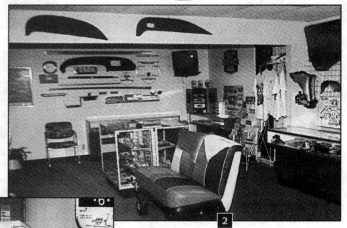

C.A.R.S. Inc. has been providing Chevy interiors, parts, manuals and memorabilia from its Berkley, Mich. headquarters for years, but now the veteran supplier has expanded westward.

Actually, it was a couple of years ago that Don Hickey packed his bags, loaded up the old Chevy, and headed west to seek his fortune. In the process, Hickey, a long-time employee of C.A.R.S. (dating back to the days when the company was known as Can-Am Restoration Supplies), has also expanded the fortunes of his employer. That, of course, has delighted co-owners Bob Chauvin and Larry Wallie, and kept shop manager Dave Pena busy keeping the West Coast outlet supplied with an adequate inventory.

Much of the business at C.A.R.S. West, which is located in suburban Fullerton, Calif., walks through the front door, but a lot is also transacted over the phone and through the mail. Many West Coast orders processed at the home office in Michigan are routed through Hickey's western operation. As

3. Don Hickey, western manager for C.A.R.S., answers a customer's questions over the phone. Much of the store's business is still handled by phone and mail, although walk-in traffic has increased dramatically in the past year or so.

4. One end of the spacious showroom presents the company's interior products, including seat covers, door panels, armrests, etc.

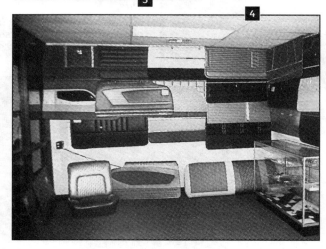

for Hickey, he's very comfortable in his new surroundings, He prefers the more temperate year-round climate of California to Michigan's frigid and salty winter. His old Chevys don't rust, and his Harley is a lot more fun to ride on dry, ice-free roadways. The western opera-

tion also gives owner Bob Chauvin a good excuse to periodically visit California and check out the rust-free tin of the Golden State, some of which he ships home to Michigan for his own collection.

C.A.R.S. West is a success in more ways than one.

About the shop

Carrying the company's complete line of Chevy, Impala, Camaro, Monte Carlo, Nova, El Camino, Malibu and Chevy truck products, including a wide range of interiors, C.A.R.S. West is located at 525 Raymond Ave., Fullerton, Calif. 92631. The phone number is 714-525-1956, 1-800-451-1955 (easy to remember numbers - 1956 and 1955 - since the company's main line is focused on 1955-57 Chevys). Don Hickey is the western branch manager. The bulk of the company's business is still transacted through the main operation in Michigan, which is located at 1964 W. 11 Mile Rd., Berkley, Mich. 48072-1187, phone 1-800-521-2194. Dave Pena is shop manager in Motown.

Suzy Q
Vette Resto
THE DASH SPECIALIST

By Bob Stevens

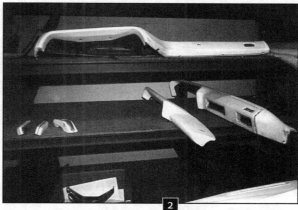

Topping off any dashboard in a collector car is the crash pad, as it was called when Suzy Q. was in her prime. It would be criminal to install perfectly restored gauges, the overhauled and cosmetically refurbished radio and new trim pieces and leave the old cracked and weathered dash pad in place. But buying a new old stock pad would only produce the same results a few years down the road, or sooner (possibly during installation as that 30-year-old vinyl could crack or split easily).

The only logical solution was a completely new pad, which is the house specialty at Just Dashes in Van Nuys, Calif. Although the shop's owner, Irwin Tessler, got his start reproducing only dash pads, hence the name Just Dashes, the firm today supplies much more than dash pads. Its product lineup includes vinyl-covered console lids, armrest pads, factory headrests, door panels, and vinyl cleaners and preservatives.

Most of Just Dashes' products are the direct result of a Thermo-Vacuum forming process that is quick, efficient and produces outstanding results. The days of hand molding, hand stretching and hand stapling vinyl to dash pads, door panels, etc., are happily over. The process, which will be presented in detail next month, is a fascinating one.

Just Dashes opened in 1981, specializing in dash pads from the 1950s up through the '80s. Today, pads are made for cars up to the current model year, but the bulk of the firm's business is still vintage cars. Since federal law required dash pads beginning in the 1966 model year, there are a lot of dashes out there in need of replacement covers.

Materials used today are far superior to those in use some 20 to 40 years ago. Just Dashes uses top quality vinyl of correct grain and texture for the applica-

Photos by the author

1. Inside the reception area at Just Dashes, Van Nuys, Calif., numerous examples of the shop's capabilities line the walls. The firm is located in a commercial/light industrial section of the northern L.A. suburb.

2. Incoming dashes await recovering. The firm is running a backlog of several weeks, but orders are handled as promptly as possible. Quality is still the key, and the company offers a lifetime guarantee on its dash recovering work.

3. Freshly recovered dashes are ready for pick up by the customer, or shipping to out-of-town car owners.

4. Hobbyists in the greater Los Angeles area can take advantage of Just Dashes' curbside service, as the owner of this 1961 banana-nose Thunderbird hardtop did. The dash restoration outfit will remove the dash, or more likely just the foam padding to make a pattern, and then install the freshly manufactured dash pad, often on the same day.

5. *A masked worker sands a core. The shop is divided into several sections to accommodate the different types of work.*

6. *The dash pad for the '61 T-Bird is recovered with brand new vinyl. Only new materials are used; NOS vinyl is just too old to depend on for current installations.*

7. *George Ramos, shop foreman, separates the new pad from its core. The vacuum process is quite amazing, pulling the new vinyl into precise form over the mold.*

8. *The finished pad has been trimmed and is ready for installation in the T-Bird.*

9. *Irwin Tessler, owner of Just Dashes, is an old car hobbyist himself; he's shown here with his pride and joy, a restored '57 Cadillac Coupe de Ville.*

the hobbyist takes photos or makes drawings of all dash trim pieces, hardware, moldings, clips, radio speaker grilles, knobs, etc., before removing the dash so that reassembly won't be a problem. Also, dashes should be carefully packed. Most are shipped via UPS.

Years ago there was little to be done about cracked dash pads; few trim shops would even mess with them and NOS pads were usually too brittle from age to be used. Today, brand new pads are available that exceed OEM quality (then or now). As Tessler, a vintage car owner and hobbyist himself, explains: "It's getting easier and easier to restore a car today, thanks to the huge network of suppliers of specialty parts and services now available."

Next Month
Suzy Q.'s new dash pad

---

tion, applied over a high-density polyethylene foam. The finished product is guaranteed as long as the customer owns the car, which is amazing considering that OEM pads are usually good only for about five years in regular, daily use.

The business currently has 10 full-time employees, and all are very busy as the shop runs about a four-week backlog of orders, although four to six weeks is not uncommon. About 75 percent of the incoming business is mail-order (mail, phone, fax, etc.), with about 25 percent walk-in (or drive-in, actually). Expansion plans are already being finalized to help

the shop accommodate its growth over the past few years, since the addition of Thermo-Vacuum forming to the operation.

Tessler adopted the process about three years ago. "When I found out that the original OEM materials were still available from the original suppliers, I knew that was the way to go because that's the way restorers and collectors prefer it," Tessler said, explaining that the base materials are dyed to match original colors. The new foam padding then assures long service life.

The dash specialist recommends that

About the shop
Just Dashes, 5941 Lemona St., Van Nuys, Calif. 91411, operates normal business hours, and can be reached at 818-780-9005 (orders can be placed toll free at 1-800-247-3274), or a fax can be directed to 818-780-9014. Irwin Tessler is the proprietor, and Jason Gabbert is the front counterman.

Vette Resto

MOLDING A NEW DASH PAD

By Bob Stevens

Thermo-Vacuum forming is a process by which vinyl is permanently attached to a dash core by means of suction. It's advanced the art of vintage car dash restoration immensely. In fact, it's one reason that Just Dashes has expanded tremendously in recent years to accommodate the growth in demand for dash restoration.

It used to be that a car restorer either stripped away the old cracked and weathered dash pad and simply repainted the dash, or searched for a 30-year-old new-old-stock dash pad that probably cracked upon installation or a few months later. Today, a completely new pad, using a new superior form of padding and an original style but better quality and thicker vinyl, can be made in virtually any dash shape using the Thermo-Vacuum method, which is depicted in the accompanying photos.

The process begins with an actual dash frame, or dash core, stripped and cleaned and fitted with a new pad. It's then propped up in the Thermo-Vacuum machine and it rises onto hot vinyl that is suctioned down over the dash. It's an amazing process, and one that takes only minutes to complete.

Before that, though, the experts at Just Dashes go over every inch of a dash frame, checking for cracks or other imperfections, which are remedied before the dash is recovered. If a frame is beyond reuse (which is unlikely because they are rarely exposed to the elements), a new core can usually be provided by Just Dashes. In some cases, dash pads for many popular models are kept in stock for immediate shipment; no need to even send in the core.

Once the frame is cleaned and approved for use, a base layer of closed-cell, high-density foam is applied. This material is better and more durable than the original foam used (it's the foam that expands and contracts, causing a dash pad to tear, separate, bloat, etc.). Then the vinyl material is applied in the Thermo-Vacuum machine. The vinyl is heavier than original equipment for longer service life. Excess material is then trimmed away and the dash is allowed to "cure" for a few hours.

Then a technician takes a power drill and opens the holes for the heater and radio controls, the gauges, the radio speaker grille, etc.

The finished product is a thing of beauty with the correct grain and a taut fit. The pad is then dyed to match the original color, or whatever color the customer prefers. The shop has a complete set of interior color trim books from the '50s up through the '80s to properly match colors. The dye is a permanent application.

The finished pad not only tops off any dash restoration, but it also enhances safety. Furthermore, the materials and craftsmanship represented in each dash pad are guaranteed for as long as the original customer owns the car. Fortunately, car collectors tend to own several cars, otherwise Tessler wouldn't be realizing much repeat business.

Now that the dash is recovered in better than new padding and vinyl, the futuristic look of the Sting Ray cockpit has been restored to its original beauty, complete with fresh gauges, rebuilt radio and new controls. 📷

About the shop

Just Dashes, 5941 Lemona St., Van Nuys, Calif. 91411, has a full complement of contact numbers: Information line, 818-780-9005; orders, 1-800-247-3274; and fax, 818-780-9014. Irwin Tessler is the owner-manager.

Photos by the author

1. *Upon entering the production system, each dash unit is marked with the owner's name and the year and model of the car to ensure that mixups do not occur and to help track the order. This inscription reads: "Cars & Parts '63 Vette - Project Suzy Q."*

2. *Irwin Tessler (right), owner of Just Dashes, Van Nuys, Calif., explains to noted automotive author,* Jim McGowan, how the Thermo-Vacuum forming process secures the vinyl covering to the dash core.

3. *George Ramos, shop foreman for Just Dashes, does a little sanding work on the core. Each piece is fully prepared before receiving the new pad and vinyl covering.*

4. *The two individual pods for the driver and passenger sides are ready for prep work.*

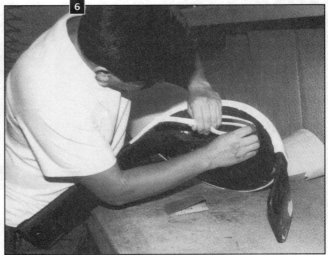

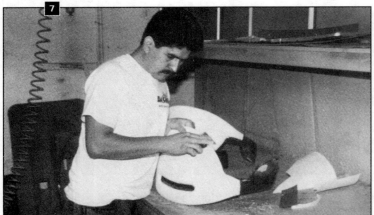

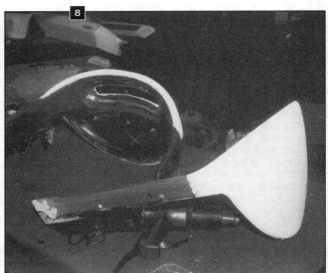

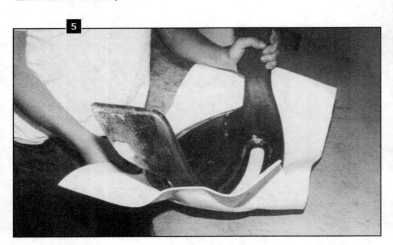

5. *New padding is fitted to the passenger side pod, which has a built-in hand grab that will have to be accommodated.*

6. *Ramos affixes the padding to one of the half shells. The padding in use today is far superior to what was used in the original installation.*

7. *Ramos fits the padding to the two dash pods, sanding them into form.*

8. *The two housings are now trimmed and ready for the vacuum-forming operation.*

9. *Each dash piece is fitted for mounting blocks that will hold the units steady during the vacuum operation.*

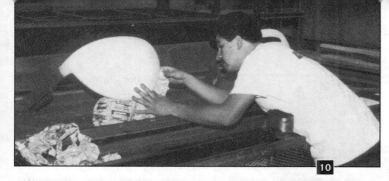

10. *The two dash pods, which will be treated simultaneously, are positioned on their wooden blocks with old newspapers used for cushioning.*

11. *The two dash pods are ready to receive their new covers.*

12. *The machine accepts the two dash pods, which are lowered into the unit,* and then workers place a fresh sheet of newly made vinyl of the correct style and grain over the top of the work bed.

13. *The Thermo-Vacuum process begins with the vinyl being sucked down over the dash pods as the pods are raised upward. It's a fascinating process, and one requiring some expensive equipment.*

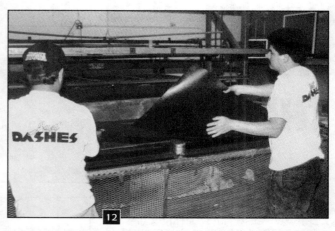

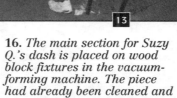

14. *The workmen check to make sure that the process has been effective all the way around. The dash pieces are virtually sealed by the vinyl without a ripple, a crack or a crevice. The process is thorough.*

15. *Ramos inspects the finished product, although it still needs to be trimmed. It will also be allowed to "cure" for a few hours.*

16. *The main section for Suzy Q.'s dash is placed on wood block fixtures in the vacuum-forming machine. The piece had already been cleaned and inspected for any cracks or other problems. It was in fine shape.*

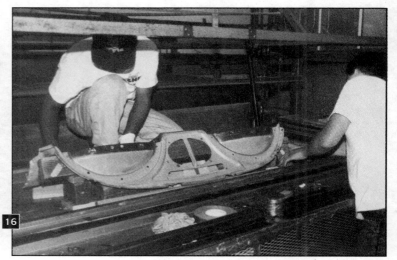

Suzy Q
Vette Resto

INSTALLING THE DASH

By Eric Brockman

1. *Our "dashing" restorer at D&D Classic Auto Restoration, Tim Henderson, first bolted the new defroster duct, supplied by Corvette Central, to the underside of the dash.*

2. *With the windshield and interior out of the car, it greatly simplified positioning the dash.*

3. *Once he had it in the car, Henderson maneuvered the bulky unit into its correct position.*

4. *A series of bolts along the top edge of the dash secured it in place. Again, having the windshield out of the car aided this step.*

5. *On each side of the car, a series of rivets was installed to secure the dash to the door pillars.*

Suzy Q.'s dash is a bit on the fragile side. But installing the unit is a relatively easy and straightforward process with the interior and windshield out of the car. After we had it restored by Just Dashes in California (covered elsewhere in this issue), D&D Classic Auto Restoration handled the installation.

Once in position in the car, several bolts along the top of the dash secure it to the cowl. Panels attached to either side of the dash must be riveted to the door posts. The riveting tool is the only specialized equipment needed for the installation.

For convenience sake, the defroster ductwork, radio speaker, radio and clock could be bolted in place prior to installation. If you go that route, be careful not to damage these items while maneuvering the dash into place. 📷

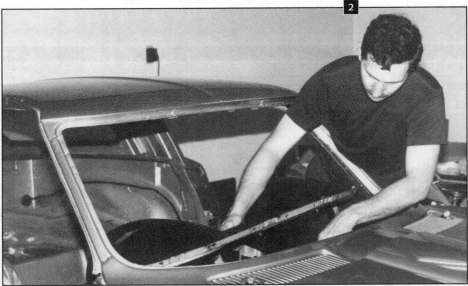

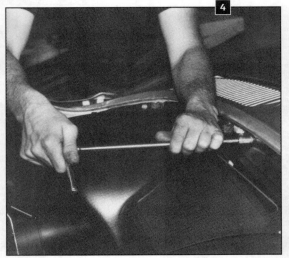

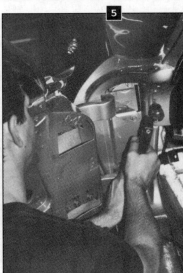

Suzy Q Vette Resto

INSTALLING THE DASH INSTRUMENTS

By Eric Brockman

With the wiring and newly recovered dash in place, installation of the gauges, clock, radio, etc., could commence.

There's no great mystery to most of this reassembly — everything is pretty straightforward. With the gauge cluster, a wiring diagram is helpful in determining the correct placement of the various instrument lights and some of the gauge connections.

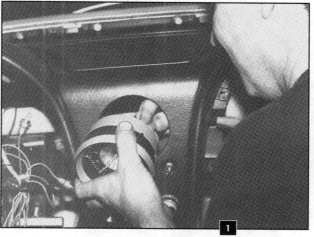

Photos by the author

1. *The clock was held in place in the center of the dash by a pair of clips.*

2. *Space was a bit tight when reconnecting the gauges. D&D's Tim Henderson connected part of the wiring before mounting the gauge cluster in place, then completed the installation after mounting the cluster.*

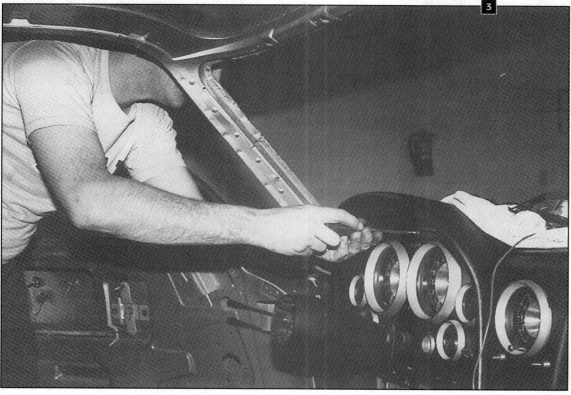

3. *Once positioned in place, a series of screws around its perimeter held the gauge cluster in place.*

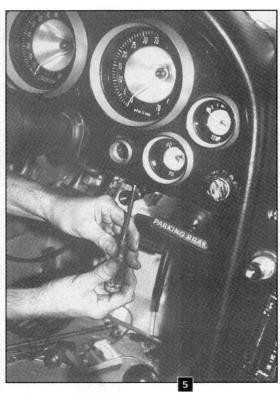

4-5. *With the cluster in place, Henderson attached the headlight motor switch and vent control cables to the underside of the cluster.*

6. *The antenna cable was laid into place along the door sill.*

7. *The bezels and knobs for the heater controls were installed in the center of the dash, along with the trim piece for the radio.*

8. *The radio was then slid into place and the knobs and bezels installed.*

9. *The new grab rail molding was installed at this point, too.*

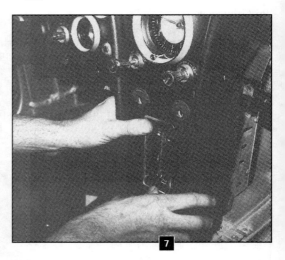

Suzy Q

Vette Resto

O.E.M. GLASS

By Dean Shipley

That familiar phrase, "necessity is the mother of invention," certainly holds true in the instance of Dale Smith of O.E.M. Glass. Smith, of Bloomington, Ill., had been involved with the Bloomington Gold Corvette extravaganza for a number of years. He had also been involved in the auto glass business since the late '60s.

Someone came to Smith and said something like, "Hey, it sure would be nice if we could get correctly marked glass for our Corvettes."

That set Smith to thinking and doing some research. The product thereof was glass, correctly marked with the proper logo and date code for Corvettes from 1956-62. From that point, Original Etchings and Markings Glass (O.E.M.) was born.

Just as a baby is born small and grows with proper care and feeding, so did O.E.M. Glass. Smith continued his research and expansion beyond doing glass for just a few years of Corvette.

He has photographed the glass of numerous original automobiles to verify the appearance of originally marked glass. Smith said he photographed one car out of the '30s that had glass from six different manufacturers.

The glass itself is made to modern industry standards. Windshields, straight or curved, are, of course, laminated. Rick Peek, spokesman for O.E.M., said they have become lighter in weight and stronger over the years. Side glass is of the tempered variety. It will not discolor or bubble as old laminated side glass will. Tempered glass is also a much safer product for side windows than laminated glass.

Having good glass is one aspect, but cutting it to the correct size and shape is also necessary. O.E.M. Glass holds in their files, literally thousands of patterns, cataloged by number. Peek said if

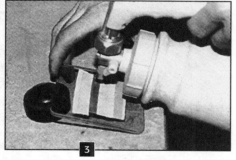

About the shop

O.E.M. Glass is located in Bloomington, Ill. Dale Smith is the owner. The company sells windshields, side glass and rear glass. Address: P.O. Box 362, Bloomington, IL 61702. Phone: 309-662-2122.

Photos by the author

1. *Dale Smith, owner of O.E.M. Glass, Bloomington, Ill., is always looking to provide restorers with correct glass for their cars. Here he examines the left half of a windshield for a '47 Cadillac.*

2. *Smith displays a sampling of the more than 3,000 patterns in the O.E.M. collection used for cutting glass to the correct shapes. Numerous makes are included. Shown here are patterns for Chevrolet, Ford, Chrysler and Packard.*

3-4. *Smith demonstrates the etching process. A mask is placed on a piece of glass in the correct position. Fine sand under pressure is sprayed onto the glass. The result is seen in photo 4.*

a customer calls and, for example, needs side glass for a '32 Packard, O.E.M. only has to pull the appropriate pattern from the catalog and use it to guide the cutter.

Once the glass has the proper shape, it is etched with the proper logo. O.E.M. holds hundreds of masks that bear the logos of various makers — L O F (Libbey-Owens-Ford) to name one. Peek said he can combine the correct masks to give the new glass the proper code to correspond with the build date of the automobile. Peek said information provided by the customer is used to mark the glass.

Once the process is completed, the glass is shipped to the customer. The glass is placed in a box. Then a liquid packing chemical is sprayed into the box. The chemical, when it reacts with ambient air, forms around the glass in the box and becomes solid. The glass is completely surrounded and protected for shipment to anywhere in the world. Smith said though it is expensive, it thoroughly protects the product and breakage has been virtually eliminated — percent of breakage is in the hundredths of a percent. O.E.M. has shipped its products literally all around the globe.

Vette Resto

INSTALLING A NEW WINDSHIELD

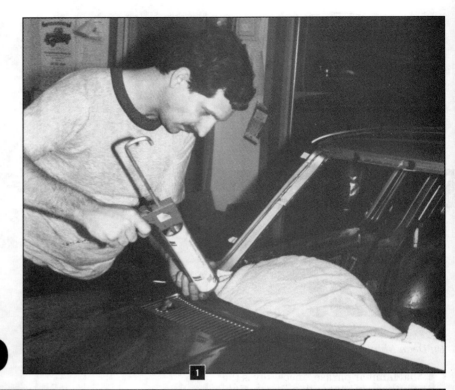

By Eric Brockman

Installing glass can seem like a daunting job to the restorer who's never attempted it. After all, the margin for error is pretty slim, and automotive glass can be expensive to replace if an accident occurs. In addition, if a window doesn't properly seal, the resulting water leak could cause untold damage.

D&D Classic Auto Restoration showed us that no great magic surrounds installing a windshield. But it does take patience and careful attention to detail to do the job correctly. Tim Henderson and Roger James skillfully installed Suzy Q.'s new windshield, which was supplied by O.E.M. Glass of Bloomington, Ill. (The firm also provided new side glass, vent windows and back glass to the project.)

With the Corvette, the installation procedure was fairly straightforward. First, the windshield molding clips were installed, and a bead of windshield sealant applied. The windshield seal goes over the windshield, and the unit is then put into place. The accompanying photos detail some tricks for getting the windshield seal into place. In a future issue, we will detail the installation of the rear and side glass.

Photos by the author

1. *After installing the molding clips, Tim Henderson laid down a bead of windshield sealant along the lower edge of the windshield mounting lip.*

2. *Henderson and Roger James then installed the windshield seal, supplied by Corvette Rubber Co., on the windshield, making certain to get the proper side installed against the edge of the windshield. The windshield seal does not come with the regular weatherstripping kit, and must be ordered separately.*

3. *Henderson applied a little dish washing soap into the groove of the seal. This served as a lubricant, and helped make it easier to get the seal pulled over the mounting lip during installation.*

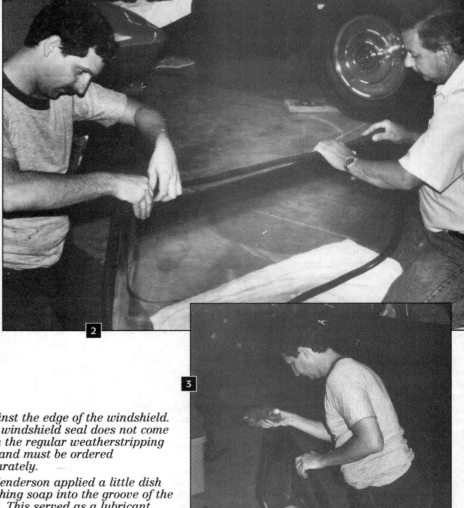

4. *Ever wonder how the pros get the seal over that mounting lip? Here's the answer, a simple piece of string. Henderson pushed it down into the groove all the way around the window, with the two ends left hanging out at the bottom center of the windshield. Once the windshield was in place, the string ends were carefully pulled out at the same time, moving around and up toward the top of the glass. This pulled the rubber seal over the mounting lip.*

5. *James and Henderson carefully lowered the windshield into place. They put the bottom in first, and as installation progressed, pushed the windshield down, eventually moving the top in its place.*

6. *Starting at the bottom of the windshield, Henderson carefully pulled the two ends of the string out simultaneously. This pulled the rubber seal over the lip. James pushed down on the top portion of the windshield at the same time, helping to seat it in place.*

7-8. *In a few spots, the seal needed a little extra help getting past the mounting lip and molding clips. Henderson used a hook tool to gently pull it into place.*

9. *A bead of sealant was run between the upper mounting lip and the seal. This step could be done prior to the installation of the windshield, but things might get a little messy during installation.*

10-11. *With the windshield in place, Henderson installed the stainless steel trim moldings.*

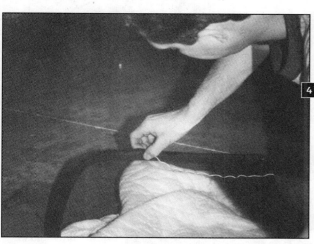

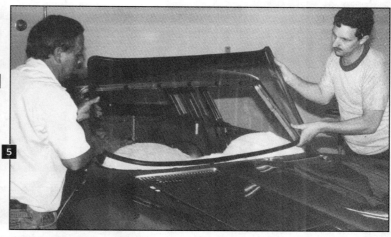

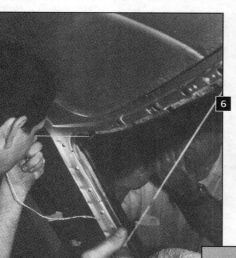

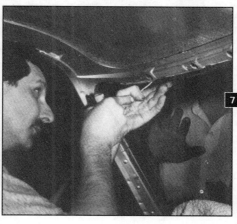

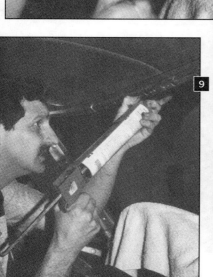

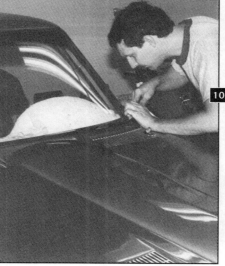

Suzy Q Vette Resto

INSTALLING THE SIDE AND REAR GLASS

By Eric Brockman

Previously, D&D Classic Auto Restoration installed Suzy Q.'s new windshield, supplied by OEM Glass. This month, we will detail the installation of the rear and side glass, which were also supplied by OEM Glass, Bloomington, Ill.

Once you've seen the windshield installed, there's not much to the back glass installation. It follows the same basic procedure as the windshield, so we'll just hit the high points of the installation.

The side glass, on the other hand, is a bit more complicated. The window regulator assemblies must be installed, along with the new window channels, the vent windows and their regulator mechanisms. Notes and photographs during disassembly are a definite plus here. If nothing else, make notes of the order of installation for the various pieces. Otherwise, trial and error, along with some inevitable disassembly to correct errors, will be necessary. 🚗

Photos by the author

1. *The new window molding retainer clips were installed. The marks left in the fiberglass by the old clips were used as an installation guideline.*

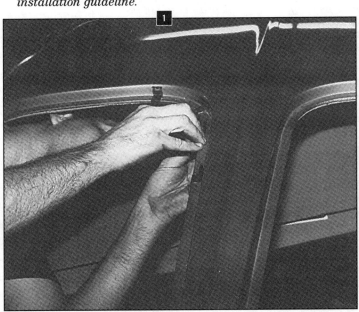

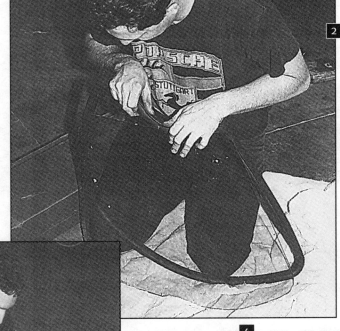

2. *Tim Henderson pressed the rubber seal over the edge of the back glass. With the '63, there are, obviously, two halves to deal with.*

3. *As with the windshield, a little bit of liquid dish soap was applied into the seal's groove to ease installation. Then a length of string was inserted in the groove to help pull the seal over the rear window lip.*

4. *Henderson and Jim Dotson carefully lowered one half of the split rear window into place.*

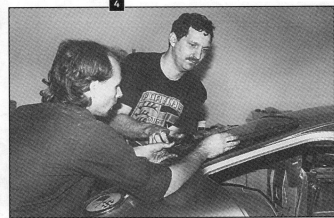

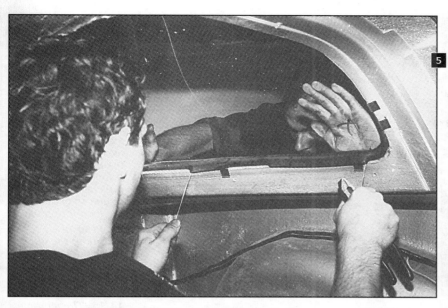

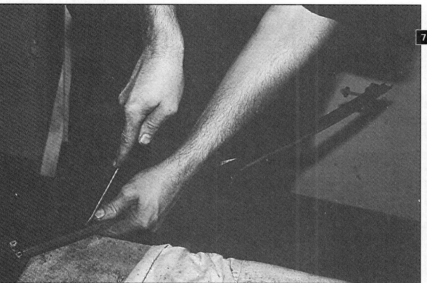

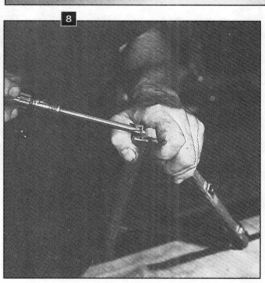

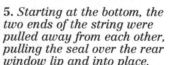

5. *Starting at the bottom, the two ends of the string were pulled away from each other, pulling the seal over the rear window lip and into place. Dotson pushed down on the window from the outside while Henderson pulled the string.*

6. *With the rear glass securely in place, the stainless steel trim moldings were pressed into place over the retaining clips.*

7. *Moving to the side glass, new front channel felts were installed. The felts are pushed into place over clips that protrude through the channel from the opposite side. The front channel for the side glass serves as part of the vent window frame as well.*

8. *The rest of the vent window frame was reattached to the window channel.*

9. *Henderson then installed new vent window seals.*

10. *In addition to new side glass, OEM Glass also supplied new vent window glass. The new glass was installed into the vent window molding, and the excess was trimmed from the new seal used between the two.*

11. *The vent window was then installed in the frame.*

12. *The rail that attaches to the window regulator was pressed onto the new side glass. It took a few gentle taps with a rubber mallet to get it all the way into place.*

13. *Prior to installing the glass, the window channel and outer reveal molding were installed.*

14-15. *The window regulator assembly (photo 14), followed by the lower guide rail (photo 15), were installed and mounted in the door. The regulator has to be installed prior to the installation of the vent window assembly.*

16. *The vent window assembly was then slid into place in the door. It took a bit of maneuvering to put it in its proper place.*

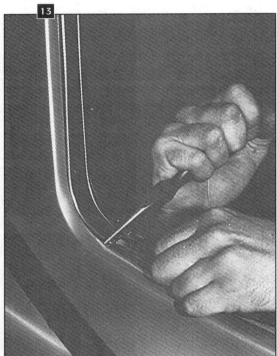

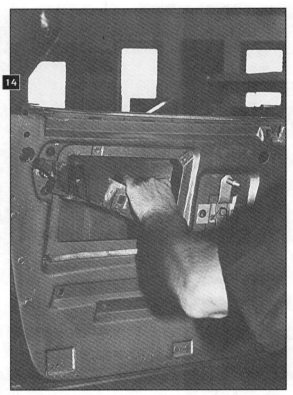

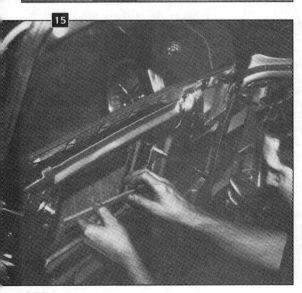

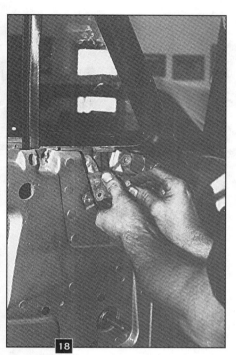

17. *The vent window frame is secured to the door via a series of screws.*

18-20. *The regulator mechanism for the vent windows is then installed and bolted into place.*

21. *Finally, the side glass is lowered into place, attached to the regulator mechanism, and adjusted.*

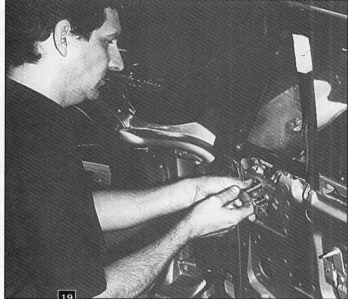

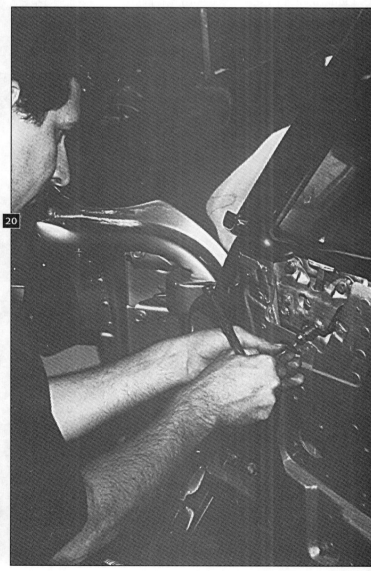

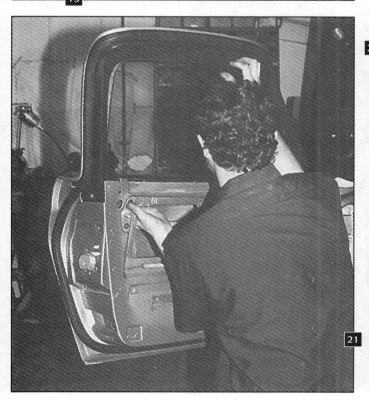

Suzy Q
Vette Resto
TRIM PARTS

By Bob Stevens

If you've ever bought a replacement Chevrolet tail lamp lens, a reproduction plastic Corvette emblem, a new speedometer or gauge face for your Camaro, or a freshly made chromed logo for a Chevelle or Nova, chances are you dealt with TrimParts ... probably without realizing it.

TrimParts, Milford, Ohio, manufactures a huge line of reproduction automotive plastic and metal parts for Chevrolet products, including full-size Bel Air and Impala models, El Caminos, Camaros, Corvettes, Novas, and Monte Carlos. Items produced include emblems, door handles, instrument faces, wheel spinners, engine badges, horn buttons, hood and fender ornaments, body trim pieces, taillight lenses, clock and radio faces, tail lamp bezels, sill plates, dome lights, etc. The list is almost endless, covering more than 1,100 different parts. In addition, 100 new parts are added to the line each year.

But it was only recently that TrimParts went public with its operation. In the past, the company dealt almost exclusively with individual parts vendors. Now, though, one can order directly from TrimParts. However, Darryl Bowman explains that the company is not really setup to accommodate walk-in traffic, so most individual orders are handled by phone, fax or through the mail.

A trip through the TrimParts operation is impressive. Bowman, who is sales manager for the firm, says that the company's name is self-explanatory in that its specialty is trim parts of all types. Bowman boasts that his plant is a full-service plastic parts producer with all the in-house equipment and expertise needed to completely design, tool and produce a plastic automotive replacement part. This includes manufacturing the tools, dies and molds; producing the part from raw materials; painting, cleaning, and buffing the final product; and then shipping it to the retailer, or selling it directly to the end user.

The company opened its current facili-

Photos by the author

1. *TrimParts is quartered in a modern one-story structure in Milford, Ohio, just north of Cincinnati. The old car parts manufacturer moved into the building in 1986 when it had 5,000 sq. ft., but another 5,000 sq. ft. were added a year later, in 1987, and then a 6,500-sq.-ft. expansion was undertaken in 1990. Another expansion is currently in the planning stages.*

2. *The lobby and offices are decorated in an automotive motif. The firm does now sell directly to hobbyists, but walk-in traffic is discouraged as the firm does not have a showroom or counter personnel. Phone and mail orders are preferred when dealing directly with TrimParts.*

3. *Darryl Bowman (left), sales manager of TrimParts, Inc., shows a newly minted emblem to Walt Reed, publisher of Cars & Parts.*

4. *The plant is expansive (this is only a small portion of the overall operation), yet it's well organized and very clean throughout.*

5. *Rick Holzclaw paints a gauge face in TrimPart's paint shop. Sometimes, a part must be masked off three, four or five times to get all the different colors correctly applied.*

7. *A Toolmaker, Mark Windle manufactures a special tool to produce a Pontiac GTO part, a small plastic cap that goes over the exposed screws in the trunk.*

6. *These are just a few of the dozens of templates in the paint shop that are used for masking instruments faces, clock lenses, gauge faces, etc.*

8. *Dave Castle uses a buffing wheel to clean up a '57 Chevy clock face. Buffing removes surface imperfections picked up during painting and other operations. The process also produces a high sheen.*

ty in Milford, Ohio, in 1986 and doubled its size a year later to 10,000 sq. ft. Then a second expansion added yet another 6,500 sq. ft. in 1990, and plans call for yet another building expansion in the near future.

The plant is fully equipped and includes a vacuum metalizer for laying chrome on plastic pieces, a 400-ton die cast machine that will make just about anything except grille and hood bars, and a series of plastic parts equipment for all types of specialized work. An example of the latter is a huge machine that makes clear plastic pieces only, such as a clear plastic emblem for an Edsel hub cap. We saw other machines cranking out taillight lenses for '55 and '63 Chevys during our tour.

TrimParts is now selling directly to the public, but it still conducts special runs of specific parts for vendors on an exclusive basis. The aforementioned Edsel hub cap emblem was such a piece. In such an instance, the vendor buys the entire run of parts. Occasionally, the firm even does contract work for vendors, making the molds, tools, dies, fixtures, and whatever, for a fixed cost. That, of course, is not an inexpensive proposition, but the vendor is the one putting up the money and taking the risk, speculating that he can sell enough of a particular piece to cover the high tooling costs.

Bowman says that his company attempts to provide the complete package on a part, including mounting hardware, instructions, etc. All 21 of the company's employees are trained to watch for any quality problems along the way as a part is cast, machined, buffed, packed and shipped.

TrimParts has expanded its offerings, moving into several new areas, including Chevy and GMC pickup trucks, Pontiac, GTO, Firebird, Corvair, Buick, Olds, Cadillac and now Mopar. The latter is just now coming on board, and is currently limited to a few window trim pieces and tail lamp lenses, but more Mopar parts are planned, mostly plastic items.

A number of items made by TrimParts are helping complete the restoration of Suzy Q., including a few smaller pieces that are used as parts of larger components, such as the face plate on the AM-FM radio and the lenses for the gauges. As someone once said, the fine details are what separate a first-class restoration from a runner-up.

About the shop
TrimParts, Inc., is headquartered at 5161 Wolfpen-Pleasant Hill Rd., Milford, Ohio 45150, and the phone number is 513-831-1472. Darryl Bowman is the company's sales manager, and Fred Wieck is the in-house technical expert. The company operates normal business hours, 7:00 a.m. to 5:00 p.m., Monday through Friday, and has a 24-hour fax line, 513-248-3402.

Vette Resto

INSTALLING EXTERIOR TRIM AND BUMPERS

By Eric Brockman

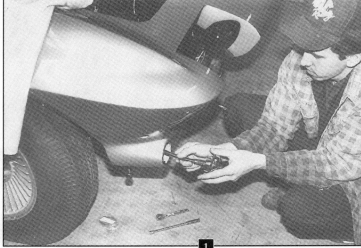

Photos by the author

1. The turn signals are available from GM as a complete assembly (except for the mounting hardware) ready for installation. Jeff Mitchell of D&D slid the assembly into place.

2. Emblems are understated — rear deck script, front fender flags and nose flag.

3. The gas filler door and its trim ring are held in place by screws.

4. The base for the outside mirror bolts to the door. The mirror itself then attaches to the base.

5. Tim Henderson screwed the lens onto the license plate light assembly, then mounted it in place after connecting it to the wiring harness.

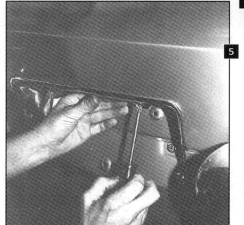

Compared to some of its immediate predecessors, the '63 Sting Ray was fairly restrained in its display of chrome and trim. However, when compared to a *'67* Sting Ray, the '63 positively drips with the stuff.

Installing most of Suzy Q.'s trim was a fairly straightforward operation. The only really tricky parts are the front bumpers; it takes a bit of fiddling and tweaking to get the two halves level. But there's no great science to that procedure — it just takes time and patience. A *lot* of patience.

In our case, the grille required a bit of fabricating, as there had been a good bit of damage in that area when we got the car. Several grille mounting tabs had to be fabricated during the body work, and later drilled out to accept the mounting screws.

While the quality of the reproduction parts we've gathered for the project has been outstanding, a couple of trim items purchased from GM bear mentioning at this point. The General can still supply parking lamp assemblies and the large aluminum rocker panel trim pieces, so

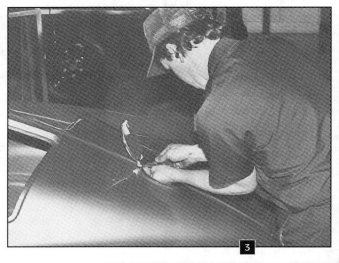

we acquired those parts from GM. One of the parking lamp assemblies had mismatched screws — one polished, one luster finish — holding the parking lamp lens in place. No big deal to remedy, but kind of annoying. On the rocker panels, the black accent paint between the panel ribs was so poorly done that we opted to have the resto shop repaint the panels for a more uniform appearence. Other than the cosmetic problems, the quality of the parts was just fine.

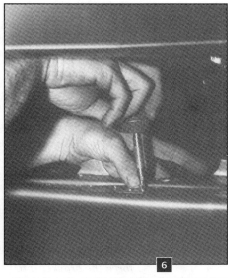

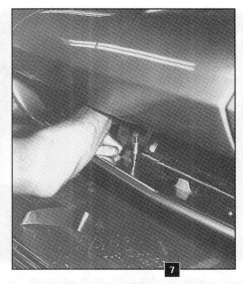

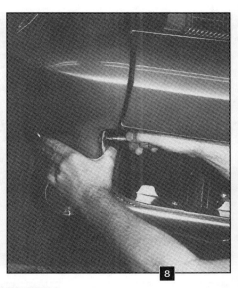

The installation of all the exterior trim really goes a long way toward making a car look completed. Suzy Q. is starting to look like a real car again.

6. *Before the grille could be installed, the anodized aluminum grille molding had to be installed. First, the retaining clips for the molding were installed.*

7. *The retaining clips hold the front portion of the trim piece in place, and the back of the piece is held in place by a series of screws.*

8. *With the center piece installed, the two side pieces were installed.*

9. *Most of the lower grille tabs had been broken when we acquired Suzy Q. New ones were fabricated when the body work was done. As a result, the mounting holes had to be drilled. After drilling the holes, a mounted clip was installed over the top of each tab. With the grille in place, screws secure it to the lower mounting tabs.*

10. *At the top, brackets bolt to the nose and extend down. Again, screws secure the upper mounting points in the grille to these brackets.*

11. *Front bumper installation began by bolting the inner and center mounting brackets in their proper positions. A third outer bracket mounts between the inner fender and fender.*

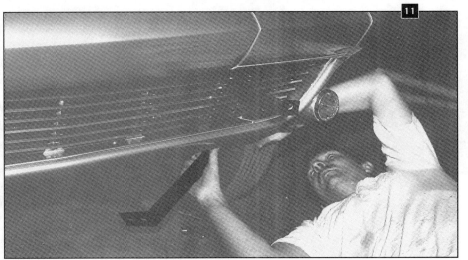

12-13. *The bumpers were then put into place, and the bolts for the three mounting points installed. The shop manual recommends adjusting the bumper assemblies to their proper position before tightening any of the mounting bolts.*

14. *After getting everything in place, we discovered that the inner bracket on the driver's side was slightly bent, making proper alignment of the bumpers difficult. A few gentle mallet blows managed to force the bracket into an acceptable position.*

15-16. *As adjustments were made, Henderson took measurements to compare the distance of the bumper halves from the body. Once everything was even, the mounting bolts were tightened.*

17. *When the rocker panel moldings were taken from the package, they were found to have inconsistent painting in the grooves. So Roger James repainted them.*

18. *After the paint had dried, Jeff Mitchell used a cloth dipped in lacquer thinner to remove the paint from the high spots and places where it should not be.*

19. *Mitchell screwed the rocker molding mounting bracket into clips that had been tapped into place. The molding was fitted over the top lip of the bracket. It was further secured with screws on the underside of the rocker area.*

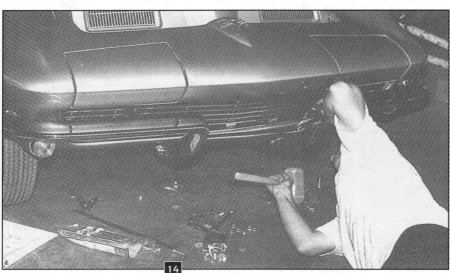

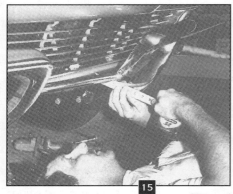

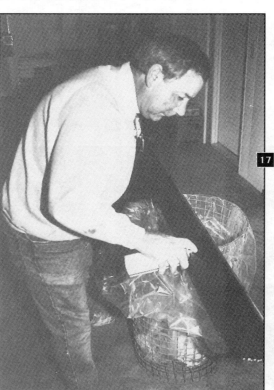

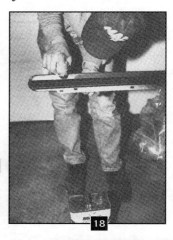

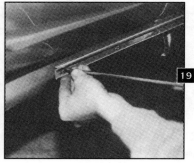

COOLING SYSTEM RESTO

By Eric Brockman

Stop and take a look at the cooling system on a mid-year Vette sometime, then try to figure out how to fill it.

The cooling system on the '63-67 Vettes is quite a piece of work — sort of a love it or hate it thing. There wasn't room under the hood for the supply tank to be a part of the radiator, as in a normal cooling system. So Chevy's engineers just removed it from the radiator and mounted it to the inner fender!

As a result, there is no radiator cap on the actual radiator; it's part of the supply tank. If you tried to fill the whole cooling system via the supply tank, you could spend days trying to get it completely full.

Ah, but here's a "little trick." Use the upper radiator hose, attached to the radiator inlet neck, as a "filler tube." Then top off the supply tank.

With a freshly rebuilt engine, we didn't want to take any chances when it came to engine cooling. So Suzy Q. got a new supply tank, correct aluminum radiator, radiator cap, hoses and clamps. Hopefully she won't "lose her cool" anytime soon. 📷

Photos by the author

1-2. *The heater hoses were installed on the water pump (photo 1) and the firewall (photo 2) with the correct clamps.*

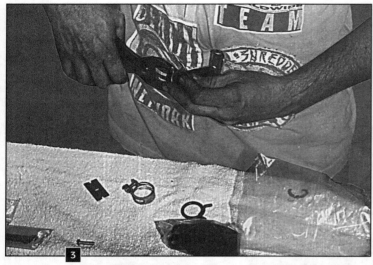

3

4

5

6

7

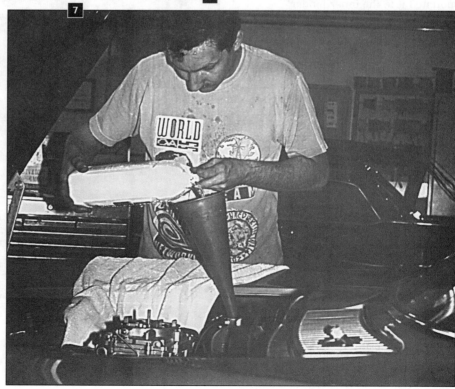

3. *A special "T" fitting connects one of the heater hoses with an outlet on the bottom of the supply tank. Tim Henderson of D&D Classic Auto Restoration first fitted the section of hose to the fitting that will run to the supply tank.*

4. *He then cut the heater hose, installed the fitting, and connected it to the supply tank. The old supply tank had received a number of crude patches over the years, so a reproduction supply tank, with the correct date code, was installed.*

5. *A small hose runs from the supply tank neck to the radiator. Here, Henderson tightens the hose clamp at the supply tank neck. The additional fitting protruding from the supply tank neck is for the overflow line.*

6-7. *With all hoses installed, the cooling system was filled. With the upper radiator hose connected to the radiator inlet neck, Henderson used the other end of the hose as a makeshift funnel to fill the cooling system. Henderson then finished installing the upper radiator hose, and filled the supply tank.*

Vette Resto

Installing the Ignition Shielding

By Eric Brockman

There is one drawback to the fiberglass body of the Corvette — a lack of shielding for the radio to operate properly.

The electrical system of a car will generate "noise" that can cause an excessive amount of interference on the car's radio. With metal-bodied cars, the metal provides a certain amount of shielding from this interference; the fiberglass-bodied Corvette lacks this "natural" shielding.

To compensate for that, grounding straps are located throughout the chassis to help prevent radio interference. The greatest source of noise, though, is the car's ignition system. It's for this reason that Corvettes have metal shielding covering the ignition systems.

While this prevented radio "noise," the shielding had its drawbacks. First of all, it was a hassle to remove in order to change spark plugs, spark plug wires, breaker points, etc. In fact, any time something in the ignition system needed attention, the shielding had to come off. Also, as plug wires got older, they tended to short against the metal shielding. As a result, many Corvette owners said, "Oh well," and trashed the shielding.

Such was the case with Suzy Q., which lacked *all* of the ignition shielding, including the plug wire heat shields. Fortunately, as with many mid-year Vette parts, these items are available as reproductions. With a new set of shields procured from Corvette Central, Tim Henderson at D&D Classic Auto Restoration set about installing the shielding. It consists of lower horizontal shields — a one-piece shield on the passenger side, a two-piece shield on the

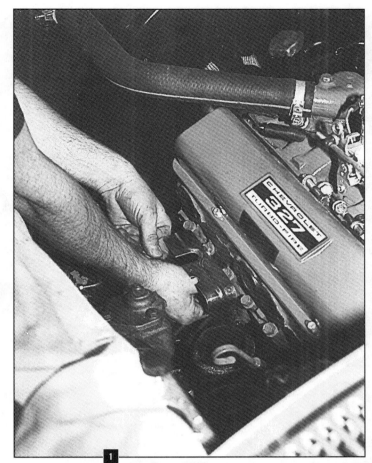

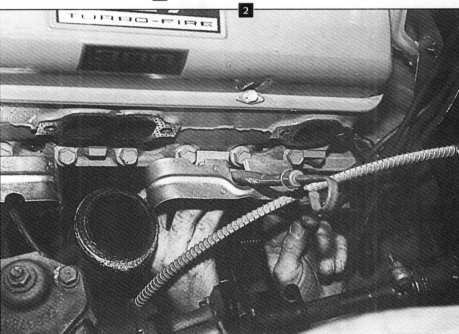

driver's side — vertical shields, and the top shield which covers the distributor. Mounting tabs held in place by exhaust manifold bolts secure the horizontal shields, while the vertical shields and top shield attach to brackets bolted to the engine block.

Photos by the author

1. *The heat shield for the front pair of ignition wires was bolted into place. Having the exhaust manifold off the motor simplified the installation, but it wasn't absolutely necessary.*

2. *To get the rear heat shield bolted into place, it was necessary to crawl under the car to get the bolts started into their holes.*

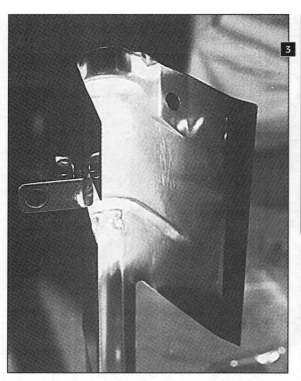

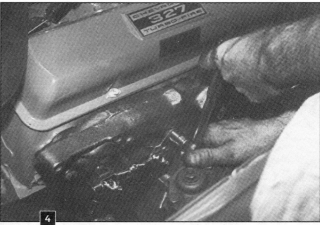

3. The lower horizontal portions of the ignition shielding are held to mounting tabs via wing nuts. The tabs are held in place by the exhaust manifold bolts.

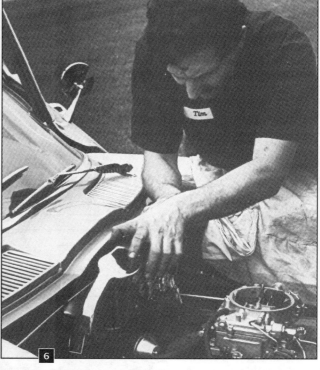

4. With the exhaust manifold back in place, the shields, already attached to the mounting tabs, were put in place and the manifold bolts were tightened. There are separate shields for the front and rear pairs of spark plug wires on the driver's side. A one-piece shield covers the ignition wiring on the other side of the motor.

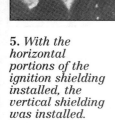

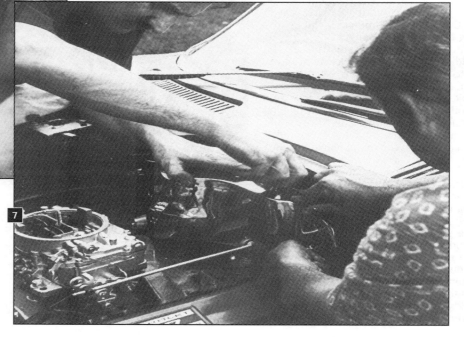

5. With the horizontal portions of the ignition shielding installed, the vertical shielding was installed.

6-7. Finally, the top shield, which covers the distributor, was installed, and fastened in place.

Suzy Q
Vette Resto
AL KNOCH INTERIORS

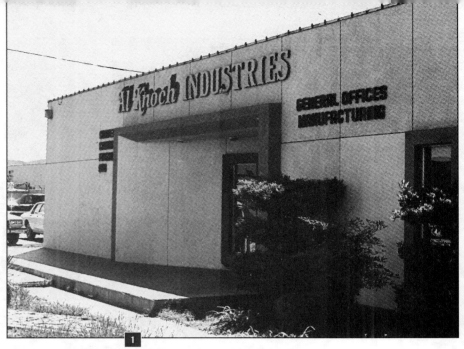

1

By Eric Brockman

Compared to most of her other components, Suzy Q.'s interior wasn't too bad when we bought her.

But "wasn't too bad" just wouldn't cut it for the major rebuild Suzy Q. received. She had to have a new interior, and one of the highest possible quality. When you're talking high-quality interiors and Corvettes, there's really only one place to turn to: Al Knoch Interiors of El Paso, Texas. The company is the recognized leader when it comes to reproduction Corvette interiors, and it supplied the kit for Suzy Q.

In business for more than 30 years, Al Knoch Interiors makes its interior items in-house at the company's facility located outside of El Paso, Texas. Al Knoch Interiors offers interiors for nearly every Corvette made, from 1953 to 1991. These items include convertible tops, seat covers, door panels, dash pads, carpet, headliners and kick panels. In many instances, such as with door panels, the company has original assembly jigs on hand to make certain the parts fit properly.

The company also offers installation hardware, and has recently begun selling various other Corvette restoration parts produced by other companies. In addition to Corvettes, the company offers interior items for 1967-69 Camaros and Firebirds as well as Corvairs, Chevelles and GTOs.

Unlike some parts suppliers, who just sell you the parts and then you're on your own, Al Knoch also offers in-house installation of many interior items, such as seat covers. If El Paso is a little out of your way, the company sets up booths at most of the major Corvette shows, as well as numerous other large swap meets, and offers installation services right at the show.

2

3

Photos by the author

1. *Behind these walls, Al Knoch Industries makes interior kits for just about any Corvette ever made. The company's headquarters is located near El Paso, Texas.*

2. *To insure that items such as door panels fit properly, the company has original Corvette door jigs for the purposes of test fitting.*

3. *An employee removes a newly made door panel backing from its mold. All interior items are custom made at the El Paso factory.*

4

5

4. *Rear windows for convertible tops are cut to size and made ready for installation.*

5-6. *In addition to its manufacturing facilities, Al Knoch Interiors has extensive warehouse space for raw materials (photo 5), and finished items ready to be shipped (photo 6).*

7. *A door panel skin is prepared for stitching.*

6

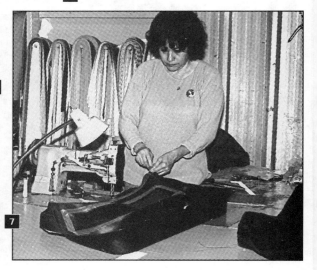

7

8

9

About the shop

Al Knoch Interiors is located at 130 Montoya Rd., El Paso, Texas 79932. To order call toll free 1-800-880-8080; fax 915-581-1545. The company offers a wide range of interior items for Corvette, as well as interior components for Camaro, Firebird, Corvair, Chevelle and GTO. In addition, Al Knoch Interiors offers an installation service for many of its interior components, both at the El Paso location and at the various shows the company attends each year.

8. *You can either order interior items and install them yourself, or send your interior to Al Knoch's, and they'll install the items for you. Here, a seat cover is installed.*

9. *Displayed here is a mold for a dash pad.*

Suzy Q Vette Resto

RECOVERING THE SEATS

By Bob Stevens

One of the most critical facets of any restoration is the recovering of the seats. Quality materials, precision sewing and stitching, correct color and proper installation are all necessary to produce a show quality interior restoration. And that's just what Suzy Q. received: a professional installation of the first order.

Specifying a complete '63 Corvette coupe interior kit in dark blue (also called midnight blue in the trade) from Al Knoch Interiors, Inc., El Paso, Tex., we headed for Detroit, Mich., where we connected with Dave Pena, of C.A.R.S., Inc., and his installer, ABA Trim, Troy, Mich. Pena explained that many of his customers buying C.A.R.S. upholstery kits were unable to get them installed locally, and were unable to install the kits themselves. So, C.A.R.S. arranged with ABA to install the kits on customers' seats, which are shipped to C.A.R.S. at its Berkley, Mich., showroom and warehouse. The setup, which is relatively new, has been working quite well, with customers receiving their seats recovered and ready to install.

At ABA Trim, owner Ron Horecki explained that the bulk of his shop's business is in the form of leather conversions for new cars, either directly from new car buyers, or through new car dealers whose customers have requested leather trim for cars not offered with the upgraded upholstery. Horecki opened his shop five years ago. Prior to that Horecki worked for a major OEM supplier and had been a supervisor for General Motors in the color and trim section. He had been with GM 18 years before going to the OEM supplier and then subsequently opening his own shop.

ABA Trim, which is short for Automobile-Boat-Airplane Trim, also performs upholstery and trim work on

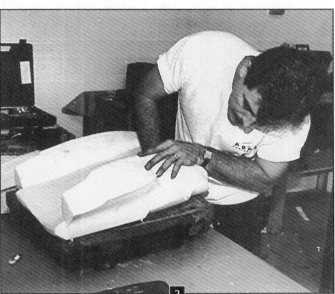

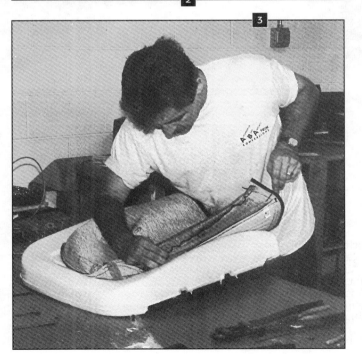

Photos by the author

1. *In comparing the old seat foam (left) with a fresh Al Knoch pad (right), it was easy to see why we're sitting so low in Suzy Q. She definitely lacked means of support, even if they were invisible.*

2. *Upholstery installer Mark Ogden fitted the new foam padding onto the seat. The seats, it was determined, had been recovered not all that long ago, but the original foam had been reused. The foam had been patched, however.*

3. *The skilled hands of an installer "work" the material, molding it into the desired shape.*

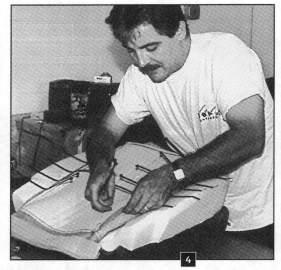

4

5

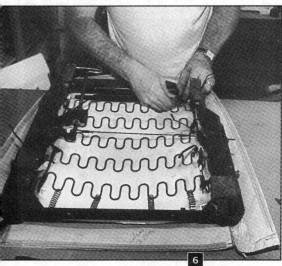

6

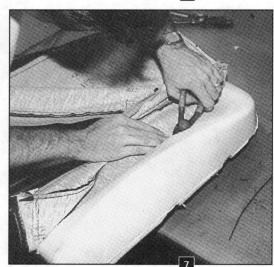

7

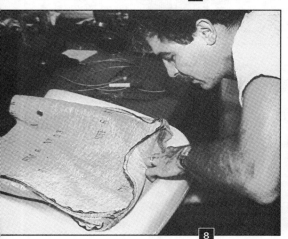

8

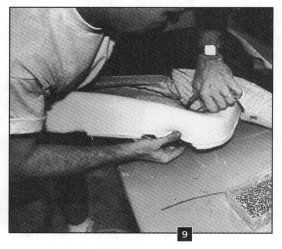

9

4. *Mark Ogden laces up the vinyl on the seat bottom, preparing to secure the cover around the foam to the seat frame. The strings are used to pull the upholstery down tight, but this method can create lumps in the beading, but there's a fix for that also.*

5. *The seat is turned upside down to check for proper mating of the vinyl cover and the foam cushion to the frame.*

6. *Using conventional plastic ties, Ogden secures the vinyl cover to the frame at several points.*

7. *Working on the seat back, the upholsterer uses small pliers to work the hog rigs into position. This was repeated all the way around the circumference of the seat back.*

8. *The material must be worked slowly to avoid tearing it or punching holes in the wrong locations. Patience and perseverance are rewarded in this task.*

9. *Once again, the specialist doesn't hurry the job, taking it one hog ring at a time until the entire seat back is covered in fresh vinyl.*

boats and airplanes, specializing, again, in leather work, but also offering vinyl, fabric and other materials. The shop also performs custom work. And, of course, it performs most of C.A.R.S.'s upholstery and related installation work. That alone was good enough for us.

C.A.R.S. doesn't handle Corvette interiors, even though it supplies interior kits for just about every other kind of Chevy from 1955 up through the early '70s. But they took delivery of the Al Knoch kit directly from Texas, where it was shipped by Al Knoch's right-hand man, Dale Robertson. With a name like that, we knew he'd be a square-shooter, and he was.

The installation, which was approached cautiously and deliberately to avoid any damage to an expensive set of seat covers, was handled smoothly and efficiently. The results were very rewarding visually, and proved to be comfortable, too. 📷

About the shop

ABA Trim can be reached at 810-588-3460. The shop is located at 1205 Chicago Rd., Troy, Mich. 48083. Ron Horecki owns and manages the specialty upholstery business.

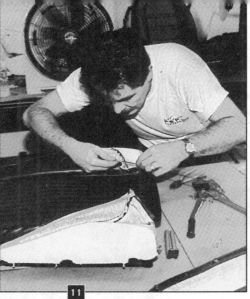

10. *Metal rods are inserted to hold the beading down and effect a more uniform installation.*

11. *Ogden feeds another reinforcing rod into the bead. It keeps the bead crisp and straight with no sagging or zig-zagging.*

12. *The seat back nears completion as one side is secured. Note the small vent in the seat back.*

13. *Mark Ogden (left) and Roger St. Louis put the finishing touches on a seat back. The high-quality material covered beautifully and was easy to work with in fitting, stretching, etc. The metal side trim was then screwed into place. The new chromed side pieces were acquired from Corvette Central in Sawyer, Mich. There's nothing like new chrome set against fresh vinyl, in this case dark blue, to create a visual sensation.*

14. *A close inspection and a couple of minor adjustments and the seat reupholstering job was completed.*

15. *The newly refurbished bucket seat is loosely bolted into position for one final check. Everything came together on cue!*

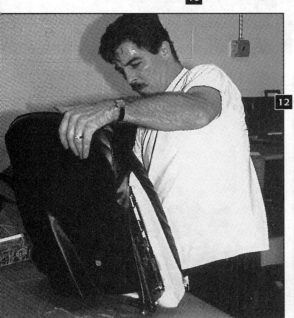

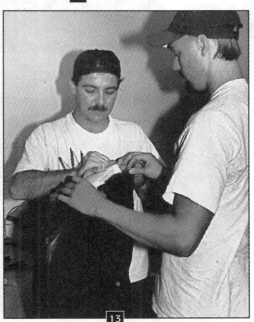

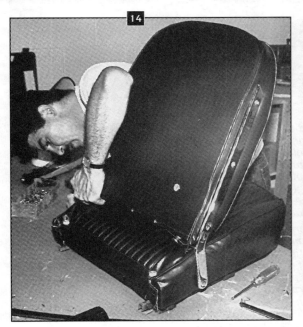

Suzy Q. Vette Resto

INSTALLING CARPETING, DOOR PANELS

By Bob Stevens

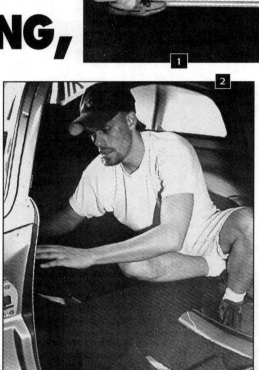

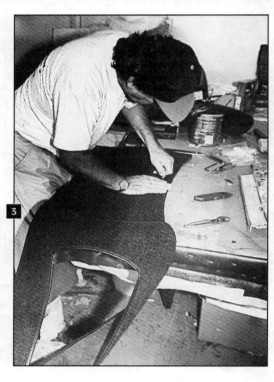

The interior kit suppied by Al Knoch, Al Knoch Interiors, El Paso, Tex., was complete and of high quality. All we needed now was an installation commensurate with the quality of the materials for both the door panels and the carpeting. The answer was found at C.A.R.S. Inc., Berkley, Mich., where shop manager Dave Pena offered to handle the installation through a supplier that has been installing seat covers and other interior products for C.A.R.S. Inc. customers.

The company, ABA Trim, Troy, Mich., handled the installation with ease, combining it with the installation of the seat covers on the same day. Follow along as Ron Horecki and his ABA Trim crew refurbish Suzy Q.'s dark blue interior. 📷

Photos by the author

1. Ron Horecki, owner of ABA Trim, Troy, Mich., surveys the many interior parts and pieces needed to make Suzy Q.'s interior delightful to inhabit. The Al Knoch carpeting and door panels were easy to work with and very attractive once installed.

2. Roger St. Louis, an installer with ABA Trim, checks the fit on the carpeting. A total of 18 pieces came in the Al Knoch carpet kit. St. Louis

suggested that car owners, who replace their carpeting, keep the old pieces intact until the new carpeting can be set in place. It's a bit like solving a jigsaw puzzle with each piece to be put in its proper place.

3. Ron Horecki does a little light trimming. Be careful when cutting the carpeting, because if you cut too much, you can't put it back. The Al Knoch carpeting fit extremely well, but holes and slits must be made for such items as the headlight dimmer switch,

the accelerator pedal mount, etc.

4. Roger St. Louis secures the carpeting in place. After a proper fit was determined, the back of the carpeting was coated with 3M's Super 74 Foam Fast Adhesive, then laid one final time. Laying carpeting is a lot more involved and tedious than one anticipates, especially when dealing with so many pre-cut pieces.

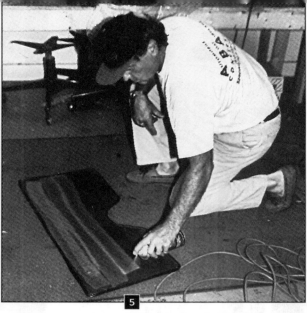

5. Some adhesive is sprayed on the carpeting piece that trims out the cover in the luggage compartment. Cuts were needed for a hole for the finger hold in the lid, which was then trimmed with a small, round chrome bezel. The new board was a repro from Corvette Central, Sawyer, Mich.

6. With the carpeting in place and glued down, the interior looks more finished.

7. Ron Horecki checked the mounting hardware for the door handle, window and vent crank handles, etc., before the door panel was trimmed and installed.

8. A screwdriver was used to bend the tabs on the door panel trim and other pieces.

The panels are precut to accept the various pieces of hardware, but it is necessary to cut some holes for the reflectors, door lock, etc., and occasionally some holes must be custom trimmed because of ill-fitting hardware, warped doors, etc. Our installation was fairly clean on both sides.

9. The finished installation lacks only a single piece of stainless trim (which we forgot to take to the trim shop). It was installed at a later date.

Vette Resto

INSTALLING THE HEADLINER

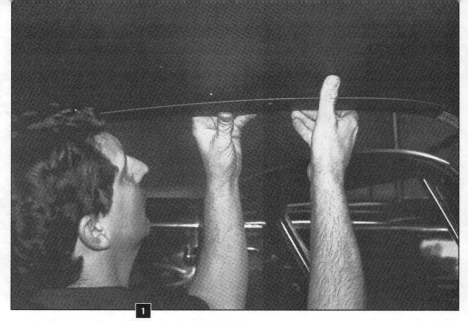

By Eric Brockman

In the restoration process, Corvette coupes have one obvious advantage over their convertible brethren: restorers don't have to deal with the hassle of installing a convertible top.

Midyear coupes do, of course, have a headliner, but it's a simple piece of work compared to the type of headliner used in most automobiles. Above the seats is a one-piece headliner held in place by the interior trim moldings. The dome light is contained in a large "halo" molding that mounts to the mid section of the interior. Covering the split between the rear windows and the area below the rear windows are four separate pieces of vinyl that are glued to the fiberglass.

It takes only a small amount of time and some patience to install the pieces. As with the rest of the interior, the headliner was supplied by Al Knoch Interiors of El Paso, Texas.

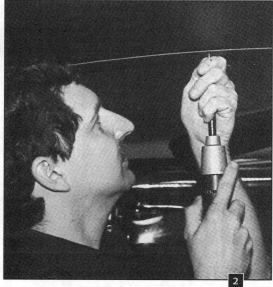

Photos by the author

1. *Tim Henderson at D&D Classic Auto Restoration handled the installation of the headliner. With the headliner in position, Henderson placed one of the side trim pieces that holds it in place.*

2. *Once the trim piece was in place, Henderson installed the screws that hold it down. A little trick to get the holes in the trim piece to line up with the mounting holes is to insert a small punch or awl through the hole and feel around for the mounting hole. Once you find it, you can use the punch to pull the trim piece into alignment with the mounting hole.*

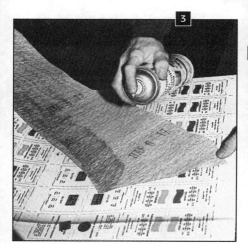

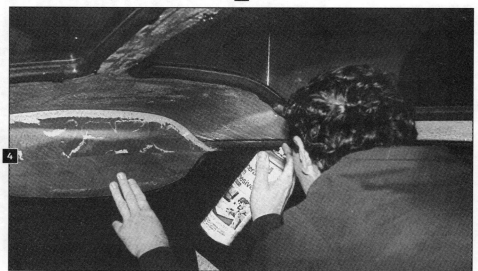

3. *The "split" between the rear windows and the area below the rear windows are covered by pieces of vinyl — in this case colored dark blue. Trim adhesive was sprayed on the back of the vinyl pieces.*

4. *To insure a good bond, Henderson also coated the fiberglass below the rear window with the trim adhesive.*

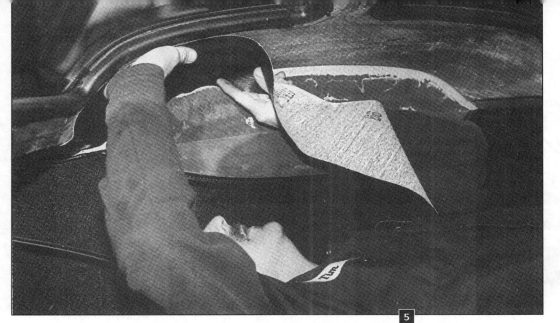

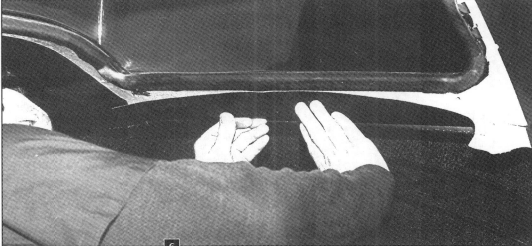

5-7. *Henderson then carefully installed the pieces of vinyl. Before beginning, he held the rear window trim moldings in place and marked their edges on the fiberglass. He then test-fitted the vinyl pieces to make certain the moldings would cover the edges of the vinyl. Any excess vinyl was trimmed after installation.*

8. *With the vinyl pieces securely in place, the final step was installing the moldings around the rear windows.*

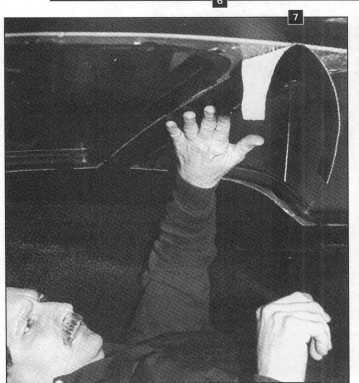

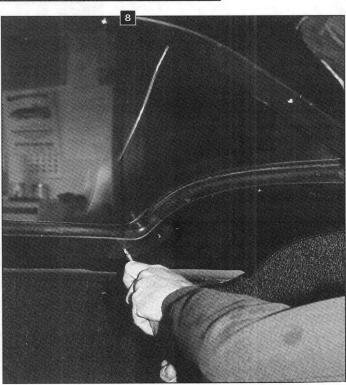

Vette Resto

Suzy Q. Goes 'Home'

By Bob Stevens

It's really appropriate that Suzy Q.'s new home is in Kingman, Ariz., where the Route 66 legend is kept alive on a daily basis. The famous Chicago-to-Los Angeles artery carried many Americans and their dreams westward during the Great Depression on up through the '50s and '60s. It served as the inspiration for the classic television series *Route 66* starring Martin Milner and George Maharis as two adventurers who got their kicks on Route 66 while touring the 2,400-mile-long ribbon of highway.

The stars of *Route 66*, Tod and Buz, hit the Mother Road in what else but a Corvette. So Suzy Q., *Cars & Parts'* '63 Corvette split window coupe project car, should feel right at home roaming the legendary strip of Route 66 that still courses through Kingman. That stretch of highway, in fact, is the longest active strip of Route 66 still in operation.

Suzy Q. was presented Oct. 27 to Doyle Kash, who won the *Cars & Parts* Corvette Sweepstakes, in Railroad Park right alongside Route 66. It's not far from the huge Route 66 tower and adjacent to a diner, Mr. D'z, fashioned after the restaurants that served Route 66 travelers some 40 years ago. Two area newspapers, *The Standard* and the *Kingman Daily Miner*, both ran illustrated reports of the Kingman resident accepting his sweepstakes prize.

Doyle Kash, a diesel mechanic for IWX in Kingman, was surrounded by family and well-wishers as he took delivery of Suzy Q. from the author, who had trailered the '63 Corvette from *Cars & Parts'* headquarters in Sidney, Ohio to Kingman. Doyle's parents, Jim and Teddi, were present for the occasion.

Weeks earlier, his mother had accompanied him to Hershey, Pa., for the formal presentation of the keys to Suzy Q. with Publisher Walt Reed presiding.

Suzy Q. has joined a varied stable of vehicles in Kingman, ranging from a '41 Chevy coupe and '42 Chevy pickup to '69 and '70 Dodge Chargers. Doyle also owns several other trucks from the '50s and '60s, plus a '45 military vehicle and a '46 Chevy 1 1/2-ton truck. He cleared a special spot in the garage for Suzy Q., but is having a new garage built to house his prize, which he intends to keep forever. "When he dies, he'll probably be cremated in the car," his mother said.

With the car in Kingman and the keys

in his hand, Doyle was finally coming to the realization that Suzy Q. was indeed his car. When the magazine's publisher called him back in September to notify him he had won the car, he couldn't believe it. In fact, he called the *Cars & Parts* office an hour or so later just to make sure a friend wasn't pulling a prank on him.

Doyle plans to show the car frequently, and participate in as many cruise-ins and rallies as he can.

The Sunday after taking delivery of Suzy Q., he entered the silver blue beauty in a local show, and won a first-place trophy. His life-long romance with Suzy Q. was off to a winning start!

Photos by the author

1. Doyle Kash (third from left), Suzy Q.'s new owner, is surrounded by family shortly after taking delivery of his prize in Kingman, Ariz. From left are: Jim Kash, Doyle's father; Teddi Kash, mother; Doyle; Jeff Kash, brother; Bradley Kash, nephew; Brian Kash (background), brother; Michael Kash (foreground), nephew; Julie Kash, sister; and Sherry Kash, sister-in-law. This fine-looking group was made even finer by the addition of Suzy Q. to the family. Doyle's relatives, especially his dad and mom, were as excited about winning the car as he was ... well, almost.

2. The Kash family poses once again with Suzy Q., this time for a newspaper photographer. Two area newspapers covered the event and ran stories on it. It's not everyday that a small town resident wins a national sweepstakes, especially one with such an incredible grand prize.

3. Back in 1963, Chevrolet touted the all-new Corvette with this challenge: "Only a man with a heart of stone could withstand temptation like this! The new Sting Ray is about all the car a red-blooded America male enthusiast could want." Speaking as a red-blooded American male enthusiast, Doyle Kash heartily agrees with that sentiment, especially since becoming a Sting Ray owner himself.

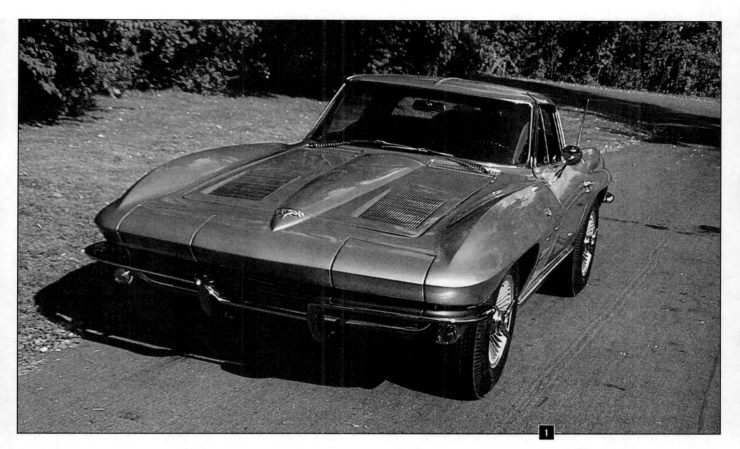

1

THE FIRST STING RAY
CHEVY SERVES UP A WORLD CLASS SPORTS CAR

By Bob Stevens

Rumors of a new Corvette had circulated for years, much of the talk fueled by Chevy engineers themselves. The Corvette had been around for 10 years, the first one appearing in 1953, but it was only toward the end of that first decade that the car earned its place in Chevy's lineup with production hitting the 10,000-unit plateau. The common dream of such men as Ed Cole, Zora Arkus-Duntov, Bill Mitchell, and many others had become a reality.

It's no secret that many within General Motors, and even a few within Chevrolet itself, had conspired to axe the fiberglass-bodied sports car. Their arguments were strong, and keyed mostly to the car's low volume, lack of profitability, manufacturing complications, etc. But the image that Corvette brought to Chevrolet, especially during the years when the ban on racing was in effect at GM, was immeasurable. Besides, it was a healthy car for the sporting enthusiast, and there were many of them at GM.

Harley Earl, who headed up the styling department at GM when the original Corvette arrived in '53, had always

admired sports cars for their pure shape, and their fun of operation. Ed Cole, who was Chevy's top engineer at the time, was a sports car enthusiast of the first order. He had owned a Cadillac-powered Allard and a Jaguar XK-120, so he was a natural to become the standard-bearer for the Corvette program from the very beginning, something he did with earnest and purpose. Zora Arkus-Duntov, the legendary chief Corvette engineer who retired in 1974 after some 20 years with Chevy, was quite possible the Corvette's savior, along with Cole and Bill Mitchell, who succeeded Harley Earl as GM's design boss in 1958.

Mitchell was also a sports car fan, and a Harley-Davidson motorcycle enthusiast ("He'd fire up his big Harley at two or three in the morning and head out for a brisk ride through the empty streets of suburban Detroit," recalled a less-than-enthused neighbor of Mitchell's). He was also a major proponent of the Corvette, and another executive on whom the car's survival would hinge.

Ed Cole, still the primary player in keeping the Corvette alive despite a

Photos by the author

1. *Revolutionary by American standards, the fresh, vibrant and racy design that had its debut with the '63 model year catapulted the Corvette from contemporary to almost futuristic. Its sleek lines and menacing stance made its new name, Sting Ray, a most appropriate moniker. This specific example, of course, is our own Suzy Q., the latest* Cars & Parts *project car.*

growing contingent of detractors, mostly bean-counter, was elevated to Chevy's top post, general manager, in 1956. Cole would be elevated into the corporate executive ranks in late 1961, turning the reigns of Chevrolet over to Semon E. Knudsen, who would also become a supporter of the Corvette concept and programs. This was fortunate, because the car was still living on the edge, financially.

Duntov, who joined Chevy engineering shortly after the Corvette's initial debut, had eased into the top Corvette engineering spot in 1957. So, with this set of tal-

2

2. *The dark blue interior provides contrast and complement to Suzy Q.'s silver blue exterior.*

3. *Corvette Sting Ray emblem helped people identify the radically redesigned sports car, which at first glance appeared more European in flavor, specifically Italian than anything American inspired. With all the performance options available, most observers only got a glimpse of this emblem as it flashed by.*

4. *Crossed flags decorate the flip-up gas lid on the rear deck.*

5. *On the coupe version, which also had its debut in the Corvette series in '63, the rear window featured the now-famous "split." Though it enhanced the rear styling, it created a rear-view blind spot and was removed after one year. The split window coupe has become one of the Corvette hobby's most cherished collectibles.*

3

4

5

6. *Powering this '63 Corvette split window coupe is the optional 300-hp edition of Chevy's durable 327 V-8.*

7. *Chevy's crossed flags logo appears in a fresh design on the nose of the first Sting Ray.*

ented, but temperamental and self-styled characters in place, development work on an all-new Corvette began in earnest in the late '50s, becoming quite focused by the early '60s.

There was some disparaging over the name selected to identify the new Corvette slated to debut in the fall of 1963. Mitchell, a deep sea fisherman who was enamored with the shape of sharks, sting rays and other creatures of the deep and how they flowed so smoothly and quickly through the water, had selected Sting Ray and pushed hard for its adoption. There was some opposition. For instance, Zora Arkus-Duntov responded: "It's a dumb fish." Nevertheless, Mitchell prevailed.

Duntov, of course, guided the engineering effort, with considerable help from a very dedicated and intelligent staff. Mitchell handled the car's interior and exterior design, with a young Japanese-American, Larry Shinoda, being the primary stylist on the body. The result, modeled before you by *Cars & Parts* own Suzy Q., our most recent restoration project, was sensational. Remember, this design was developed more than 30 years ago, without the aid of computers, extensive wind-tunnel testing, etc.

One look at Suzy Q. in her mirror-like finish of silver blue is enough to tantalize the senses and yearn for an open, twisting road snaking through some scenic rural terrain. The car's engineering

prowess would prove up to the task. In other words, Duntov, Mitchell, Shinoda and their respective crews succeeded in serving up a new Corvette that was, indeed, "new."

The sensational Sting Ray styling was an instant success. Sales of the new Corvette soared to 21,513, up more than 6,000 from the previous year. In fact, 1962 would be the last year that Corvette

sales were ever under 20,000, except for a one-year dip to about 17,000 in 1971 (also, there was no Corvette for 1983). The year 1962 would also be the last one in which the Corvette came with a built-in trunk, the last for the solid axle design, the final season for exposed headlamps, and the last year that the Corvette would not have a coupe in the lineup.

VEHICLE IDENTIFICATION NUMBER

```
┌─────────────────────────────┐
│  C H E V R O L E T          │
│ • 30867S100001 •            │
└─────────────────────────────┘
```

Commonly referred to as the VIN NUMBER, this series of numbers and letters is embossed on a metal plate spot welded to a horizontal body support. The plate is visible just under the glove box door.

FIRST DIGIT: Identifies the model year (3 = 1963)

SECOND & THIRD DIGITS: Identify the series (08 = Corvette)

FOURTH & FIFTH DIGITS: Identify the body style

BODY STYLE	CODE
2-Door Sport Coupe	37
2-Door Convertible	67

SIXTH DIGIT: Identifies the assembly plant (S = St. Louis, MO)

LAST SIX DIGITS: Represent the basic production number. Starting number 100001 to 121513.

BODY NUMBER PLATE

Located on the crossbrace under the dash, it is visible just under the glove box door. It identifies the month and day built, model year, body style, body number, trim combination and paint color.

EXAMPLE:

```
┌──────────────────────────────────────┐
│ H2                                    │
│ STYLE   63 837  │ 1234   BODY         │
│ TRIM    STD     │ 923    PAINT        │
│        BODY BY CHEVROLET              │
└──────────────────────────────────────┘
```

H2	Build Date (April, 2nd week)
63	Model Year (1963)
837	Body Style (Coupe)
1234	Body Number
STD	Trim Combination (Black vinyl)
923	Paint Color (Riverside Red)

THE BUILD DATE identifies the month and week the vehicle was built.

MONTH	CODE
September 1962	A
October	B
November	C
December	D
January 1963	E
February	F
March	G
April	H
May	I
June	J
July	K
August	L

WEEK	CODE
1st Week	1
2nd Week	2
3rd Week	3
4th Week	4
5th Week	5

BODY STYLE

BODY STYLE	CODE
Coupe	837
Convertible	867

THE BODY NUMBER is the production serial number of the body. Starting number 001.

THE TRIM NUMBER is the key to the interior trim color and material.

COUPE

COLOR	VIN.	LTHR.	CODE
Black	•		STD,BLK
Dark Blue		490	A,J,S,XE,XG
Red		490	C,L,Q,XA,XC
Saddle		490	E,N,U,XJ,XL
Saddle		• 898	A,E,Q,G,S

CONVERTIBLE

COLOR	VIN.	LTHR.	CODE
Black	•		STD,BLK
Dark Blue		490	B,K,T,XF,XH
Red		498	D,M,R,XB,XD
Saddle		490	F,P,V,XK,XM
Saddle		• 898	B,F,R,H,T

THE PAINT CODE is the key to the exterior paint color.

COLOR	CODE
Tuxedo Black	900
Silver Blue	912
Daytona Blue	916
Riverside Red	923
Saddle Tan	932
Ermine White	936
Sebring Silver	941

THE TRANSMISSION NUMBER on manual and Powerglide transmissions indicates the type, month and day produced and the shift on which it was assembled. The code for the 3-speed is located on the rear face of the case in the upper right hand corner. The code for the 4-speed is located on the left side of the case at the rear of the cover. The Powerglide is located on the bottom center of the transmission oil pan.

EXAMPLE: C1120N (3-speed, 4-speed Muncie and Powerglide)

C	Cleveland Powerglide
11	Month built (November)
20	Day built (20th)
D or N	Shift built (D = Day, N = Night)

(1 or 2) 4-speed Shift built
(1 = Day, 2 = Night)
(Day shift transmissions may not have a shift code suffix).

WARNER 4-SPEED

EXAMPLE: WF1763-2

W	Warner Gear
F	Month Built (June)
17	Day Built (17th)
63	Year Built (1963)
1 or 2	Shift Built (1 = Day, 2 = Night)

(Day shift transmissions may not have "1" code).

TRANSMISSION CODES

TYPE	PLANT	CODE
Powerglide	Cleveland	C
4-Speed	Muncie	P
Powerglide	Toledo	T
3-Speed	Saginaw	S
4-Speed	Warner	W

THE REAR AXLE NUMBER identifies the gear ratio, the build month and day. The code is located on the bottom of the differential carrier housing by the cover.

EXAMPLE: CD0629

CD	3.70 ratio w/Positraction
06	June
29	29th day of month

DESCRIPTION	CODE
3-Speed (3.36 ratio)	CA
Positraction (3.08 ratio)	CJ
Positraction (3.36 ratio)	CB
Positraction (3.55 ratio)	CC
Positraction (3.70 ratio)	CD
Positraction (4.11 ratio)	CE
Positraction (4.56 ratio)	CF
4-Speed (3.08 ratio)	CZ
4-Speed (3.70 ratio)	CX

REGULAR PRODUCTION OPTIONS (RPO)

DESCRIPTION	RPO NO.
Windows, electric control	A31
Folding Top Equipment	C05
Auxiliary Top Equipment	C07
Less Heater Equipment	C48
Air Conditioning	C60
Differential Carrier, Positraction	C81
Differential Carrier, 3.08 ratio	C91
Power Brake Equipment	J50
Metallic Brake Facing Equipment	J65
Engine, V-8 327 - Hi-Perf.	L75
Engine, V-8 327 - Special Hi-Perf.	L76
Engine, V-8 327 - Fuel Injection	L84
4-Speed Transmission	M20
Powerglide Transmission	M35
Power Steering Equipment	N40
15X6L Aluminum Wheel, Quick Take-off	P48
6.70-15-4 PR Tires, whitewall	P92
Radio Equipment, signal seeking	U65
Radio AM-FM	U69
Special Performance Equipment	Z06
Tinted Glass, all-windows	A01
Tinted Glass, windshield	A02
Gas Tank 36.5 gallon	N03
Off Road Service Exhaust	N11
Steering Wheel, woodgrain	N34
6.70-15 Tires, blackwall	P91
Backup Lamp Equipment	T86

THE ENGINE NUMBER is located on a raised pad - actually an extension of the head mounting surface - on the right front of the engine block. All Chevrolet Corvette engines are stamped with an assembly plant code, month and day produced and engine application suffix.

EXAMPLE: F0I18RC

F	Flint Plant
0I	Month built (January)
I8	Day built (18th)
RC	Engine Type 327, 250 HP

ASSEMBLY PLANT   **CODE**

Flint (motor) . . . . F

ENGINE CODE	NO. CYL	CID	HORSE-POWER	COMP. RATIO	CARB	TRANS
RC	8	327	250	10.5:1	4 BC	MAN
RD	8	327	300	10.5:1	4 BC	MAN
RE	8	327	340	11.25:1	4 BC	MAN/SHP
RF	8	327	360	11.25:1	F.I.	MAN/SHP
SC	8	327	250	10.5:1	4 BC	AUTO
SD	8	327	300	10.5:1	4 BC	AUTO

SHP - Special High Performance

All engines also have the model year and production sequence number (last 6 digits) of the Vehicle Identification Number stamped on the engine.

EXAMPLE: 3112072

3	Model Year (1963)
112072	Production Sequence Number

THE ENGINE CASTING NUMBER for 1963 was 3782870. The casting number is located under the master cylinder.

Among the new features introduced in '63 were four-wheel independent suspension, retractable headlamps, the addition of a coupe to the Corvette series (and one with a "split personality" at that), cockpit-style interior, and the unveiling of a host of new options, including a hot Z06 performance package, beautiful knock-off wheels, air conditioning, and the arrival of the Muncie four-speed transmission.

Other improvements for '63 included a beefed-up frame, quicker steering, self-adjusting brakes with 18 percent more lining area, additional steel reinforcing for the fiberglass body, a lower stance, and a tighter tread for better stability. The new model was also shorter and narrower.

The coupe, distinguished by its split rear window, was an overwhelming success, almost equalling the convertible in production (10,594 coupes vs. 10,919 ragtops). Through the ensuing midyears, plus the newly designed 1968 model, the coupe was not as popular as the convertible. However in '69, coupe production shot by the convertible and remains the more popular body style.

In addition to air conditioning, which was very expensive at $422 and ordered on only 278 cars in '63, and knock-off wheels, which retailed for $323 and were sold essentially over the counter at the local Chevy dealer (as opposed to being factory installed), there were several other interesting options offered on Corvette for the first time. Among them were power steering, power brakes, leather upholstery, AM-FM radio (midyear intro), off-road exhaust, woodgrain steering wheel and the aforementioned Z06 performance package.

The Z06 special performance option included the 360-hp fuel-injected engine, knock-off wheels, a 36-gallon fuel tank, Positraction, four-speed manual tranny,

8. *Chevy bow-tie is cast into the mirror head. Early '63 Corvettes used an outside mirror with a slightly different design. The second version, which is seen here, was kept in production all the way through the '67 model year.*

9. *Found on the door panels were a built-in armrest, two reflectors, crank handles for the window and vent window, and the sliding, ball-shaped door release.*

10. *Crossed flags emblem with a red, white and blue bar is found on the front fenders to indicate a 327 V-8 lurks under the hood.*

11. *A large "stinger" rose from the hood and continued onto the nose. The hood held a pair of fake louver panels in the recesses. The panels, also called hood grilles, were a one-year feature and disappeared in '64.*

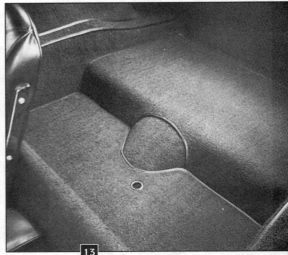

12

13

14

15

16

power heavy duty brakes, dual-circuit master brake cylinder, sintered metallic brake linings, front brake air scoops, heavy duty stabilizer, and heavy duty springs and shocks, front and rear. The package listed for $1,818. A later Z06 kit, excluding knock-offs and the big tank, was offered for convertibles at about $1,300.

The base engine was a 250-horse version of the 327-cid V-8, the only block available in the Corvette that year. Other editions of the 327 included three options producing 300 hp, 340 hp (performance cam and solid lifters) and 360 hp (fuel-injected). The three engine options were $54, $108 and $430, respectively. The standard transmission was a three-speed manual, but a four-speed and Powerglide automatic were optional at $188 and $199, respectively. Only 2,621 elected for the Powerglide, while 17,973 spread an extra $188 over their 36-payment loan schedule to add the four-speed (only $5.22 a month).

Suzy Q. is modestly attired, with knock-off wheels, the optional nylon tires, 300-hp engine, four-speed, Positraction, AM-FM radio, and tinted glass in the windshield and all windows. The fully restored beauty is now owned by the winner of the *Cars & Parts* Suzy Q. Sweepstakes (see Editor's Stop, page 6).

Chevrolet was justifiably proud of its latest accomplishment. In ads, the automaker proclaimed its new Sting Ray "the winnah" in announcing that the car was the recipient of *Car Life* magazine's award for engineering excellence. Chevy further described its freshly restyled Corvette as also a winner on the road with "handling that's far and away the best thing ever to come from Detroit and performance that's on par with any production sports car built."

Motor Trend agreed, describing the new Corvette as being "far in advance, both in ride and handling, of anything now being built in the United States."

Also infatuated with the new Vette was *Car and Driver*, which observed: "Steering effort is very low, cornering behavior is extremely stable, and the car

12. *Four taillamps were incorporated into the '63 design, with two to each side. If the optional backup lamps were ordered, they occupied the inboard housings. The dual exhaust was routed through the rear valance, beneath the bumper, with one pipe on each side.*

13. *The coupe is well endowed with luggage capacity, some 10.5 cubic feet of it, thanks to its spacious and carpeted rear cargo area.*

14. *The two-place cockpit was pure sports car, and was actually quite roomy. Adding to the cockpit-feel of the Corvette's interior were two large hoods that shielded the instrument panel and the glove box. The passenger side dash hood came with a built-in grab bar for when the driver opted to exercise those horses corralled up front.*

15. *Another appearance by the crossed flags emblem is made on the hub of the steering wheel.*

16. *The transmission selector/shifter is floor-mounted, of course, and comes with a diagram showing its shift pattern, which in this case is for a four-speed. An ashtray is also found in the console; and there's an armrest pad to the rear of the console.*

SPECIFICATIONS
1963 CHEVROLET CORVETTE

GENERAL DATA
Model: 0837
Body style: 2-dr. coupe
Production: 21,513, incl.
  10,594 coupes,
  10,919 convertibles
Passenger capacity: 2
Base price: $4,257; $4,037
  (convertible)
Price as equipped: $5,071
Options: L-75 300-hp 327,
  $54; 4-spd. manual,
  $188; Positraction, $43;
  knock-off wheels, $323;
  blackwall nylon tires,
  6.70x15, $16; AM-FM
  radio, $174; tinted glass,
  all windows, $16

BASIC SPECIFICATIONS
Wheelbase: 98"
Length: 175.3"
Width: 69.6"
Height: 49.8"
Weight: 3,000 lbs.
  (convertible, 3,020 lbs.);
  curb, 3,140 lbs. (convert-
  ible, 3,150 lbs.)
Front tread: 56.3"
Rear tread: 57"
Ground clearance: 5"

**INTERIOR
SPECIFICATIONS**
Headroom: 38.5"
Legroom: 42.7"
Hip room: 50.9"
Shoulder room: 48.4"
Cargo capacity: 10.5 cu. ft.

ENGINE
Model: L75
Type: OHV V-8
Features: Cast-iron block,
  special camshaft
Displacement: 327 cu. in.
HP @ RPM: 300 @ 5,000
Torque @ RPM:
  360 lbs.-ft. @ 3,200
Compression ratio: 10.5:1
Bore x stroke: 4 x 3.25"
Induction: Carter 3460S
  AFB 4-bbl. carb
Fuel: Leaded premium
Exhaust: Dual
Valve configuration:
  Overhead

Lifters: Hydraulic
Main bearings: 5
Ignition system:
  Delco 12 volt
Oil pressure: 40 psi

TRANSMISSION
Type: 3-spd. manual
Ratios:
  1st - 2.10
  2nd - 1.76
  3rd - 1.00
Opt.: 4-spd. manual
Ratios:
  1st - 2.54
  2nd - 1.89
  3rd - 1.51
  4th - 1.00
  Reverse - 2.61
Opt.: Powerglide
  2-spd. automatic
Ratios:
  1st - 1.76
  2nd - 1.00
  Reverse - 1.76

REAR AXLE
Type: Semi-floating
  overhead pinion
Opt.: Positraction
Ratio: 3.36 (w/auto);
  3.70 (w/4-spd.);
  3.36 (w/3-spd.)
Opt. ratios: 3.08, 3.36,
  3.55, 4.11, 4.56

SUSPENSION
Front: Independent, coil
  springs, stabilizer bar,
  hydraulic shock
  absorbers
Rear: Independent, multi-
  leaf springs, hydraulic
  shock absorbers

FRAME
Type: All-welded steel,
  ladder style w/5
  crossmembers

STEERING
Type: Semireversible,
  recirculating ball nut
Make: Saginaw
Opt.: Power assist
Ratio: 20.2 (w/power, 17.6)
Turning circle:
  (diam.): 39.9'
Turns, lock to lock: 2.92

BRAKES
Type: Drum, 4-wheel
  hydraulic
Size: 11" drums
Lining area: 185.2 sq. in.
Opt.: Power assist; sintered
  metallic linings

TIRES
Size: 6.70 x 15
Type: Blackwall
  tubeless, 4-ply
Opt.: 6.70 x 15 nylon
  blackwalls, 6.70 x 15
  rayon whitewalls

CAPACITIES
Cooling system: 15.5 qts.
  (16.5 qts. w/heater)
Gasoline tank: 20 gals.
Engine oil: 4 qts.
  (5 qts. w/filter)
Manual transmission:
  3-spd., 2 pts.; 4-spd.,
  2.5 pts.; automatic, 3.5
  qts. refill, 10.5 qts. total
Rear axle: 4 pts.

CALCULATED DATA
HP/CID: .917
LBS/HP: 10.00
LBS/CID: 9.17

PERFORMANCE*
Acceleration:
  0-30 .... 3.0 sec.
  0-40 .... 4.2 sec.
  0-50 .... 5.6 sec.
  0-60 .... 7.2 sec.
  0-70 .... 9.8 sec.
  0-80 .... 13.0 sec.
  0-100 .... 22.9 sec.
Standing 1/4 mile:
  15.5 sec. @ 86 mph
Top speed: 130 mph
Stopping distance:
  60 to 0 ... 134'
  30 to 0 ... 30'
Fuel mileage: 12-16 mpg

*Source: *Car Life*,
Dec. 1962 road test
of a '63 Corvette
coupe w/300-hp V-8,
Powerglide,
3.36 rear end

---

inspires a high degree of confidence." The magazine appreciated the car's new suspension, especially the rigid front anti-roll bar, but noted that even with its nice ride and remarkable cornering stability, the car still did not feel perfectly stable, especially on rougher pavement.

The scribes at *Car and Driver* liked the new heater-defroster system, the larger improved brakes (adding that the car still deserved disc brakes, something that would arrive in the '65 model year), a quiet ride with less wind and road noise, and precise handling. The magazine quoted Zora Arkus-Duntov as saying: "For the first time I now have a Corvette I can be proud to drive in Europe." The author injected, "We are happy to agree that the Sting Ray is a fine showpiece for the American auto industry."

The Corvette even found a receptive audience at *Road & Track*, the import-oriented publication that was often over-critical of American sports car efforts. A few things the editors at *R&T* liked were the curved side glass, redesigned windshield, improved heater, spare tire mounted in its own housing underneath the car (a necessity since there was no longer a trunk), better weight distribution with 48 percent front and 52 percent rear (vs. 53 front and 47 rear in '62), the front crossmember welded rather than bolted to the frame, and all the new options, from the Z06 package to the genuine leather seats.

Road & Track tested the new Sting Ray on the "infamous ride and handling road" at the General Motors Proving Ground, and also out on the streets and at the dragstrip. Its most stirring conclusion was: "Whether you slam the car through an S-bend at 85 mph or pop the clutch at 5,000 rpm at the dragstrip, the result is the same — great gripping gobs of traction." The buff book tested a 360-hp fuelie, running it through the quarter in 14.9 seconds at 95 mph, and sprinting from 0-to-60 in 5.9 seconds, then hitting 100 mph in 16.5 seconds. Top speed was 142 mph, with first gear winding out to 65 mph, second to 85 mph and third to 108 mph.

The editors at *R&T* were so impressed with the Vette's overall performance that they uncharacteristically composed the following compliment: "As a purely sporting car, the new Corvette will know few peers on the road or track. In its shiny new concept, it ought to be nearly unbeatable."

Chevrolet was buoyed by the grand reception its newest creation was accorded by the press and the public. The division's enthusiasm for the Corvette was rekindled with the new model of 1963. The country's top automaker announced: "The new Corvette Sting Ray is a 100 percent improvement over the old Corvette, and we're pretty sure everybody remembers how good *that* was!"

Yes, we do. And we also remember how good the '63 Sting Ray was when it blasted onto the scene more than 33 years ago. That's the way it is with legends ... people never forget them.

Vette Resto

SUZY Q. IN REVIEW

By Bob Stevens

Asking any *Cars & Parts* editorial staff member what the next project car will be is akin to asking a woman who has just given birth when she's going to have her next baby. The pain is still too fresh.

Actually, the restoration of Suzy Q., our 1963 Corvette coupe project car, was relatively painless, thanks in great measure to the corps of first-rate suppliers and restoration specialists supporting the venture. All three restoration shops involved did a superb job, and the many parts suppliers provided only the best stuff. Also, the specialty outfits that rebuilt the engine, transmission, radio, etc., were all top drawer, as evidenced in the finished product, modeled last month in the special cover feature on the '63 Corvette ... silver blue Suzy Q.

Without the dedication and quality service afforded by the companies supporting the restoration project, it might not have been possible, and we certainly couldn't have produced such a stunning beauty in such a relatively short time. The companies and individuals involved in the restoration effort are acknowledged in the accompanying Suzy Q. Project Honor Roll. They deserve a great deal of credit for the success of the project.

The point man on the Suzy Q. project at *Cars & Parts* was our own tech expert, staff writer Eric Brockman. Also making major contributions were staff writer Dean Shipley and the author, Editor Bob Stevens. Helping out in primary support roles were Publisher Walt Reed, Art Director Ken New, and staff artist Jeff Gunderman. Bruce Henderson from the ad department also contributed much to the project, hauling the car from shop to shop and show to show, running parts to different shops, and taking Suzy Q. on her maiden voyage, the big shakedown cruise. He teamed with Sidney mechanic

Photos by the author

1. *Within weeks after Suzy Q.'s arrival, the office looked like a parts warehouse.*

2. *Project point man Eric Brockman surveys the freshly refurbished frame, wondering if the old girl will ever regain her dignity.*

3-4. Cars & Parts' *24-foot enclosed trailer has been a God-send, and a beautiful hauler, but it can be a handful in tight quarters, as Editor Stevens discovered after punching a hole in her side when a dumpster proved to be a nearly immovable object.*

5. *Show duty proved strenuous and dangerous to Suzy Q. She barely missed being in the path of a mini tornado that leveled the* Cars & Parts *booth at the Bloomington Gold Corvette show in June of '95. We were going to leave her under the tent overnight, but at the last minute changed our minds and decided to load her back in the trailer. Half an hour after we left the show site, the storm hit. Damage to the car would have been substantial.*

Earl Duty to work out any bugs.

It was a rewarding project, but it had its pitfalls. The wrong parts were shipped a couple of times, and sometimes the correct parts were sent but they still wouldn't fit for one reason or another (usually something we had done). A little "custom" fitting generally took care of the problem. Suzy Q. got filthy dirty at every show she was dragged to over the last year and a half, so we did a lot of cleaning and detailing ... over and over again. It got old pretty fast, but we had to keep her pretty side pretty. And pretty it was!

We did have a couple of mishaps. In one, we did a little hydroplaning while hauling the nearly completed project car in the safe confines of our 24-foot enclosed trailer. The entire rig — Chevy Suburban towing the loaded trailer — moved sideways a couple of feet. We slowed down.

Then, the author, while attempting to negotiate a tight pathway through a crowded, narrow parking lot in suburban Detroit, encountered a dumpster with the trailer, moving the dumpster several feet and punching a hole in the side of the trailer. He hadn't even realized what he'd done until much later. The car was unhurt.

There was the usual assortment of bruised knuckles, skinned shins, and wounded egos, but overall the project progressed quite well. We were more than satisfied with the results, and feedback from readers was very positive and encouraging, for the most part. Those who were most critical were readers who objected to the choice of project vehicle more than anything.

Some readers took us to task for not revealing the costs involved in each facet of restoration. Such figures would prove fruitless for most hobbyists, as we generally supplied our own parts and materials, occasionally did some of the work ourselves, and had to work under special circumstances for which major allowances had to be made. For instance, it takes a lot longer to complete a given task when the restorer is being asked a zillion questions and must pause frequently for photos, etc.

Will *Cars & Parts* undertake another body-off-frame, ground-up restoration? In all likelihood, yes. Despite the tremendous cost involved, and the incredible commitment of staff time, resto projects are worthwhile. But it will be at least a couple of years before another similar project is launched. A little breather is in order.

It has been an honor to be associated with the three *Cars & Parts* projects ... Miss Vicky, the '55 Ford Crown Victoria; Peggy Sue, the '57 Chevy Bel Air convertible; and the latest, Suzy Q., the '63 Corvette coupe. All three are fitting testaments to the old car hobby, the art of modern restoration, and the dedication of *Cars & Parts* to the actual preservation of vintage cars, as well as automotive history.

SUZY Q. PROJECT HONOR ROLL

American Metal Cleaning
James Taylor
475 Northland Road
Cincinnati, OH 45240
513-825-1171
• Stripping of frame, engine oil pan, timing chain cover, etc.

Antique Auto Battery
Dave Lane
2320 Old Mill Road
Hudson, OH 44236
800-426-7580
• Battery

Antique Auto Shop
Terry Kesselring
P.O. Box 18217
Elsmere, KY 41018
606-342-8363
• Chassis restoration

AE Clevite Engine Parts
325 E. Eisenhower Parkway
Ann Arbor, MI 48108
313-663-6400
• Engine rod and main bearings; engine overhaul gasket set

Beverly Hills Motoring Accessories
200 S. Robertson Blvd.
Beverly Hills, CA 90211
800-421-0911
• Car cover

Bud's Chevrolet-Olds-Buick, Inc.
1415 Commerce Dr.
P.O. Box 128
St. Mary's, OH 45885
• Miscellaneous OEM and NOS parts

B.W. Incorporated
316 West Broadway
Browns Valley, MN 56219
612-695-2891
• Storage preservation products

C.A.R.S., Inc.
Box 721185
1964 W. 11-mile Rd.
Berkley, MI 48072
313-398-7100
800-521-2194
• Interior installation

Chicago Corvette Supply
7322 South Archer Rd.
Justice, IL 60458
708-563-0400
• Restored Carter 3461 AFB carburetor, rebuilt starter, remanufactured alternator, rebuilt headlight motors

Classic Car Radio Co.
Jim Sheldon
John Sheldon
2718 Koper Dr.
Sterling Hts., MI 48310
810-977-7979
810-268-2918
• Radio rebuild; speaker reconing

Comer & Culp Engines
Glen Culp, Earl Comer
1604 Wapakoneta Ave.
Sidney, OH 45365
513-498-9879
• Engine rebuild

Corvette Central
5865 Sawyer Road
Sawyer, MI 49125
616-426-3342
• Miscellaneous parts, including knock-off wheels, radiator, hood, grille, air cleaner, etc.

Corvette Rubber Co.
10640 W. Cadillac Rd.
Cadillac, MI 49601
616-779-2888
• Weatherstripping

D & D Classic Auto Restoration
Dave Myers, Dale Sotzing, and Roger James
2300 Mote Drive,
Covington, OH 45318
513-473-2229
• Final assembly of car

EDCO Automotive, Inc.
Earl Duty
2304 Fair Rd.
Sidney, OH 45365
513-498-4384
• Troubleshooting, fine tuning

Fine Lines
650 West Smith Rd.,
Unit #2
Medina, OH 44256
216-722-7641
• Fuel lines, brake lines

4-Speeds by Darrell
Div. of J.T. Piper's Automotive Specialties
P.O. Box 140
Vermilion, IL 61955
800-637-6111
• Transmission overhaul

Instrument Services Inc.
11765 Main Street
Roscoe, IL 61073
815-623-2993
• Clock restoration

Just Dashes
5941 Lemona Ave.
Van Nuys, CA 91411
800-247-3274
in Calif. 818-780-9005
• Dash pad restoration

Kanter Auto Products
76 Monroe Street
Boonton, NJ 07005
201-334-9575
• Front and rear suspension, brakes

Kepich Exhaust
John Kepich
17370 Alico Center Rd.
Ft. Myers, FL 33912
813-433-1150
• Exhaust system

Al Knoch Interiors
Al Knoch, Dale Robertson
130 Montoya Rd.
El Paso, TX 79932
1-800-880-8080
• Complete interior kit

Lectric Limited
7322 South Archer Rd.
Justice, IL 60458
708-563-0400
• Complete wiring harness, T-3 headlights, battery cables

Lucas Automotive
2850 Temple
Long Beach, CA 90806
310-595-6721
• Tires

Maple Hill Body Shop
Jeremy C. Turner
Route 1, Box 74
Broadway, VA 22815
703-896-9024
• Stripping the body (plastic media blasting)

Meguiar's, Inc.
P.O. Box 17177
Irvine, CA 92713
714-752-8000
• Wax

Mershon's World of Cars
Dan Mershon
201 E. North St.
Springfield, OH 45503
513-324-8899
• Spare wheel

Mid-America Designs
One Mid-America Place
Effingham, IL 62401
217-347-5591
• Miscellaneous parts

O.E.M Glass
P.O. Box 362
Bloomington, IL 61702
309-662-2122
• Windshield, side glass, rear glass

Paul's Chrome Plating
Mars Valencia Road
Mars, PA 16046
412-625-3135
• Chrome plating

PPG Industries Inc.
Main Office
One PPG Place
Pittsburgh, PA 15272
412-434-2445
District Office
Mike Sloop
5010 Glenvar Heights Boulevard
Salem, VA 24153
703-380-2752
• Paint and primer

Quanta Restoration & Preservation Products
45 Cissel Drive
North East, MD 21901
410-658-5700
• Fan belt, touch-up paint, wheel well paint, fuel tank resto kit

Trailer World
800 Three Springs Rd.
Bowling Green, KY 42101
502-843-4587
• Car hauler, trailering equipment

TrimParts
5161 Wolfpen-Pleasant Hill Road
Milford, OH 45150
513-831-1472
• Taillight lenses, gas filler lid, glove box door, door handle kit, horn button, turn signal lever, radio face lens, etc.

Vintage Vette
14831 Honor Court
Woodbridge, VA 22193
703-670-7489
• Restoration of gauges

Virginia Vettes
110 Maid Marion Place
Williamsburg, VA 23185
804-229-0011
• Exhaust manifold dressing

WW Motor Cars & Parts
Jack Wenger
P.O. Box 667
Broadway, VA 22815
703-896-8243
• Body restoration & painting